THE MYTHOLOGY OF
SOUTH AMERICA

Gods and Heroes
of the New World

THE MYTHOLOGY OF NORTH AMERICA

THE MYTHOLOGY OF SOUTH AMERICA

THE MYTHOLOGY OF MEXICO AND CENTRAL AMERICA

John Bierhorst

The Mythology
of South America

QUILL
WILLIAM MORROW
NEW YORK

Recognizing the importance of preserving what has been written, it is the policy of
William Morrow and Company, Inc., and its imprints and affiliates to have the books
it publishes printed on acid-free paper, and we exert our best efforts to that end.

Printed in the United States of America.
Designed by Jane Byers Bierhorst
2 4 6 8 10 9 7 5 3 1

First Quill Edition

Library of Congress Cataloging in Publication Data

Bierhorst, John
The mythology of South America /John Bierhorst
p.   cm.
Summary / Discusses the mythology from Indians of various regions of
South America, describing origins, comparing the similar tales,
and presenting some of the myths themselves.
ISBN 0-688-10739-7
1. Indians of South America—Religion and mythology. [1. Indians
of South America—Religion and mythology.]   I. Title.
F2230.1.R3B54   1988
299'.8—dc19 87–26237   CIP   AC

Sources for the illustrations, unless given in the captions, are as follows (for full au-
thors' names, titles, and publication data, see References in the back of this book). Page
7 / Bororo drawing: Steinen 1894, pl. 18. Page 9 / Cubeo drawings: Koch-Grünberg
1967 2, figs. 66a and 67. Page 29 / Shipaya twins: Nimuendajú 1919–20, 1017. Page
37 / Ancestors: Reichel-Dolmatoff 1978, 63 (by permission of the UCLA Latin American Center). Page 43 / *Kúwai* and his two brothers: Koch-Grünberg 1967 2, fig. 93.
Page 47 / Water-spirit masks: *left, Povos e Culturas* 1972, fig. 19 (copyright Junta de In-
vestigações do Ultramar, Lisbon); *right*, Hartmann 1967, fig. 46; cf. Steinen 1894,
310–15. Page 51 / *Yurupari* mask: Biocca 1965–66 1, pl. 3 (by permission of the Consiglio Nazionale delle Ricerche, Rome). Page 69 / Myth of the sky people: Couture-Brunette and Saffirio, 1. Page 77 / Hunters: Koch-Grünberg 1923, pl. 32. Page 85 / Animals
and people: ibid., pls. 28, 31, and 32. Page 109 / *Kokrít* body-mask with horns: negative
no. 81–4608–21, cat. nos. 404909 and 404910, Dept. of Anthropology, Smithsonian
Institution. Page 141 / Man on horse: Nordenskiöld 1912, fig. 65b. Page 181 / Sun
mask: Hartmann 1967, fig. 331. Page 185 / Shaman's rattles: Petrullo 1939, pl. 24. Page
223 / Mountain scene with feline god: Schmidt 1929, 165. Page 225 / Revolt of the utensils?: Kutscher 1950, 44–45 (by permission of Ulf Bankmann for the estate of Gerdt
Kutscher). Page 227 / Water monsters: Schmidt 1929, 217. Page 229 / Staff God: Preuss
1929, pl. 87. Page 231 / Fox head: Collection of Raymond and Laura Wielgus, on ex-
tended loan to the Indiana University Art Museum.

Frontispiece / Kokrít body-mask, Canela, collected 1934 (Hartmann, *Masken
südamerikanischer Naturvölker*, Museum für Völkerkunde, Berlin, 1967, fig. 30).

Contents

ILLUSTRATIONS

MAPS

—————————

A NOTE ON PRONUNCIATION

Names of mythological persons and certain other words from Indian languages have been printed in italics to indicate that they may be pronounced according to a simplified system. The rules are that consonants and consonant combinations have their usual English values; vowels are as in Spanish or Italian (*a* = *ah*, *e* = *eh*, *i* = *ee*, *o* = *oh*, *u* = *oo*). There is one exception: the letter *h* at the end of a syllable, as in *Tokwah* or *Tséhmataki*, has the guttural sound of a Spanish *j* or a German *ch* as in *ach*. The accent mark, if present, shows which syllable should receive the main stress. Such a system does not give correct native pronunciation but only a rough substitute for speakers of English.

Introduction

A continent apart

More than any other of the six inhabited continents, South America has preserved the conditions that allow mythology to be freely produced. In Asia and Africa, and perhaps in remote corners of Europe, old-style communities may be distinguished where traditional lore, including myth, remains alive. But in South America it is possible to speak of parks devoted to the proposition that Indian cultures, along with plants and animals, can be kept intact as living museums. This is quite different from the North American concept of the Indian reservation with its self-governing features and its history of treaties.

To be sure, the situation is not uniform throughout the continent. In Uruguay there are no Indian cultures left to preserve. In Ecuador, by contrast, the politically aware Shuar Indians, better known as the Jívaro, have formed a native federation with its own program of self-advancement. But opportunities for establishing the so-called parks still exist in eastern Peru, in parts of Bolivia, Colombia, and Venezuela, and, especially, in Brazil.

Best known of these all-embracing nature preserves is the Xingu National Park in south central Brazil, where some twenty small tribes are given the freedom to pursue a traditional way of life. Vaccinations against selected diseases and the distant roar of construction crews laying roads through the forest are not unknown. Yet here, deep in the Amazonian wilderness, myths and ceremonies of great purity continue to be rehearsed, revised, and performed.

The watershed of the Amazon, the greatest of the world's rivers, forms the heartland of South America and the principal stronghold of its mythic traditions. With or without the protection of parks, tribes in many parts of this vast region have managed to survive, preserving their Indianness.

Elsewhere on the continent native cultures and their mythologies have fared less well. Little of significance for our subject has remained along Brazil's lower coast, now dominated by Rio de Janeiro, São Paulo, and other metropolitan areas.

Directly south of Amazonia, however, lies the interesting Gran Chaco of southern Bolivia, western Paraguay, and northern Argentina. In this inhospitable region, partly arid, partly swampy, Indian cultures have continued to find refuge.

South of the Chaco the continent begins to narrow. The land is drier, cooler, nearly treeless—and excellent for ranching. In the late nineteenth century, faced with a policy of extermination and having no place to retreat, Indians of southern Argentina yielded not only their land but their lives to Europeans who had come to raise cattle. The oral traditions of at least two tribes, the Yamana and the Selknam, were given up a generation later by a few survivors, but the myths of other groups went unrecorded.

The Andes, the backbone of South America, lie just west of the Chaco and the Amazon lowlands and extend in both directions to the northern and southern tips of the continent. The ancient civilizations of the Inca in Peru and of various groups in Colombia developed in the high valleys of this ribbonlike region. Today their town-and-village-dwelling descendants, though converted to Christianity, are producing noteworthy new mythologies in the native tradition.

East of the Colombian Andes and north of Amazonia, we again find Indian cultures that have survived in a relatively undisturbed state. Among the Cariban tribes of eastern Venezuela, in particular, the native way of life has persisted, and mythmaking remains a valued art.

From Amazonia itself the world still hears reports of small tribes that have remained "uncontacted," that is, completely untouched by civilization. For the present the Brazilian interior is spacious enough to give these people the choice of not coming forward unless they wish to learn about outsiders. If or when they do, they will discover, eventually, that there are outsiders who wish to learn from them.

The learning process

If the islands of the Caribbean are included with South America (as they usually are in discussions of Indian culture), then the desire to find out about South American lore can be dated from 1495, the year the Taino Indians attacked the small colony Christopher Columbus had founded on the island of Hispaniola. In the hope of preventing further trouble, Columbus decided to learn more about these people and ordered his chaplain, Father Ramón Pané, to investigate their beliefs. Pané thus became the New World's first collector of myths.

A generation later, Peter Martyr d'Anghiera, the royal chronicler of Spain, was able to record several myths from the kingdom of Dabaiba in what is now Colombia, and these were published in the year 1530.

Somewhat more detailed were the Tupinamba myths collected

near Rio de Janeiro by the French historian André Thevet in the 1550s. At about the same time and continuing through the middle of the seventeenth century, missionaries, conquistadors, and assorted chroniclers filed reports from the central and northern Andes, many of which included information about religious beliefs and mythology. Among these writers were Fray Pedro Simón for the Muisca of Colombia, and Pedro de Cieza de León, Cristóbal de Molina, Juan de Betanzos, and Francisco de Avila for the cultures of Peru and Ecuador.

Two outstanding Peruvian chroniclers, of Indian ancestry themselves, were Garcilaso de la Vega, called El Inca, and Waman Puma (falcon lion).

In part the investigators of this period were simply satisfying Europe's curiosity about the New World. But in seeking out Indian myths, they were also hoping to aid the work of conversion. Indeed, missionaries felt that learning native beliefs was a necessary step toward replacing them with Christian doctrine. Garcilaso and Waman Puma, on the other hand, were attempting to convince Europeans of the dignity and inherent worth of Indian tradition.

By the end of the seventeenth century the mood of Europe had changed, as people became less receptive to news and ideas from abroad. Not until the mid-1800s did the pace of discovery again quicken, and with the dawn of modern anthropology in the 1880s the study of South American culture, including mythology, became a serious enterprise.

At this time scholars and fieldworkers from Germany took the lead. Among the most important expeditions were those of Karl von den Steinen and Paul Ehrenreich, who published small, though choice, samplings of mythology from southern Amazonia. In 1918 Theodor Koch-Grünberg completed the first comprehensive collection of the myths of a single South American tribe, the Arekuna of the Mount Roraima region of Venezuela and what is now Guyana. Two years later Konrad Theodor Preuss finished his researches among the Witoto of Colombia, resulting in a two-volume report on the religion and mythology of that group.

Thus well begun, myth studies progressed steadily under the leadership of a growing band of workers, among whom may be mentioned two prominent anthropologists who were also folk-lorists, Curt Nimuendajú, noted for his Brazilian researches, and Alfred Métraux, the foremost South Americanist of the second quarter of the twentieth century.

Needless to say, observations throughout the years were being made on both sides. In the words of an Aguaruna informant, the visitors were "tall and substantial-looking. They wore special coats, and when they walked the coats sounded like this: saku, saku. They were great talkers, and they loved to joke around." As noticed by a Guajiro of northern Colombia, the strangers "wore black clothing, or white, and often their hats shone brightly, as did their revolvers and their rings."

Some of the actual portraits made by Indians, however, give a more penetrating view. In a Bororo drawing of von den Steinen, possibly the earliest South American portrait of an anthropologist, we see the bearded European as nature intended, though with his pipe in his mouth and his notebook in his right hand.

Open hostility was expressed by many tribes, especially in the Chaco region, where among some groups myths in quantity were not obtained until the 1960s and 1970s. But even where narrators were cooperative, problems arose that cannot always be detected in published myth collections.

Few fieldworkers have been as candid as Erland Norden-skiöld, who tells of listening to Chocó myths at night after climbing into bed and pulling up the covers. As the evening wore on, the anthropologist and his companions would drift off to sleep. The next morning, the narrator would be willing to reconstruct his performance, but it would always be done in a less spontaneous way, with the result that details were lost.

Nevertheless, by the 1960s enough stories of reasonably good quality had accumulated to make possible Claude Lévi-Strauss's very full anthology of South American myth, *The Raw and the Cooked*, which was soon followed by a sequel, *From Honey to Ashes*. Together the two volumes covered 353 myths, accompanied by a running commentary of great delicacy and far-ranging scholarship, linking myth to music, philosophy, and modern anxieties. This remarkable work drew worldwide attention to the lore of South America and in itself inspired a new generation of myth collectors.

Lévi-Strauss had argued that myths were rugged enough to survive bad translation and, presumably, imperfect collecting methods. Yet at the same time, fieldworkers were refining the art of using compact, battery-operated tape recorders, which enabled them to capture oral texts more perfectly than ever before.

Among the notable publications of the 1970s was the volume of Shavante narratives entitled *Jerônimo Xavante Conta* (Geronimo the Shavante narrates). These texts were transcribed from tape recordings made by a Shavante attending a native myth recital with no outside investigators present. Here then, with a minimum of contamination, were myths direct from their natural environment.

Jerônimo Xavante Conta, not surprisingly, was brought out in Portuguese, the official language of Brazil. Yet the material itself is of international significance, potentially valuable to scholars around the world. Its publication in Portuguese calls attention to a continuing difficulty for the study of South American lore, which over the years has been collected by fieldworkers of several different nationalities.

Many of the available texts, still, are in Portuguese, Italian, or French. Even more are in Spanish, German, or English, not to mention occasional sources in Swedish or Dutch. Few scholars command all these languages, and those who do are inconvenienced by the rarity of the publications themselves, many of which cannot be found even in large libraries.

Addressing this problem, the South Americanist Johannes Wilbert initiated in 1970 a series that has come to be known as The Folk Literature of South American Indians, designed to

Bororo drawing of Karl von den Steinen, shown with cap, mustache (above the eyes), pipe at mouth, notebook in right hand, beard, navel, and belt. 1887.

bring together the myths of particular tribes in a single language—English. As of 1986, twelve volumes had appeared and several more were planned. The tribes covered were the Warrau, Selknam, Yamana, Mataco, Toba, Bororo, Tehuelche, Chorote, Guajiro, and various Ge-speaking groups of the Brazilian Highlands. When the series is complete, the process of learning about South American myth, at least for readers of English, should go forward more smoothly.

The stem of the story

Among the Witoto it has been said that the story of Creation was brought up out of the earth by the first ancestors when they emerged. Similarly, the Kogi of northern Colombia say that myths were handed down by the four priests who participated in the Creation and that the telling of these stories today "goes by a thread," or umbilical cord, connecting the storyteller to the Creator herself.

No doubt stories of this sort are to be distinguished from ordinary folktales. In fact, among the Quechua of highland Peru two distinct types of stories are recognized: true and make-believe. True stories are those that tell of origins. Similarly, the Shuar of Ecuador used to say that stories of creation belonged to a category known as *nuhinyo* (earth story), from which lesser tales were excluded.

In other tribes, however, there is no distinction between myth and tale. Among the Suyá, for instance, all narratives are simply "what the old people told." The Yekuana, likewise, consider all stories *watunna* (a word derived from the verb "to tell"), which includes origin myths, folktales, and legends about recent historical events. For the Mataco, stories of various kinds, including light anecdotes, are *onkey* (our way), meaning that the narratives

---

Cubeo drawings of Theodor Koch-Grünberg,
standing and in his hammock 1905.

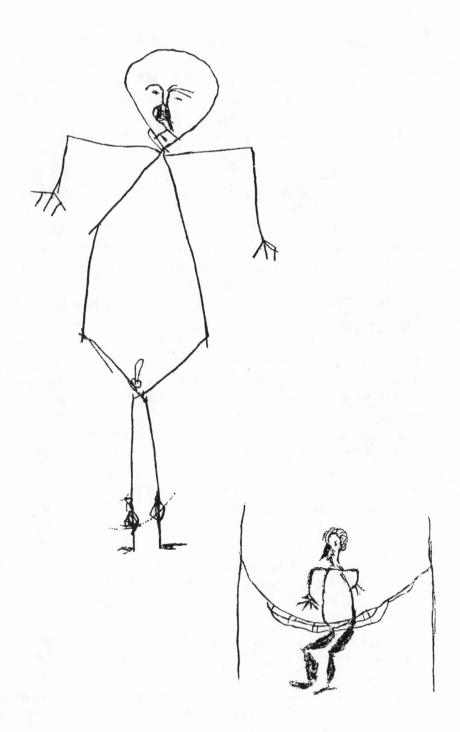

explain and reinforce the Mataco way of life, whether or not they are myths in a strict sense.

A useful point of view comes from the Ufaina of the Northwest Amazon, who see a difference between the "stem of the story" and its "branches," thus keeping to a twofold division while not denying the unity of narrative lore. The "stem" has to do with the deeds of the immortals, who created plants and animals, learned to hunt, started rivers, released the night, discovered the dangers of sex, built the first house, and, in short, established the Ufaina way of life.

Borrowing the Ufaina phrase, we may say that the science of mythology concerns itself with the "stem" of narrative lore.

Among the people themselves this essential lore—or mythology—is taken seriously. But it need not be serious in the telling. The folklorist who observed that the Acawai of Guyana repeated their Creation story "while striving to maintain a very grave aspect" was reporting an unusual attitude. Generally, South American myths are told with animated gestures and voice modification. Characters are mimicked, animal sounds are produced, and the audience frequently interrupts with laughter or questions.

In nearly all tribes, myths are a principal form of entertainment, and storytelling sessions may last for hours, even all night. The eagerness of audiences is itself the subject of a little myth from the Kogi accounting for the origin of tobacco.

Tobacco plants, it seems, were formerly people. They loved stories and would stand around outside the houses, waiting to hear if any were going to be told. Whenever they heard talking from inside, they pressed against the walls and listened. Therefore the Creator commanded that they grow around houses, right next to the walls, as in fact tobacco plants do today. This way they can hear all the stories.

Though entertaining, myths can also be educational—and in many cultures thoroughly uninhibited. The anthropologist Janet Siskind, who lived with the Sharanahua of western Amazonia, has told of small children lying on the floor, laughing as they watched the dramatic gestures of their father telling a myth about the origin of menstruation.

Among the Cubeo of southeastern Colombia it has been told that *Kúwai*, the culture hero, was the first to plant a hair from his head on his wife's genitals (thus the origin of pubic hair). He then performed sexual intercourse with her for the first time, asking a small boy to watch, so that he could learn how it was done.

The modern debate whether sex education belongs in the home or the school has not reached the tribes of Amazonia. For them, myths and schooling are one and the same.

Generally the teacher, or entertainer, is a man, often an older man. But women, again older women, are accomplished story-tellers in many cultures. In Mataco villages male narrators are corrected by women listeners and must accept this criticism. The reason is that Mataco society is matrilocal. In other words, men leave their home villages to come live with the women they marry, not the reverse. Therefore the man, in a sense, is an outsider, who must tell a myth according to the locally accepted version. In this way the underlying seriousness of myth is recognized at the same time that it is valued as entertainment.

Elements of mythology

The myths of virtually every tribe or nation, South American or otherwise, consist of themes, tale types, motifs, a cast of charac-ters, and a historical frame. These are the elements that deter-mine how rich, or poor, a particular mythology will be.

Among basic themes, the origin of food, fire, sex, work, and death may be mentioned first. Often two or more of these are said to have come at the same time, and it is made clear that the world was never again the same.

The creation of the universe, prominent in biblical lore, is widely ignored in South America. But the separation of night and day and the establishment of the heavenly bodies are themes that receive attention in many of the native cultures. The origin of the first people is not overlooked, and numerous stories account for the beginnings of particular mammals, birds, fish, trees, and herbs. The slaying of monsters also plays a role, along with the discovery of ceremonies, medicines, and the art of healing.

The various themes give a mythology its subject matter. But its distinctive shape comes from what folklorists call tale types. These are story plots that remain much the same from one culture to the next. The details may vary, but not enough to obscure the essential outline. In South America there are two that stand out, the so-called Twin Myth and the story that will here be referred to as The Tree and the Flood.

The Twin Myth, the most popular of all the stories, tells of a pregnant woman whose husband has left her. Wandering through the forest, the woman comes to the house of a jaguar, who eats her after cutting her open and delivering her twin sons. The jaguar's wife assists in the murder but spares the twins, whom she proceeds to bring up as though they were her own children. When the boys have grown, a bird tells them the truth about their parents. The twins then avenge their mother's death, killing the jaguar and his wife. Afterward they set out through the forest to find their father.

Basically no more than a folktale, the story is almost always loaded with mythological themes and becomes a principal myth for many tribes.

The other of the two widely distributed tales, here called The Tree and the Flood, has to do with the selfish owner of a valuable tree. This tree, located deep in the forest, bears a nutritious fruit or, in some cases, all kinds of fruits and vegetables. Although everybody else is hungry, the owner does not share his secret. Suspicious, the others follow him, discover the tree, and try to cut it down. But with every ax stroke the tree magically heals itself. When the people have at last overcome this difficulty, water from the trunk or the stump unexpectedly gushes forth, spoiling the whole project. Often told to explain how rivers began, the story has a deeper significance in that the loss of the food tree implies the need to plant gardens, hence the origin of work.

Tale types like The Twin Myth and The Tree and the Flood

contribute to mythology on a grand scale. Smaller elements, called motifs, help to fill out the picture. These lesser components, like the self-healing tree or the telltale bird (in The Twin Myth), are mere details, which may recur in stories of different types. Characteristic South American motifs include the birth of children from the knee of a male deity, the hero hatched from an egg, utensils that rebel against their human owners, and night held in a sealed container.

The cast of characters, if it is kept the same from story to story, can lift mythology to the rank of a tribal doctrine. The principal figure becomes the culture hero, whose deeds are followed through a cycle of tales. Often the hero has a companion, who may be weaker or less admirable. The companion, or the hero himself, may be a trickster or have trickster tendencies. Sometimes, as in the case of the Inca god *Wirakocha*, the hero is a deity, who is worshipped and receives prayers.

Finally, myths are placed within a historical frame, even if only by stating that the events happened in the distant past. The Wapishana, for example, begin their myths by saying, "A long time ago when the world was still close." This means that the action took place while the culture hero was still on earth and while people were more like gods and could change themselves into other beings.

In the lore of many tribes the mythic flood, said to have covered the earth, serves as a turning point, which marks the beginning of the world as it is known today. Others hark back to the world fire. For some, including the now extinct tribes of Tierra del Fuego, time is divided by the origin of male domination, and it is said that particular mythic events occurred in the days when society was ruled by women.

One of the mysteries associated with mythology is the belief that powerful forces operative during the ancient time may be felt again in the present, especially at annual feasts or during important ceremonies. This is true even among the Quechua of Peru, who envision an elaborate time frame of several ages, suggesting a view of the world's past that approaches the modern concept of history.

South American traits

With the exception of Australia, South America is the most isolated of the continents. More so than with North America, its plant and animal life and its human cultures have developed independently of the rest of the world. Accordingly, its myths, at least at first glance, appear to have a life all their own.

This is attributable in part to the peculiar animals that inhabit some of the stories, among which are to be found the flesh-eating piranha of the Amazon and its tributaries, the giant anteater, the four-foot-long capybara (the world's largest rodent), the tapir, the sloth, the rhea or South American ostrich, and the guanaco, a kind of woolly camel of the Andes and the Argentine grasslands.

Less peculiar, but nonetheless impressive, are the western hemisphere's largest snake, the anaconda, and its largest cat, the jaguar (which in fact ranges northward through Mexico). Acknowledged to be prime sources of supernatural power, the "serpent" and the jaguar play significant roles in mythology.

On close inspection, however, South American myths turn out to be not quite so odd after all. Reviewing the available material in the 1960s, the folklorist Stith Thompson was able to identify 150 South American motifs found throughout the world. A few are listed here.

Brothers as creators	Man created from seeds
Supreme god	Theft of light
Mother of the gods	Fire drill invented
Twin gods	Theft of fire
Sun god	Forbidden tree
God of thunder	Fountain of youth
Culture hero as trickster	Vampire
Primeval chaos	Reincarnation
Raising of sky	Sky window
Tree to heaven	Toothed vagina

Man in moon	Mysterious housekeeper
World flood	Murder punished
World fire	Adultery punished

Enough to suggest that the general features of mythology, and even some fine points, are of world occurrence.

If the first South Americans reached the continent by way of the Isthmus of Panama, as archaeologists believe, there is a possibility that these elements and perhaps whole myths came with them from Central and North America. But if myths arrived with the earliest migrants, proceeding along the isthmus, it would be hard to prove that these were the same myths that have survived. There are no tale types today with a continuous distribution through the Americas.

In Mexico there are faint echoes of myths common among United States tribes, but they die out in Guatemala. From the south a story identifiable as The Tree and the Flood (but without the flood) seems to have traveled up through Central America as far as Belize, but no farther.

A limited number of eye-catching motifs, such as the revolt of the utensils, are spotted here and there in the hemisphere, but without a pattern that argues strongly for diffusion.

A few important tales, absent from Central America, have clusters of distribution both in the north and in the south. The Twin Myth, for instance, has a North American parallel in the story of Lodge Boy and Thrown Away. In the northern tale a pregnant woman, left by her husband, is visited by a stranger, sometimes a monster, who demands food. At his insistence the woman serves him meat on her abdomen. Promptly carving into it, the stranger kills her and in the process delivers her twin sons, throwing one of them aside before leaving. The woman's husband returns and brings up the twins, who soon set out to slay monsters, including, in some variants, the monster who killed their mother.

There are significant differences between this and The Twin Myth, but an overall sameness would allow either to be regarded as at least a subtype of the other.

Another example is Moon and His Sister, the story of Moon's incest and how he got his spots. In the northern variants only, the sister is Sun. Still another type is The Bird Nester, the tale of a hero treacherously abandoned in the top of a tree. Scattered through North America, The Bird Nester has a cluster of variants in the Coast-Plateau region, centering on Washington and Oregon. The myth is also clustered in the Brazilian Highlands. Although independent invention cannot be ruled out, it would seem that the complex and largely unknown history of Indian migration had allowed these clusters to become separated.

There is, then, a basis for claiming a common mythological heritage. But the truth remains that the lore of the southern continent has gone its own way. Aside from distinctive tale types, such as The Tree and the Flood, and forgetting for a moment such animal characters as Sloth and Tapir, we find underlying themes that give the mythology a peculiarly South American orientation. These include the influence of shamanism and the pervasive tension between men and women.

Shamanism, often regarded as another name for primitive religion, is better treated as a special kind of religious activity, in which the practitioner, or shaman, induces in himself a state of ecstasy and enters the spirit world. In the northern half of the continent, east of the Andes, the spirit world is often the same as the world of myth, and the spirits sought are the culture heroes. In many cases the heroes themselves are thought to have been shamans.

Independent of shamanism, the cult figures of Andean religion, likewise, are the principal figures in myth. Even in a remote society such as the Yamana of the far south, the culture heroes are regarded as messengers of the supreme deity.

The net result is that the connection between religion and mythology is probably stronger here than it is in North America, though many exceptions would have to be examined before a general statement could be accepted.

With regard to the tension between men and women, mythology usually has little or nothing to say. But not in South America. From the bottom of the continent to the islands of the Caribbean come myths that illuminate the conflict between the sexes. In the Northwest Amazon and in the Upper Xingu, major ceremonies are organized around it, and in Tierra del Fuego, formerly, it was also a central theme.

Of the various myths that treat this subject the most important are those that account for men's dominance over women, the idea being that women were at one time the stronger sex and held men under their control. Related to these stories are the so-called Amazon myths, which tell of an ancient or faraway tribe of warrior women.

The creation of humanity itself is told by many tribes as two separate events, the origin of men and the origin of women, most always from different causes. In western Amazonia and in the Andes, goddesses sometimes take precedence over gods. Clearly impressed by female power, mythmakers in South America offer the rest of the world an opportunity to witness the open expression of attitudes that remain latent elsewhere.

Regional divisions

Though it may be isolated, South America is extraordinarily rich in its diversity of life-forms. Amounting to roughly a tenth of the earth's land area, it holds a quarter of all the animal species. Its birds are so numerous that ornithologists have nicknamed it the "bird continent." More than two thousand kinds of trees are to be found in its forests, along with probably more orchids than will ever be named.

The variety of human cultures is equally impressive. Estimates of the number of South American languages range as high as three thousand, with perhaps as many as four hundred still spoken today. The reason for uncertainty is that only a few of the languages have been carefully studied, and probably some of them should not be differentiated. Nevertheless, at least sixty-five language families have been identified, among which the best known are Quechuan, Tupian (including Guaraní), Cari ban, Arawakan, Chibchan, and the Ge group. None of these is related to any of the languages of North America.

To bring a semblance of order to the subject, the great seven-volume *Handbook of South American Indians,* prepared by the Smithsonian Institution in the 1940s, recognized four cultural divisions: Andean, Tropical Forest, Circum-Caribbean, and Marginal. The Andean cultures are distinguished by intensive agriculture, permanent architecture, and systems of government that control large populations. At the other end of the spectrum, the Marginal societies, mostly confined to the Gran Chaco, Argentina, and southern Chile, depend on fishing, hunting, and gathering and tend to be nomadic. The Tropical Forest and Circum-Caribbean groups fall between these extremes.

One problem is that a few "Marginal" cultures are scattered here and there through the Tropical Forest, which encompasses Amazonia and the entire region east of the Orinoco. Even the Ge tribes of the Brazilian Highlands, whose living arrangements are more complex than those of the Gran Chaco, have been classed as Marginal. Thus the fourfold classification would seem in need of refinement.

In fact, both before and since the *Handbook* more detailed schemes for grouping the South American cultures have been advanced. But since none has taken mythology seriously into account, these are of little use for the purpose at hand. What follows, then, is a very rough, somewhat new method of dividing the continent, based on mythological relationships between cultures.

Greater Brazil.   In this region the Tupian languages, including the intertribal language called lingua geral, are of first importance. The Twin Myth is widespread. Other common tales include Moon and His Sister, The Origin of Night, Amazons, and The Theft of Fire from the Vulture. Emergence myths and myths of the origin of male domination are noteworthy. The Tree and the Flood occurs in the extreme west.

Guiana.   Most tribes speak Cariban languages. Here The Twin Myth, typically with the addition of the fire toad, shares importance with The Tree and the Flood. Other types: The

SOUTH AMERICA
showing proposed
mythological regions

MILES

0   500   1000

NORTHWEST   GUIANA   ?

CENTRAL ANDES

GREATER BRAZIL

BRAZILIAN
HIGHLANDS

GRAN
CHACO

?

?

?

FAR SOUTH

Underwater Woman, The Vulture Wife, The Descent from the Sky, The Gourd and the Flood, Amazons, and The Origin of the Carib Warrior.

Brazilian Highlands.   This is the region of the Ge languages. There is no Twin Myth. A recurring pattern of mythic adventures involves the tricksterlike heroes, Sun and Moon. Other myths, unrelated to Sun and Moon, include The Bird Nester and the Jaguar, The Star Woman, and The Corn Tree. Myths accounting for the origins of ceremonies are characteristic.

Gran Chaco.   No language predominates, and The Twin Myth is rare or lacking. The region is famous for its trickster cycles, in which the hero is usually Fox or Carancho (a kind of hawk). Myths of world cataclysms are significant. Typical stories include The Women from the Sky, The Bird Nester's Wife, The Star Woman, and The Tree and the Flood.

Far South.   No principal language. No Twin Myth. Narratives exhibit considerable freedom from standard tale types. A myth of the origin of male domination recurs with some frequency. Of special interest is the cult of a supreme male deity.

Northwest.   Chibchan languages are concentrated in this region. Several groups have important myths that recognize mother spirits or a supreme female deity. The Twin Myth is weakly represented. Other types: The Tree and the Flood, The Food-Inhaler Bride.

Central Andes.   Quechua is the major language. There is a tendency to place myths within a framework of several world ages. Interesting motifs include the loathly god and the god born from an egg. Typical tales: The Parrot Brides, The Twin Myth, the *chullpa* myth, and The Underwater Woman.

The regional maps accompanying each of the seven parts of this book, corresponding to the seven areas described above, will show that some difficult choices have been made. For example, the Muisca, which might just as well have been assigned to the Central Andes, have been put with the Northwest. The Bororo, whose mythology is thematically linked with the Brazilian Highlands, have been grouped with Greater Brazil on account of tale types. And the Mapuche, whose myths have been all but replaced by campfire tales, appear in the Far South region for lack of better information on which to base a decision.

Mythologically speaking, the most coherent regions are Gran Chaco and Brazilian Highlands, with Guiana not far behind. Least successful are Northwest and Far South, where data are spotty because many of the cultures have become extinct.

At the very least the maps should help keep the reader from getting lost in a welter of unfamiliar tribal names. For the uninitiated it may be comforting to know that even dedicated South Americanists have to stop and think a moment when confronted with a name like Tucano, also written Tukano, which might best be reserved for the Tucano proper but is often applied to other Tucanoan tribes, such as the Barasana, and which, moreover, must never be confused with the Tacana, nor with the equally different Tukuna, also spelled Tucuna or Tikuna. It is to be hoped that these and some of the other tribal names will become less strange as the myths unfold.

All myths, in a sense, are unique, and each belongs to a particular people. To be told that a version is from the Tucano or the Bororo or the Incas of Cuzco is to be given a word of assurance that the tale is authentic and that it may be related to the people's other stories and to their customs and ideas.

At the same time it is well to keep in mind that even the most isolated tribe has, or has had, neighbors. Those neighbors themselves have had neighbors, and the chain extends through countries and across continents.

For all of us there is a feeling that the myths we tell, even those from distant places, form a common bond. We save them and retell them, convinced that they bring us news about ourselves. For those of us who are farthest removed, the myths of South America hold a special attraction. We turn to them expecting flashes of recognition, and we are not disappointed. Yet these stories from the southern part of the world, however familiar they may be, offer a freshness and a vivacity that give us a sense of having things revealed that were not known before.

PART ONE

Greater Brazil

═══════════

Culture Heroes and
Their Deeds

═══════════

Fathers and sons

Seen from the air as an apparently limitless expanse of green,
the Amazon forest, despite inroads, still lives up to its reputation
as the world's last wilderness. The carpet of treetops stretches
mile after mile, seemingly broken by nothing but an occasional
river. The air is clean. No cities are visible on the horizon, only
variations in the weather or perhaps a flock of birds.

Yet this wilderness is the home ground of societies that have
built a substantial, stylish way of life.

In rare, temporary clearings, gardens can be seen, planted

with corn, cotton, tobacco, special palms, and manioc. Elegant basketry and featherwork are among the refinements to be found in the adjoining villages, whose people also excel in making frame houses and musical instruments. Although these features are simplified or lacking in some cultures, and already destroyed in others, a well-developed, even elaborate life-style is the traditional norm throughout the heartland of the continent.

According to the stories, it all began in the ancient time when the supernaturals created or stumbled upon certain improvements that reshaped the world. These powerful figures—the culture heroes—are sometimes said to have been shamans or to have worked their magic by blowing tobacco smoke, a common shamanic technique. In some tribes, such as the Shipaya and the Desana, the culture hero is identified with the jaguar, the king of South American beasts.

But even if he is a great shaman or a jaguar, the culture hero is seldom able to act on his own. Usually he has a companion, often a twin brother. In the Upper Xingu and among a few tribes elsewhere, these two are identified as Sun and Moon (not to be confused with the Sun and Moon of the Ge tribes of the Brazilian Highlands, whose adventures are somewhat different). In the Northwest Amazon there is a tendency to recognize a group of three or more heroes, as among the Tatuyo and the Cubeo, who tell of three brothers, or the Ufaina, who have the four "immortals."

An idea common among the Tupian-speaking tribes is that twin heroes are descended from a father who himself is a creator or hero. Such an arrangement fits in neatly with the widespread tale known as The Twin Myth, in which a man and his two sons are among the chief characters. The tale is the single most important story told in the Greater Brazil region, sometimes serving as the narrative framework for a tribe's entire mythology.

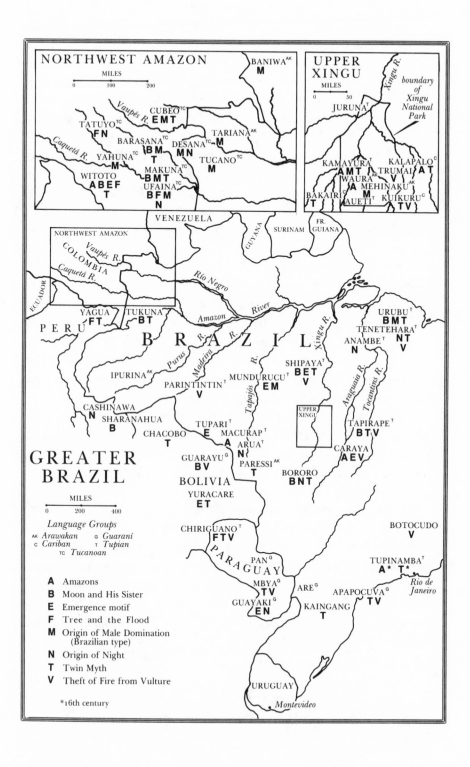

NORTHWEST AMAZON

MILES
0   100   200

BANIWA^{AK}
M

CUBEO^{TC}
EMT
TATUYO^{TC}
FN
TARIANA^{AK}
BARASANA^{TC}   DESANA^{TC}
M
YAHUNA^{TC}   BM   MN
M
TUCANO^{TC}
M
WITOTO   MAKUNA^{TC}
ABEF   BMT
T   UFAINA^{TC}
BFM
N

Vaupés R.
Caquetá R.

UPPER
XINGU

MILES
0   50

Xingu R.

boundary
of
Xingu
National
Park

JURUNA^T

KAMAYURA^T   KALAPALO^C
AMT   TRUMAI   AT
WAURA^{AK}   V
A   MEHINAKU^{AK}
BAKAIRI^C   M
T   AUETI   KUIKURU^C
TV

VENEZUELA

GUYANA   SURINAM   FR.
GUIANA

NORTHWEST AMAZON

COLOMBIA
Vaupés R.
Caquetá R.

ECUADOR

Rio Negro

YAGUA   TUKUNA
FT   BT

PERU

Amazon   River

B   R   A   Z   I   L

URUBU^T
BMT
TENETEHARA^T
ANAMBE^T   NT
N   V

Purus R.   Madeira R.

IPURINA^{AK}

Tapajós R.

SHIPAYA^T
BET
PARINTINTIN^T   MUNDURUCU^T   V
V   EM

Xingu R.   Araguaia R.   Tocantins R.

CASHINAWA
N
SHARANAHUA
B
CHACOBO   TUPARI^T
T   E   MACURAP^T
A   ARUA^T
GUARAYU^G   N
BV   PARESSI^{AK}
T

UPPER
XINGU

TAPIRAPE^T
BTV

CARAYA
AEV

GREATER
BRAZIL

MILES
0   200   400

Language Groups
AK Arawakan   G Guaraní
C Cariban   T Tupian
TC Tucanoan

BOLIVIA
YURACARE
ET

BOTOCUDO
V

BORORO
BNT

A   Amazons
B   Moon and His Sister
E   Emergence motif
F   Tree and the Flood
M   Origin of Male Domination
     (Brazilian type)
N   Origin of Night
T   Twin Myth
V   Theft of Fire from Vulture

*16th century

CHIRIGUANO^T
FTV

PARAGUAY

PAN^G
G
MBYA^G   ARE^G
TV
GUAYAKI^G   KAINGANG
EN   T

TUPINAMBA^T
A* T*

APAPOCUVA^G
TV

Rio de
Janeiro

URUGUAY

Montevideo

The Twin Myth

Twentieth-century versions collected in eastern Brazil show that The Twin Myth, in its classic form, has changed little since the 1550s. Just as in the story heard by André Thevet from the now extinct Tupinamba, the father of the principal twin is still the god *Maíra,* and the trickster Opossum is still said to have fathered the brother.

According to the modern Tenetehara, it began in this way: *Maíra,* having impregnated his wife, set out to travel and never came back; speaking from the womb, *Maíra*'s Child (*maíra ira*) suggested that the mother go in search of the father, and when the woman complained that she did not know the way, the child promised to direct her.

As the woman was walking through the forest, the unborn child asked her to pick a flower for him. But when the mother reached for it, a wasp stung her stomach and she slapped it, hurting the child inside. Angry, the little boy refused to give her any further directions. The woman soon became lost, took the wrong trail, and arrived at Opossum's house.

Opossum heard her story and invited her to spend the night. The woman hung her hammock in one corner of the house, while Opossum, unnoticed by the woman, made a hole in the roof directly over her head. During the night, when it rained, she got wet.

Opossum urged her to move her hammock next to his, where things were dry. She acted on his suggestion, then allowed him to persuade her that there was no need to continue sleeping in a wet hammock when she could just as easily share his. As she slept with Opossum, he made her pregnant with a second child.

The next morning the mother continued her journey, traveling until she reached the village of the jaguars. There an old jaguar woman hid her under a pot so that her jaguar son would not eat the guest. Later, when the son came in, he sensed the

---

The twins and their father. Shipaya drawing, 1917.

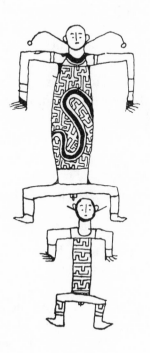

presence of a stranger and discovered *Maíra*'s wife under the pot.

Transforming herself into a doe, the woman fled. But the jaguar called his hunting dogs. After a chase they killed her, and when they opened her stomach, they found the twins, called *Maíra*'s Child and Opossum's Child, still alive.

The jaguar, who had fire, now wanted to roast the children. But when he reached out to them, they jumped aside, and his hands landed in the hot coals. When he tried to stick them with a roasting spit, they again jumped, and the stupid jaguar stuck himself instead. When he tried to boil them, he ended up scalding himself with the boiling water.

At last the old jaguar woman took the twins and said she would raise them. She put them to sleep in a tub, and the next morning they woke up transformed into macaws. The old woman was pleased. She fed them well.

The morning after that, they woke up as parrots. Each day they changed themselves into different animals. Finally they became human again, and the jaguar woman accepted them as her own grandchildren.

One day when the old woman had gone to her garden, the twins escaped and ran into the forest. There they met a jacu (a turkeylike bird), who told them how their mother had been killed. This made them cry, and when they returned home, the jaguar woman noticed that their eyes were swollen. To prevent her from becoming suspicious, they lied to her, telling her they had been bitten by wasps.

They now decided to avenge their mother's death by killing all the jaguar people. To put their plan into action, *Maíra*'s Child sent Opossum's Child to get some straw, and with this the two boys made fire fans, which they threw into the stream. As the fans hit the water, they became piranhas.

The next time the people went to the stream to fish, Opossum's Child led them onto a swinging bridge and jumped aside. The twins then overturned the bridge, sending the people to the piranhas, who devoured them immediately.

When the skull of the jaguar who had eaten the twins' mother came floating to the surface, *Maíra*'s Child transformed himself into an insect. He flew into the skull, took the jaguar's spirit, and placed it in a bamboo container.

After traveling for many days, the twins found their father, *Maíra,* and gave him the jaguar spirit closed up in the container. When *Maíra* had satisfied himself that these twins were really his sons, all three withdrew to the "village of the gods," where they live to this day.

Further adventures of the twins

For the Tenetehara, who make *Maíra* the tribal hero, the deeds of the twins are mostly limited to their escapades among the jaguar people. Farther west, however, the two boys become more prominent—as among the Kamayurá, Kuikúru, Chacobo, Yuracaré, and Yagua—where the twins take leading roles in at least three myths of wide distribution:

The Tree and the Flood.   According to the Yagua, a tribe of the upper Amazon, the twins' grandfather had a private source of water inside the enormous lupuna tree (*Chorisia speciosa*), which he tapped with a little spigot whenever he wanted to take a bath. The twins spied on him to find out where the tree was located, and when they had found it and chopped it down, the water all gushed out at once, forming the Amazon. Then they threw in the wood chips, saying, "This is for all the people," and the chips became fish. (In eastern Brazil the myth is replaced by the story of Hummingbird, who bathed whenever he wished in water that he hoarded inside a rock. Streams and rivers originated when the water was finally released.)

The Plant from the Grave.   In a Yuracaré form of The Twin Myth the younger of the two brothers, named *Caru,* has a son who dies. Given a mysterious warning that the little boy will come back to life if the father does not eat him, *Caru* finds his son's grave, then notices that mani (the South American peanut) is growing there. Thoughtlessly he eats from the mani, with the result that permanent death comes into the world. (In other, similar myths of the region, crops grow from the body of a young man, an old woman, a chief, a slain giant, or an anaconda.)

The Theft of Fire from the Vulture.   In various parts of Brazil, fire is believed to have been stolen from vultures by a hero who attracts them, pretending to be dead. "I will make myself stink," says the older of the twins in the Apapocúva form of the myth, "and let's see if we find fire." Picking up the scent, the vultures gather around. But when they have lit their fire, the hero steals an ember and scares the birds away. In some versions the hero kicks the ember into the open mouth of a helpful toad, who holds it until the vultures disappear. Since then the people have had fire.

Not all tribes include such myths in the twin cycle. Often the stories are told of an anonymous hero, or, in some cases, they may be assigned to the twins' father. One adventure typically given to the father—or even the grandfather—is the story of the origin of peccaries, or wild pigs.

According to a Shipaya variant, the people of the early time offended the hero, who punished them by blowing on their house. This turned the house into stone and the people themselves into pigs. Thereafter, whenever pigs were needed, the door could be opened and a few would come running out. All went well until a trickster left the door open permanently, and from that time on, pigs have been scattered through the forest.

Moon and His Sister

The Twin Myth, so called, does not invariably have twin heroes. For instance, among the Mbyá, where twins are considered evil spirits sent as punishment to parents who have offended the gods, the myth has the older "twin" born singly; then he himself creates his brother from a kernel of corn—or from his toenail, as the Yuracaré tell it.

The Barasana dispense with the brother altogether. In their version of the story the solitary hero is conceived by the incestuous union of Moon and his younger sister.

Moon, it is said, used to come to his sister's hammock at night. Wondering who her lover might be, the young woman prepared a pot of black dye (made from the bark of the inga tree), and the next night she painted the man's face. In the morning Moon looked in a mirror, saw that his face had been blackened, and tried to wash off the dye. But no matter what he did, he could not get rid of it.

While Moon was struggling with his ill fortune, his sister, called Inga Woman, now pregnant with the future hero, wandered into the forest and came to the house of Opossum. Although she spent the night in Opossum's hammock, she was not impregnated a second time, as in the Tupinamba and other eastern versions. Traveling on, she came to the village of the jaguars, and from here the story continues more or less in the manner of the Tenetehara variant.

Usually told separately, not as part of the twin cycle, Moon and His Sister is one of the commonest myths of Amazonia. It accounts for the origin of the moon's spots and serves as a warning against the crime of incest.

The Origin of Night

Where The Twin Myth is lacking, the various origin stories may be assigned to a pair of nontwin heroes, whose birth seems to be of little interest, since the event is not reported. When we first meet them, these heroes are fully grown.

For the Mundurucú the two are *Karusakaibe*, the tribal deity, and his companion, Armadillo. It was *Karusakaibe* who created wild pigs, say the Mundurucú, and the irrepressible Armadillo who opened the door and scattered them in the woods.

The Bororo of south central Brazil, whose rich mythology is one of the most admired in South America, have both a well-developed Twin Myth and, like the Mundurucú, a cycle of stories about two nontwin companions. In the nontwin cycle the heroes are Sun and Moon, a pair of unrestrained tricksters who are said to have lived before the twins were born.

In the Bororo version of Moon and His Sister the crime of

incest is committed by Sun as well as Moon. The sister daubs them both with genipa (black dye from a tree of the same name), and this explains why the moon—and the sun as well—has a blotched face.

The Bororo seldom adopt a myth as their own without turning it around or giving it a distinctive twist. For example, in the common Brazilian story known as The Origin of Night, a container of darkness is obtained from its owner by a careless hero who opens it too soon. But in the Bororo variant it is the owner himself who spills the darkness.

It seems that Sun, unaccompanied by Moon, paid a visit to Heron, who owned night. At the time, Heron and his wife were out fishing, and no one was home except two heron children sound asleep. Irritated, Sun pulled at the little herons' jaws, ripping them down to their stomachs. When the parents returned and saw what had happened to their children, they immediately blamed Sun and assumed he was still in the neighborhood.

Knowing that Sun was terrified of darkness, Heron unstoppered his gourd container and spilled a little of the night. Sun's screams were heard at once. Heron went to him and made him promise to cure the two children. Sun, a great shaman, did so by blowing on the little ones and patching their wounds with white down. In exchange he was given the bottle of darkness.

Thus it is explained why herons have white streaks running from the corners of the mouth—and how Sun became the keeper of night.

Ancestors and origin chants

Among the more significant duties of the culture hero is the creation, or discovery, of the first ancestors, who are widely believed to have emerged from the earth. In some of the myths the process is reminiscent of human birth, with a stream of water delivering the ancestors from the underworld. Or, as told by the Kalapalo of the Upper Xingu, they emerge from an actual woman, of whom it is said, "from her body came many men, the grandfathers of human beings who live in the world today."

In the mythology of the Desana, a Tucanoan tribe of the Northwest Amazon, Sun created the first people in the underworld not long before the origin of night. When they had been made, he appointed a supernatural called Germinator Person to lead the emergence. Stationed in a great canoe, which was really the body of an anaconda, Germinator Person and all the ancestors traveled upriver to the present-day country of the Desana, the Barasana, and other Tucanoan tribes.

These Tucanoan ancestors, as with the Kalapalo, were all males. The creation of women came later. As explained by the Mundurucú, a Tupian tribe, the males were pulled from the earth by *Karusakaibe*, who had sent his companion, Armadillo, to burrow into the ground and find them. Armadillo had been ordered to have them grasp the end of a long cord, which *Karusakaibe* would pull from above. When the deity had lifted them out in this manner, he turned to the task of creating women, whom he fashioned from clay.

According to the Guayakí, who give the story as a chantlike narrative, the men and the women emerged together:

> *The people's first ancestors were living in a deep frightful land.*
> *The people's first ancestors left the deep frightful land.*
> *All came out.*
> *The people's first ancestors' armpits smelled bad.*
> *Their skin was bitter, skin was very dark.*
> *On a road of beautiful water the people's first ancestors left*
> *   the deep frightful land.*
> *All came out.*
> *Like armadillos the people's first ancestors scratched their way out*
> *   with their nails.*
> *The people's first ancestors had empty hands, no bows, no arrows,*
> *   no lip plugs.*
> *All the women had empty hands.*

In the villages of the Cubeo, a Tucanoan tribe whose traditions are somewhat different from those of the Desana, each clan has its own origin chant derived from a basic myth of anaconda ancestors. These first beings emerged from the earth at a particular place and became human upon shedding their skins. One of the chants, referred to as "a good mouth that is talking," begins with these words:

> the people came out
> and shed [their anaconda skins]
> they went forward
> to the place of the star-ray rock
> crossing over the milk [a place of foamy rapids]

And so on, continuing with a list of the places the people passed on their river journey.

The Kaingang of southeastern Brazil recite their origin chants in an even more stylized fashion. For them the chant is a form of recreation, referred to as the "myth-shouting game." To play it, two men sit facing each other, often so close that their legs are intertwined. One of them leads by shouting the first syllable of the chant, which the other repeats. The leader then gives the second syllable, and so forth, in rapid succession, both speakers moving their bodies rhythmically in time with the syllables.

Double-chanted greetings and conversations have been reported from several South American tribes, including the Wai-wai, the Shuar, and the Cuna. In some cases, as with the Cuna, myths are delivered by a chanter whose every phrase is seconded by an assistant saying "indeed" or "so it is." But only among the Kaingang, apparently, are actual myths given in an equally reciprocal double-chant.

———

Ancestors in the anaconda canoe. Germinator Person stands with his arms raised; the horizontal band directly above him represents the Milky Way, above which float shamans in their spirit canoes. Barasana drawing, 1968.

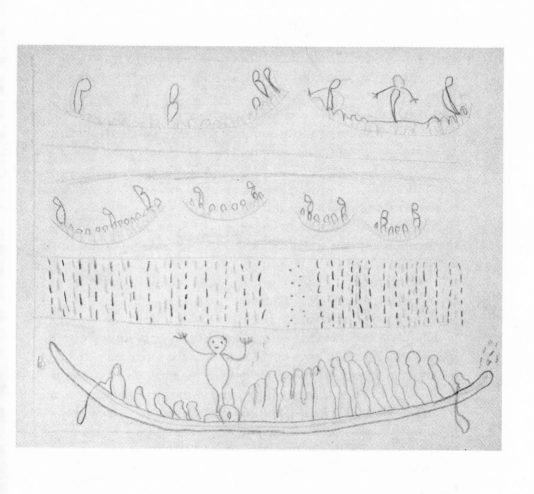

The female hero

Breaking the pattern of fathers and sons, the myths of the Desana tell of the Sun father and his daughter. As we have seen, the Sun father created the first ancestors. But it was his daughter who showed the people "how to live well."

The Daughter of the Sun, it is said, taught ceramics and basket weaving. She invented fire, then explained to the people how they could make it themselves by rotating a stick of hard wood between two pieces of soft wood. She also invented the stone ax. Moreover, it was she who taught the people how to use fish and how to care for plants.

One day when the Daughter of the Sun was cooking, her pot boiled over and nearly put out the fire. "Well then, go out!" she cried angrily, and she urinated on the embers. But in so doing she burned her pubic hair, and from this the odor of sexual desire spread through the world.

It is then told how the first death occurred. The Daughter of the Sun had a male child who was not doing well. He thought about women all the time, and this caused him to waste away. Finally his earrings, which were made of little cylinders cut in half the long way, turned so that the concave sides were toward his face, indicating that his life was no longer with him. The Daughter of the Sun tried to cure him with magic spells, but it was too late. When he died, she showed the people how to bury him, and this was the first funeral.

After her son's death, the Daughter of the Sun retired to the underworld. But the people remembered her teachings and have continued to pass them on to their children.

Why we are poor

Although the way of life established by the culture heroes has survived into the late twentieth century, there have become fewer and fewer to carry it forward. When Portuguese explorers arrived in the 1500s, the Indian population of what is now Brazil had reached one million or more; today it is only about 100,000. Once-flourishing tribes, like the Bororo and the Paressí, are now much reduced. Others, like the Tupinamba, have become extinct.

European diseases deadly to Indians and the temptations of modern civilization have played major roles in the decline of cultures. But the ultimate issue is land, and the controlling factor is the superior firepower of the non-Indian settlers.

As explained in a modern myth of the Paressí, the Supreme Being offered cattle, guns, and bows and arrows to the earliest ancestors of both the whites and the Paressí. The Paressí refused the guns because they were too heavy and the cattle because they would soil the plazas of their villages. Taking the bows and arrows, they went off into the forest.

The Carayá used to tell a similar story. The deity *Kuja*, they said, had arranged a footrace between a white and a Carayá. At the finish line were two prizes, a rifle and a bow with arrows. The Carayá came in first and took the rifle; his rival got the bow. But when the Carayá discovered how heavy the rifle was, he persuaded the other man to trade with him. From that day on, the whites have carried rifles, and the Carayá have had bows.

In the same vein, the Ufaina say that when the first ancestors of the whites and the Ufaina were hatched from eggs, God asked one of the four immortals to take care of the whites, turning the Ufaina over to the jaguar. "That's why the whites know so much and can make things."

According to the Mundurucú, it came about because the people disobeyed *Karusakaibe*, who went downriver, where his teachings were better received. "It is for this reason that the Mundurucú have little knowledge and are poor in material things, and the people downstream have so much that is wonderful."

It will be noticed that in all these myths the technology of the modern Brazilians originally belonged to the native people or their deities and was lost through default.

Typically, the proud Bororo have a story in which the loss is recouped. The civilized people, it is said, acquired knowledge from a mere monkey, who belonged to one of the Bororo clans. This monkey produced marvelous gifts by tapping his magic wand. Impressed, the modern Brazilians took what they wanted. Then, after stealing the wand, they built canoes and traveled downstream.

But the monkey had two helpers, a parrot and a little guinea pig who rode along on the parrot's back. These two flew off down the river, stole back the magic wand, and brought it home.

Whether the myth is prophetic—whether the ingenuity of the Bororo (and the conscience of modern Brazil) can bring back Bororo culture from the edge of extinction—remains to be seen.

In the late 1960s the Bororo in at least one village had reached such a state of despair that a decision was made to die out. Women began taking an herb that promotes sterility, and children stopped being born.

In the mid-1970s, however, encouraged by a program of disease control and by government promises to protect their territory, the Bororo elected new chiefs and began having children again. Tribal elders are hopeful that some of the old traditions can be regained. If a genuine revival does take place, it will be with an admixture of modern culture that will enable the Bororo to meet their Euro-Brazilian neighbors on equal terms.

=============

Men Versus Women

=============

The separation of the sexes

When the typical culture hero has finished his work, he retires
from the world and goes to live in the sky, in the underworld, or
at the edge of the earth. If he has a twin, the two may part
company, one going east, the other west. In the case of *Kúwai*,
the Cubeo hero, it is said that he is now living in the high country
to the west—without a wife.

Although it was *Kúwai* who introduced sexual relations, his
own experiences with women were constantly disappointing. At
first he and his two brothers shared a wife, and when one of the

men would go hunting or fishing, the woman would divide her favors between the two who stayed home. One of these brothers was the heroic slayer of animal people; the other was a headless monster with eyes in his chest, who eventually became the ruler of the dead. *Kúwai* got rid of them all and carved himself a new wife out of wood.

But Carved Woman, as she was called, soon found a new lover. Some say it was an anaconda, who would meet the woman when she went to the river to fetch water.

Discovering the ruse, and completely disillusioned by women's faithlessness, *Kúwai* left the world of the Cubeo, traveling upriver to the high country. He did not depart, however, until he had played the leading role in the great reversal of men's fortunes.

In the early days, it seems, the men had had to perform the domestic chores, while the women, who owned the ceremonial flutes and trumpets, did nothing but dance and play music. As explained in a Cubeo variant of the myth we are about to consider, *Kúwai* changed all this by taking the instruments away from the women and giving them to the men.

In a variant attributed to the Tariana, who live downstream from the Cubeo, the amorous adventurism of the women is repeatedly emphasized, giving the impression that the conflict between the sexes stems from sexual desire itself, as in the case of *Kúwai* and his faithless wives. Accordingly, the ritual derived from this important myth, a ritual that is felt to strengthen society, involves a temporary separation of the sexes and a brash display of male solidarity.

True to the nature of most myths that account for ceremonies, the story in many of its variants includes essential details of the ritual, as we shall see.

The culture hero *Kúwai* (top) and his two brothers.
The headless brother (lower right) has eyes
in his chest. Cubeo drawing, 1905.

The Origin of Male Domination

As told by the Mundurucú, the myth begins with the women's accidental discovery of the sacred trumpets.

While out collecting firewood, the women heard strange music and, following the sound, came to a beautiful clear lake no one had ever seen before. Using hand nets, they pulled up three of the fish that were swimming there, which, the moment they were caught, changed into trumpets.

After that, the women abandoned their housework and spent all their time playing music. The trumpets, mysteriously, gave the women power over the men.

Now it was the men who had to collect the firewood and fetch the water. They also had to make the manioc cakes (and to this day men's hands are flat from having patted the cakes into shape).

In addition, the men had to hunt, because the trumpets required meat offerings. Actually the offerings were needed by the souls of the clan ancestors, who were living inside the instruments. Before the trumpets had been found, the souls had had to live up under the roofs of houses.

Sensing an advantage, the men threatened to quit hunting unless the women handed over the sources of power. The women were obliged to do so, since they could not hunt and evidently did not wish to offend the souls. From that time on, things have been as they are today.

In a similar version of the story, told by the Kamayurá of the Upper Xingu, there are again three musical instruments, and again it is said that the three came out of the water. Here, however, it is believed that the instruments were first owned by the water spirits called *jakuí,* who could be heard playing them every day just as the sun was going down. Later, when they had fallen into the hands of the so-called *Yamuricumá* women, they were played in broad daylight in the village plaza. The men, who were forbidden even to lay eyes on these *jakuí* instruments, had to hide themselves indoors. If a man caught sight of them accidentally, the women would rape him.

The twins Sun and Moon reversed this state of affairs by scaring the women away and taking possession of the *jakuí* on behalf of the men.

Known as "flutes," the four-foot-long *jakuí* are actually reed flutes, fitted with an oboe-like mouthpiece. When they are played in the ceremony that commemorates the myth, all women must close themselves up in their family houses, and it is reliably reported that any who peek are raped by the men.

The ritual is similar among the Mundurucú. The Kamayurá, however, add dancing with special wooden masks—like the flutes, called *jakuí*—which represent the mythical water spirits.

The ceremony reaches its most elaborate expression in the Northwest Amazon, where dance masks are again used, here made of palm fiber or painted bark cloth. In this part of the region, both the rites and the associated myth have long been known by the term *Yuruparí,* a lingua geral word of uncertain derivation, which, in some cases, is also the name of the myth's principal character.

The trumpets and flutes forbidden to women are a central feature of the *Yuruparí* rites, but the emphasis of the ceremony shifts from tribe to tribe. It may variously celebrate the ancestor cult, the initiation of adolescent boys, or the ripening of the season's first fruit. Nevertheless, the myth that authorizes it usually follows the same basic story line, or at least it does in versions reported from the Baniwa, Tariana, Yahuna, Makuna, and Tucano.

As set forth in an intricate Baniwa version, the first three people on earth were created by the supreme being Nothing But Bones, who made them by "pronouncing a simple word." The three were Exhaler and Inhaler, both males, and a female, *Amaru,* who became the mother of *Yuruparí. Amaru* conceived her child by lightly touching a branch to her face.

When *Amaru*'s little boy was born, he had no mouth and could neither speak nor eat. But Exhaler nourished him by blowing on him with tobacco smoke. He grew so fast that in a single day he attained the age of six years.

Still unable to speak, he was asked by Nothing But Bones if he was man, animal, or fish. With his head the child signaled "no" each time and would not give assent until asked, "Are you *Yuruparí?*"

His body, it is said, was covered with hair like a monkey's. Only his legs, arms, and head were human. When at last his mouth was formed, he let loose a roar that could be heard all over the world.

One day he followed some little boys who were going into the forest to gather wild fruit. The children had been forbidden to eat this fruit, and when they broke the prohibition, *Yuruparí* called down thunder and opened his mouth so wide that the children thought it was a cave. Running inside to protect themselves from the storm, they were eaten alive. Later, when he returned to the village, *Yuruparí* vomited the three children, filling four baskets.

To escape the vengeance of Nothing But Bones, who now feared for the lives of the people, *Yuruparí* fled to the sky. But the deity lured him back to earth with a tempting dish of ants, tobacco fumes, and smoked fish. When he touched ground, his body emitted the cries of all the animals of the forest (just as the sacred flutes today emit the cries of the various animals).

At dawn, knowing that they would try to put an end to him, he called out, "No one can kill me, for I am the wood, I am the water, I am the knife, I am the weapon."

But as he had neglected to mention fire, Exhaler and Nothing But Bones threw him into a bonfire. He cried out once more, "Because you have killed me, henceforth people must die before they rise to the heavens." Then his belly exploded and his soul flew up through the air with a roar. In the sky he became shining white.

From his ashes grew the first poisonous plant, also the first

Water-spirit masks from the Upper Xingu. *Left*: Mehinaku mask, Museu de Etnologia do Ultramar, Lisbon. *Right*: Aueti Mask collected 1901, Museum für Völkerkunde, Berlin.

paxiuba palm, which sprang up instantly. From his entrails emerged the first mosquitoes and snakes.

A monkey cut down the paxiuba, and from this Exhaler fashioned the first flutes (ten pairs of reed flutes, ranging in length from three to six feet, each named for a different animal). The flutes are the "children" of *Yurupari* and are said to be his representatives on earth.

But when *Amaru* claimed the flutes as her "grandchildren," Nothing But Bones refused to let her have them. To resolve the conflict, a tree-climbing contest was arranged between the men and the women. Whichever side won would take possession of the instruments.

Being more agile, the men were the winners. But the women, not to be defeated so easily, decided to steal the flutes. Snatching them, they escaped by following the riverbeds, which were like dry paths, because in those days water did not yet exist.

As she ran, *Amaru* held one of the instruments close to her face and felt a rush of air against her cheek. Inspired by this, she blew into the mouthpiece and so instituted the proper manner of playing the flutes.

But Exhaler chased after the women, and because they tired quickly, he soon overtook them. Using thunder as his weapon, he killed them all except for *Amaru*. When the men's ownership of the flutes had been established, *Yurupari* or his spirit, acting through Exhaler, assembled the men and taught them the accompanying rites.

The *Yurupari* Revolt

Not only the musical instruments but also the dance masks are taboo to women; that is, the women do not wear them and may see them only in performance, at which time the masks are felt to be living spirits.

In the Northwest Amazon such masks are in fact costumes, completely covering the head and hanging down to the knees or below. Among the Tariana they are made of twisted palm fibers interwoven with human hair, recalling the Tariana myth that has the leader of the men saying, "Let us put on these garments of hair so that our mothers will not recognize us."

In a notorious incident, precipitated on October 23, 1883, one of these masks was pulled from behind the pulpit by a Franciscan priest addressing an audience of more than three hundred unsuspecting Tariana. Not only men but women and children were in attendance. There were shouts of protest from the shamans in the crowd and a general uproar in reaction to this attempt to profane the mask.

In the words of a second priest, who has left an account of the day's events, "they charged at us like jaguars in order to tear us apart." In the confusion, people were trampled and bruised, yet the two Franciscans managed to escape with the mask intact. (It is shown in the accompanying illustration.)

During the days that followed, a rebellion took shape, in which the Tariana allied themselves with several of the Tucanoan tribes. As a result the Franciscans were driven from the Northwest Amazon, and all mission activity ceased.

Known as the *Yurupari* Revolt, this episode stands as one of the few successes for native resistance in Brazil's still-unfinished war of Indian conquest.

Women without men

It must be understood that Indian women do not pass judgment on the rituals that sanctify male domination. Indeed, they are sometimes active participants. In the villages of the Mundurucú, for example, the trumpets are carried in procession three times around the houses, while the women, indoors, set up a ritual wailing to lament their having lost the sources of power.

On the other hand, it must not be supposed that the mythology is entirely one-sided. Balancing The Origin of Male Domination is the widespread Amazon myth, which tells of a tribe of powerful women never subdued by men. Extending beyond Brazil, the story has many variants in Guiana and is even known from the Andean region. It was one of the first South American myths to be retold in Europe, and indeed, in the early days of Spanish exploration it was reported more often as fact than as fiction.

Columbus at the time of his second voyage had written about a band of women in the Antilles who used the bow and the javelin and lived without men. Members of the party of Francisco de Orellana, crossing the continent from Peru to the Atlantic in 1541, claimed that they had seen the warrior women with their own eyes. Fascinated by this account, which suggested the warlike Amazons of Greek lore, Europeans gave the name "Amazon" to the great river Orellana had traveled.

Generally, the tale amounts to no more than a few scraps of hearsay to the effect that an all-female village exists on the other side of the hills or on the shores of a remote lake. Sometimes it is said that men are taken into temporary captivity in order to breed female offspring. In the Upper Xingu, however, such rumors have coalesced into a full-fledged myth.

It will be recalled that in the Upper Xingu version of The Origin of Male Domination the *jakuí* flutes were taken over by the men after Sun and Moon had driven away the mysterious *Yamuricumá* women. In the related Amazon myth these same *Yamuricumá* are said to have been abandoned by their husbands, who went on a fishing trip and never came back. The men, it seems, had turned into forest animals.

Feeling that they could no longer remain in the village, "because their husbands were not people anymore," the *Yamuricumá* got ready to leave. First they adorned themselves the way men do, putting on feathers and armbands and painting themselves with the red dye called urucú and the black dye genipa. They also spread poison over their bodies to turn themselves into spirits. For two days they sang and danced in the village.

The mask that started the *Yurupari* Revolt. Tariana, collected 1883. Museo Etnografico Pigorini, Rome.

Then, without interrupting their song, they slowly began to move away.

As they left the settlement, they seized an old man who had been left behind when the husbands went fishing. They dressed him in an armadillo shell and made him carry a manioc-cake spatula in each hand. Thus transformed into an armadillo, he led the way, scratching into the earth and bobbing up again as the women traveled along behind.

Each time they passed through a village they took all the women away from their husbands and carried them along with them. They walked day and night, constantly singing. And, supposedly, they are walking and singing still. They have no breast on one side, it is said, so that they can draw a bow without interference.

The myth, as it is given here, comes from the Kamayurá. As told by the Waurá, another of the Upper Xingu tribes, it is virtually identical, except that the women go away with three armadillos, not one.

Among the Waurá the story serves as the program for a women's ceremonial dance, in which the participants, as prescribed by the myth, decorate themselves with urucú. Dancing in two lines, those in one line moving forward with swaying hips, those in the other line taking small steps sideways, the women celebrate the myth of the *Yamuricumá*, who "learned to live without their men."

Creators and Saviors

Thinking well

The typical Brazilian culture hero is a part-time creator who sets in place no more than a few selected features of the universe. And even in these cases his acts are not always creative in the full sense, since they may result from thefts or accidents.

Nor do the storytellers place great emphasis on the hero's role as deliverer, or savior. The slaying of monsters, though regularly mentioned, is seldom a prominent theme. It is true that the twins kill the jaguar in tales reported from nearly everywhere in the region, but it is rarely suggested that they do so on behalf of humanity.

Against this background it is possible to distinguish two geographical areas, the Northwest Amazon and the Guaraní territory of southeastern Brazil, where sacred stories adopt a lofty, even mystical tone. Both areas have produced myths that exalt the power of the Creator, and both have a tradition of messianic, or savior, cults. It should also be noted that both have a long history of stressful contact with Euro-Brazilians.

By contrast, in the Upper Xingu, where tribes live more or less undisturbed, myths of a high creator, if they exist at all, are perfunctory, and messianic lore appears to be lacking. This is not to insist that the elegant Creator myths of the Guaraní and the Northwest Amazon groups are inspired by the teachings of missionaries or other outsiders. Although Christian influences can be detected in a few cases, the texts themselves will make clear that these myths are developed with great originality.

If in a general way the reader is reminded of what Europeans call philosophy, it may be useful to keep in mind the attitude of the Ufaina, who say that the ability to tell myths is necessary in order to learn how to "think" and that the mythmaker himself is one who "thinks well."

Alone in the darkness

Yuruparí myths and even The Twin Myth can be raised to a higher level of meaning by adding a preliminary account of world creation. Thus an unusual variant of The Twin Myth, collected in 1913 among the Apapocúva Guaraní, begins with these words:

"Our Great Father came alone, in the midst of the darkness he disclosed his presence alone. The eternal bats fought with one another in the midst of the darkness. Our Great Father had the sun in his breast. And he brought the eternal wooden cross, laid it in the direction of the east, trod upon it, began to make the earth. To this day the eternal wooden cross remains as the earth's support. As soon as he removes the earth's support, the earth will fall. Then he brought the water."

As the account progresses, the Creator, having formed the earth, makes the first woman, who becomes his wife and the mother of the hero twins.

In a Tariana version of the *Yuruparí* myth, told in 1963 by the shaman Mendes of Jauareté, the same situation is presented, but turned around. The Creator is a woman; she makes the first man, then forms the earth:

"When earth did not yet exist, they say, a young girl, a virgin, lived alone in the empty space. Her name was *Coadidop* [grandmother of the days].

"She said, 'I live alone in the world, I want earth and people.' She looked for tobacco, for smoke. She took the two large bones from her right and left legs to make the cigar holder, drew the tobacco from her body, and made a large cigar. She squeezed her milk onto the cigar, which she placed in the holder. She puffed on the cigar, wanting to give birth to people. She also created *ipadú* [the coca plant]. She took the *ipadú* and smoked the cigar.

"The smoke produced a thunderclap and a flash of lightning. The image of a man appeared and immediately vanished. She puffed again. Thunder and a flash of light came, then disappeared. The third time she puffed, the smoke changed into a human body. 'This one is Thunder,' she said. 'You are son of Thunder and Thunder itself. You are my grandson. I have created you. I will give you power. You will be able to make everything you wish in the world.' This Thunder was called *Enu*.

"The two lived alone. She said, 'I have made you as a man. As a man you will be able to do everything, good and evil. I am a woman. I command you to create companions for yourself in order to live well. And I will create my own companions.' "

When *Enu* had made three brother Thunders and the Creator had made two female companions for herself, she "took a cord, circled her head, laid the cord down, divided it in half, and squeezed her breast. Her milk fell into the circle and formed the earth. The next day a large field had taken shape in that earth. Then she gave the earth to the women so that they could work it. She said, 'With this earth you can live.' "

In time, one of the Creator's two female companions, impregnated by the Thunders, gave birth to the demon-hero *Yuruparí*—
and the rest of the story is similar in outline to the Baniwa
version of the *Yuruparí* myth given in the preceding chapter.

The Barasana, also, have a variant of the *Yuruparí* myth in
which the world is made, or at least shaped, by a female creator.
In the beginning the world was rock, and there was no life. *Romi
Kumu* (woman shaman) made a griddle out of clay and rested it
on three pot supports. These supports were mountains, and the
griddle was the sky.

In subsequent episodes *Romi Kumu* created the underworld
and caused the earth to be flooded. Afterward, when the land
had dried, she continued to exert her influence over the world
and all its inhabitants.

Each night *Romi Kumu* becomes old, it is said, but in the
morning she is young again. Her urine is rain, and she has fire
in her vagina. She is the mother of the sky and the mother of all
people.

The creation of space

According to the Makuna, who are neighbors of the Barasana,
Romi Kumu is the ruler of the earth, the trees, the night, and the
air space. But the actual creation of the air space is attributed, in
a separate myth, to the two *Adyawa*, or Thunders:

"In the beginning there was nothing. The first beings were
Adyawa and *Adya,* who stood on a point in the east. There was no
earth, and there was air only in the immediate vicinity of these
two, who were in the form of parrots.

"In each ear they had a plug covered with symbols. *Adyawa*,
the older of the two, said, 'This plug is to make the world with!'
Then he laid the earplug on his shoulder. And so our shoulders
were given the form they have today.

"Then *Adya* held up his plug, and it floated in the air space.
Adyawa stood up and bumped his head against the earplug, and
so the crown of our head was formed. With that the air space
trembled.

"*Adyawa* started to hum, and at the same time the plug began to spin. In this way he created new air to breathe. Then the plug stood still again. Little by little the [two] *Adyawa* expanded the air space in this manner. Now they had more room to move around."

Creation by thought

Undoubtedly the most quoted of all Northwest Amazon myths is the creation story told to K. T. Preuss in about 1914 by the Witoto shaman Rïgasedyue. Here the universe is seen to issue literally from the thoughts of the Creator:

"Was it not an illusion? The Father touched an illusory image. He touched a mystery. Nothing was there. The Father, Who-Has-an-Illusion, seized it and, dreaming, began to think.

"Had he no staff? Then with a dream-thread he held the illusion. Breathing, he held it, the void, the illusion, and felt for its earth. There was nothing to feel: 'I shall gather the void.' He felt, but there was nothing.

"Now the Father thought the word, 'Earth.' He felt of the void, the illusion, and took it into his hands. The Father then gathered the void with dream-thread and pressed it together with gum. With the dream-gum *íseike* he held it fast.

"He seized the illusion, the illusory earth, and he trampled and trampled it, seizing it, flattening it. Then as he seized it and held it, he stood himself on it, on this that he had dreamed, on this that he had flattened.

"As he held the illusion, he salivated, salivated, and salivated, and the water flowed from his mouth. Upon this the illusion, this, as he held it, he settled the sky roof. This, the illusion, he seized, entirely, and peeled off the blue sky, the white sky.

"Now in the underworld, thinking and thinking, the maker of myths permitted this story to come into being. This is the story we brought with us when we emerged."

Creation of the self

The theme of the creator who creates himself, touched upon in the Makuna account of the creation of space, is more fully developed in a myth collected by León Cadogan among the Mbyá Guaraní of eastern Paraguay. Since its publication in 1959 this mystical creation story has become widely known in Europe and in the Americas. It is worth remembering, however, that despite Cadogan's persistent questioning, the story was not given to him until he had gained the complete confidence of the Mbyá. It is, or was, regarded as secret lore:

"Our First Father, the absolute, grew from within the original darkness.

"The sacred soles of his feet and his small round standing-place, these he created as he grew from within the original darkness.

"The reflection of his sacred thoughts, his all-hearing, the sacred palm of his hand with its staff of authority, the sacred palms of his branched hands tipped with flowers, these were created by *Nyamanduí* [i.e., the First Father] as he grew from within the original darkness.

"Upon his sacred high head with its headdress of feathers were flowers like drops of dew. Among the flowers of the sacred headdress hovered the first bird, the Hummingbird.

"As he grew, creating his sacred body, our First Father lived in the primal winds. Before he had thought of his future earth-dwelling, before he had thought of his future sky—his future world as it came to be in the beginning—Hummingbird came and refreshed his mouth. It was Hummingbird who nourished *Nyamanduí* with the fruits of paradise.

"As he was growing, before he had created his future paradise, he himself, Our *Nyamandu* Father, the First Being, did not see darkness, though the sun did not yet exist. He was lit by the reflection of his own inner self. The thoughts within his sacred being, these were his sun.

"The true *Nyamandu* Father, the First Being, lived in the primal winds. He brought the screech owl to rest and made darkness. He made the cradle of darkness.

"As he grew, the true *Nyamandu* Father, the First Being, created his future paradise. He created the earth. But at first he lived in the primal winds. The primal wind in which our Father lived returns with the yearly return of the primal time-space, with the yearly recurrence of the time-space that was. As soon as the season that was has ended, the trumpet-vine tree bears flowers. The winds move on to the following time-space. New winds and a new space in time come into being. Comes the resurrection of space and time."

The land without evil

The Mbyá term *iva* (paradise), used three times in the above myth, refers either to the earth before it was "made filthy" by the "original serpent" or to the sky, the present home of the Father. Evidently this particular idea has been borrowed from Christian lore, which recognizes paradise as either the earthly Garden of Eden or heaven above.

But the Mbyá, as do most Guaraní, have another, similar concept of paradise, the so-called *ivi mará ei*, which is known to be much older. Translated "land without evil," the term refers to a place of peace and contentment, usually said to lie on the far side of the Atlantic Ocean.

Hoping to reach this destination, oppressed Guaraní led by their shamans have staged repeated migrations toward the coast, beginning as early as 1820 and reported as recently as 1947. Even earlier the Tupinamba, who lived just north of the Guaraní, staged migrations for the same purpose of escaping European rule.

Similar activity, but without the migration theme, has been typical of the Northwest Amazon, where self-appointed messiahs, sometimes calling themselves Christ, have attempted to reinforce traditional Indian values and in some cases have even tried to expel the non-Indians. The *Yuruparí* Revolt, already mentioned, may be considered a part of this long-term movement, which persisted among the Tukuna until as late as 1941.

In the Guaraní area, unlike the Northwest Amazon, messianic activity has been authorized by a special mythology. The mother of the hero twins, according to the Apapocúva, is the ruler of the land without evil, and shamans who wished to save their followers had to direct their steps toward her.

First there would be dancing "right through the year." And then, in the words of the myth, "the way would come to the shaman. When the time is ripe, the way comes to him. Then indeed we go with him toward the east and arrive at the eternal water. And our father [the shaman] goes out upon it. His children go right on the earth, and for them the water is dried up."

When they have reached the house of the mythical mother, the people are met by a parrot who offers food and a thrush who offers drink. The people are then greeted by the mother herself, who weeps and says, "Death has put an end to you on earth. Go there no more. Remain here."

In Mbyá lore the parrot acts as a judge, admitting only those who are "truly humble." In another version, again from the Apapocúva, the people rise into the air and reach "the door of heaven." A legend of the Guarayú Guaraní, which tells how the people migrated westward, explains that they corrupted themselves by accepting trade goods from the non-Indians, and as a result they cannot enter the land without evil until after their souls have reached "the death house of Our Great Father." In other words, the escape from poverty and oppression has been postponed to the afterlife.

From these various accounts it is apparent that the land without evil has been mingled with the Christian belief in heaven and that for the Guaraní the hope of a tribal refuge has been replaced by the promise of personal salvation.

Like the quest for absolute beginnings, as in the accounts of the creation of space and of the self, the search for an ultimate resolution goes beyond ordinary storytelling. For mythmakers at this higher level the immediate causes and consequences dear to the average narrator are no longer sufficient. As we attempt to follow their lines of reasoning, we are led beyond mythology and into the realm of abstract ideas that lie at the frontier of native thought.

PART TWO

Guiana

The Other World

Down from the sky

Myths in which the first humans emerge from the earth are standard lore in agricultural societies. Hunters and gatherers do not usually tell such stories, at least not in the Americas. Yet in the region north of the Amazon and east of the Orinoco, traditionally known as Guiana, emergence myths are lacking, even though many, if not most, of the native cultures have long been dependent on the growing of manioc and other crops.

If the islands of the Caribbean are included in the Guiana region, as they are here, an exception must be made for the ancient Taino chiefdoms of Hispaniola. These people traced their origin to ancestors said to have emerged from caves. Unlike the Guiana Indians of today, the Taino, known mainly from the reports of Columbus and other early observers, were a dense population with a complex system of government, reminiscent of eastern Central America and the north coast of Colombia.

More typical of Guiana, the Caribbean group known as Island Carib had an origin myth in which the culture hero Louquo descended from the sky bringing manioc roots. He then gave birth to the first ancestors through an incision in his leg (or through his nostrils, or his navel, according to variants), and later he taught the people how to cultivate manioc and prepare it as food.

Among the Cariban tribes of the mainland, the Yekuana tell of the deity *Wanadi,* who sent down from the sky a duplicate of himself, carrying a large egg filled with unborn people.

Leg birth and egg birth are two curious motifs that occur sporadically in the northern half of South America. But they are not concentrated in Guiana. Rather, it is the theme of sky descent that serves as a distinguishing feature of this region, helping to separate it, mythologically speaking, from the territory immediately to the south and west.

Among the Yanomamo, another of the mainland Cariban tribes, it is said that the sky people, fighting among themselves, broke open a hole through which everything, including themselves, fell to earth. As Yanomamo, they have continued to live on the earth's surface, while their shamans hold up the sky.

A fully developed tale type, which may be referred to as The Descent from the Sky, has been recorded among the Arawak, the Carib proper, and the Warrau. According to the oldest of the many available Warrau versions, the hero *Okonoroté* and his people originally lived in the sky world, where birds were the only game. One day, attracted by a rare bird of great beauty, *Okonoroté* ran after it and shot it, only to see it fall through a hole in the clouds.

Looking down from the edge of the opening, he could see the

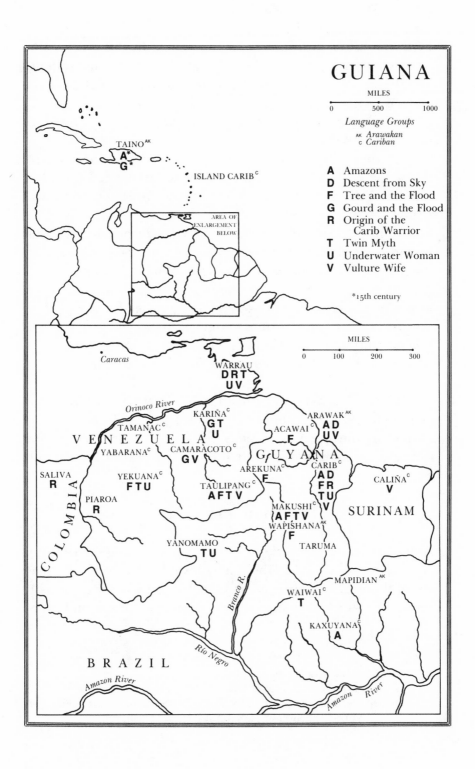

GUIANA

MILES

0 — 500 — 1000

Language Groups
AK *Arawakan*
C *Cariban*

A Amazons
D Descent from Sky
F Tree and the Flood
G Gourd and the Flood
R Origin of the
Carib Warrior
T Twin Myth
U Underwater Woman
V Vulture Wife

*15th century

TAINO^AK
A*
G*
ISLAND CARIB^C

AREA OF
ENLARGEMENT
BELOW

MILES

0 — 100 — 200 — 300

Caracas

WARRAU
D R T
U V

Orinoco River

KARIÑA^C
G T
U

ARAWAK^AK
A D
U V

ACAWAI^C
F

TAMANAC^C

V E N E Z U E L A

YABARANA^C
CAMARACOTO^C
G V

G U Y A N A

SALIVA
R

YEKUANA^C
F T U

AREKUNA^C
F

CARIB^C
A D
F R
T U
V

CALIÑA^C
V

PIAROA
R

TAULIPANG^C
A F T V

MAKUSHI^C
A F T V
WAPISHANA^AK
F

SURINAM

YANOMAMO
T U

TARUMA

C O L O M B I A

MAPIDIAN^AK

WAIWAI^C
T

Branco R.

KAXUYANA^C
A

B R A Z I L

Río Negro

Amazon River

Amazon River

earth far below with its forests and rivers. In the savannas he could see deer, peccary, and paca (a large, white-spotted rodent), and there were birds, some flying high, some flying close to the ground. After telling the other people what he had seen, he ordered them to make a rope ladder so that he could climb down and investigate.

Since there are forests of cotton growing in the upper world, the people were able to gather as much as they needed, and after some months of work the ladder, made of cotton rope, was ready.

Reaching the earth at last, *Okonoroté* shot a deer, roasted it, and brought a portion of the meat to the people above. They liked the taste of the deer and decided they would all descend.

In those days there were no old people, only young adults and children. All descended without difficulty except for one woman, the last to come, who became wedged in the sky hole. Unable to pull her through, the ancestors had to leave her, and there she remains to this day, preventing people from looking back into the upper world.

In other versions it is said that this woman was in the last stages of pregnancy. And some say it was just her thigh that became lodged in the opening. Today her leg can be seen as the constellation known in English as the Great Bear or Big Dipper.

The shaman's journey

Although ordinary people can no longer reach the sky world, it is by no means closed to the shaman, whose detached soul may travel there during dreams or trances. At these times he—or, rarely, she—makes contact with the animal masters and plant

Myth of the sky people who fought among themselves. Those who fell to earth are shown at top; at bottom are shamans holding up the broken sky. Felt-pen painting by Taniki, Yanomamo, about 1980. Carnegie Museum of Natural History, Pittsburgh.

spirits, who determine the availability of game and the success or failure of crops. Or the shaman may seek out and bring home the soul of a sick person that has been captured by hostile powers.

According to the Yekuana, it was *Wanadi* who created the means by which shamans could reach the other world. Before retiring from the earth, he made the *akuhua* (*Virola calophylla*), a tree whose resin, when dried and powdered, is used as a vision-inducing snuff.

The first shaman to make the journey was a man named *Medatia*. In a lengthy myth recounting his adventures, it is told how he entered different levels of the universe, releasing captured souls and restoring his own body to health. In one of the sky countries he discovered a rejuvenating lake, whose waters can heal wounds and revive the dead. Exhausted, he drank from it and felt his strength returning.

Evidently there may be more than one sky world. Among the Yekuana the universe in its entirety is imagined as a structure of seven levels, two below the earth's surface and four above. A somewhat simpler, four-layered model has been reported from the Yanomamo, who place the earth's surface second from the bottom. In Guiana these mental pictures are closely associated with shamanism. The Yanomamo, for instance, believe that the spirits who steal souls live on the lowest level and are constantly engaged in battle with shamans of the human world.

A variant model has been reported from the Waiwai, who assign a particular creature to each of five levels:

> 5/vulture people
> 4/various spirits
> 3/hawk(?) people
> 2/humans
> 1/cicada people

Again, earth's surface is the second level from the bottom. But the strayed souls of the sick are said to be "high up, in the house of the vulture people." In order to bring them back, the shaman seeks out a special helper from among the many spirits of the fourth layer. Presumably vultures occupy the fifth, or highest, level because these birds are observed to fly higher than all others.

The Vulture Wife

In Yekuana lore the spirits of the other world, especially the animal masters, lure people away by offering them irresistible brides or husbands from among their own animal children. As the daughter-in-law or son-in-law of an animal master, a person cannot return to the human world unless rescued by a shaman.

Such a theory finds echoes throughout Guiana and beyond. But it is also true that marriage to an animal spirit, even if dangerous, brings with it the chance to acquire power. The point is made in a Camaracoto version of one of the most popular of Guiana stories, The Vulture Wife, in which it is the culture hero himself, *Maichak*, who wishes to make contact with the chief of the vultures.

Knowing that vultures are attracted by rotten meat, *Maichak* smeared himself with foul-smelling grease and lay down next to a putrid tapir carcass. When the birds arrived, he picked out the one he thought was the chief and followed it, only to learn that this was not the chief but his daughter, who then transformed herself into a beautiful woman.

The vulture woman, eventually, led *Maichak* to her father, offering him as a son-in-law. But the chief demanded three tests. First *Maichak* had to drain an enormous lake and bring in all its fish for the chief to eat. Next he was ordered to build a house on a certain ledge, which required that holes for house posts be dug into solid stone. Finally, he had to carve a shaman's bench in the likeness of the chief himself, a seemingly impossible task since the chief always kept himself covered and no one but his daughter knew that he had two heads.

Helped by friendly animals, *Maichak* accomplished all that the chief had wanted. When he brought forth the two-headed bench, it spoke with a voice of its own, saying, "I am just like the chief." Terrified, the vulture withdrew, later confiding to his daughter that he intended to kill this son-in-law.

Warned by the daughter, *Maichak* fled. But on the way home, chased by the vulture's sons, he landed on the summit of Auyán Tepuí and could not get down. (The world's highest waterfall, Angel Falls, plunges from the massif of Auyán Tepuí.) Opportunely, a lizard appeared and carried *Maichak* to safety. Returned from his travels, "he knew everything, he could do everything." And so the dangerous marriage had indeed brought him great power.

In a version from the Warrau the hero is said to have been an apprentice shaman who had smoked so much and eaten so little that the wind practically carried him away. In an old Caliña variant the adventure is undertaken by one *Macanaholo*, regarded as the greatest of all shamans, who could "rise up from the earth and go over the trees, just as though he had wings."

The Underwater Woman

Important as it is, the sky world is not the only source of supernatural power. Spirits also exist beneath the earth's surface, especially in the underwater realm, which may be entered through whirlpools or rapids or simply by being swept into the water by a gust of wind.

Sometimes imagined as an anaconda, the chief of the water spirits is usually the fish master, and it is often said that he has one or more daughters who may take human form in order to entice unwary fishermen. In a lighthearted myth of the Ye-kuana, the hero *Wanadi* followed such a woman into the rapids and became the fish master's son-in-law. Obediently he worked for his father-in-law to "pay" for his wife, thus establishing the custom of bride service.

But in other versions of this widespread tale, the marriage to the underwater woman becomes a hopeless captivity, resulting in the death or permanent disappearance of the human victim. In a variant from the Kariña of the lower Orinoco it is told that a man offended the water spirits by shooting fish day after day. As punishment, water suddenly rose up along his shins, and a wave washed over him.

In that instant a "dream" advised the man's wife and children that he had been changed into a water spirit, and they immediately went to the spot where he had been fishing. What they saw from a distance confirmed their fears. To avoid his family, the man, now a spirit, slipped into the water.

Finding himself married to the daughter of the fish master, the man lived with her for a year. At the end of this time, wishing to visit the wife and children he had left behind, he was given permission to go. But he was warned that he must not allow his children to paint him—as a protection against spirits—or hold a torch to his face during the night. Otherwise he would never be able to rejoin his water family.

Arriving at his old home, he resumed his human form, and his wife and children greeted him joyously. That night, however, when he lay down to sleep, he again became a water creature. In the dark he called out to his children, "Don't paint me or hold a light toward me, or they'll never see me again."

"Very well," said the children. But the oldest son thought, "So it seems if he's painted he can't go back." In the dark, as his father slept, the boy began painting him, holding up a light. There, asleep in the hut, lay a huge water creature.

The next morning the father woke up in a rage. "You lighted me and painted me," he said. "Now they will not take me back." And with these words he left his earth family and was not seen again.

In a variant from the Carib of Guyana the angry man jumps into the water and is attacked and killed by the water spirits for having betrayed them. Worse, in a Warrau version the vengeful underwater father-in-law curses the earth people with sickness and death.

This last detail is echoed in the lore of the Kariña, who say that the chief of the water spirits, the anaconda, rises into the sky whenever he wishes and takes the form of the rainbow. At such times, mothers keep their children indoors, since anyone who looks at the rainbow falls sick. (Characteristic of South America, the serpent-rainbow, usually associated with illness or evil, has been reported from all regions except the Brazilian Highlands and the Far South.)

Not surprisingly, The Underwater Woman, like The Vulture Wife, is often told as a myth of shamanic initiation. In certain Carib and Caliña traditions the spirit woman is called *Amana*, and it has been said that she falls in love with the apprentice shaman and takes him all over her realm, teaching him how to deal with the underwater spirits.

In one of the Carib versions the hero is lured by not one but several beautiful women, whose singing can be heard rising up from the bottom of the river. Diving down, he disappears for three days, during which time he learns the songs and acquires the tobacco and the special gourd-rattle filled with pebbles used in shamanic rites. Afterward he teaches other men, "and that is how *piai* [shamanism] first came to the Caribs."

It should be mentioned that the popularity of the story has carried it beyond the sphere of serious mythmaking. As a simple tale type, The Underwater Woman has become a staple of Guiana folklore, forming the basis for a variety of "Fair Maid" or "Water Momma" stories. In Guyana (formerly British Guiana) such tales are now often told in English.

Myths as formulas

The songs acquired by the shaman in the Carib story of the underwater women are used for summoning spirit helpers. Words without music, spoken as a kind of incantatory poem, called a spell or a formula, may also be used by shamans and others in order to make contact with the spirit world. More specific than the usual song, the formula is calculated to treat a particular problem. Rarely, myths may be used in the same manner.

For example, when threatened by an approaching storm, the Wapishana are reminded of the story of *Kasum,* the electric eel. *Kasum,* they say, once presented himself as a suitor upon hearing that a certain shaman intended to marry off his daughter. Unimpressed by the eel, the shaman merely laughed. Then he discovered that this suitor, who had the power of electricity, could command thunder. Seeing that *Kasum* could divide rain clouds and send away a storm, he gave him his daughter, and the two were married.

In practice a shaman wishing to drive off a storm faces the clouds and addresses the following formula to *Tuminkar,* the culture hero, now retired to the other world. *"Tuminkar,* in ancient times you gave *Kasum* power over the storm cloud to turn it aside. You have more power than *Kasum.* Turn this storm away. It will do us great harm to have it come now."

The story and its accompanying formula were published in 1918 by W. C. Farabee, who implied that other Arawakan tribes in the region, not just the Wapishana, were familiar with this lore. Farabee did not say whether the story itself had magical powers or merely served as a point of reference. Be that as it may, the story with its incantatory prayer has virtually the same form as the story formulas reported from the nearby Taulipáng, who definitely consider the story a part of the spell.

The spells of the Taulipáng, of which hundreds have been reported, are called *tarén.* Each has its purpose, whether to drive off a storm, attract a lover, or cure blindness, food poisoning, snakebite, measles, or diarrhea.

If a hunter wishes to improve his luck, he utters the *tarén* about the hawks and the wasps, saying: "Some poor wasps were living together with *karará, kirirí,* and *sakutá* [different species of hawks]. All were brothers-in-law. And the hawks were great deer hunters. . . ."

As the *tarén* progresses, the hawks set out on a hunt. The wasps, intending to join them, are laggards, unable to get themselves moving until their in-laws are already returning with their catch. "Is that you?" say the hawks. "Just setting out? When today's the day for coming home?"

The wasps reply, "Well, yes. Right this moment we were just going, just to kill a little game."

"Impossible," say the hawks. "We've been all over. Where could you find game now?"

"Nevertheless and so be it, we'll just go right around here." And with these words the wasps started out. As they walked along, one of them picked up a pebble and said to the other, "What will you call yourself? How will you make your *tarén?*" Then the first one said:

> *Here*
> *it is I*
> *here*
> *it is I*
> *I restore the feathers that the good hunters plucked*
> *I raise up the blood that they spilled*
> *I pick up the ears that they pulled off*
> *I stand up the claws that they threw away*
> *I revive the eyes that they tore out*
> *I remake the bush turkeys, the deer*
> *I, I am* Makón, *the ancient one.*

Then he threw the pebble, and a deer appeared. Following his example, his companion did the same. (In closing, the speaker always identifies with one or more of the ancient ones, or ancestors; the choice of *Makón* in this case is not explained, though the term may be one of the shortened forms for the name of the culture hero, *Makunaima,* who is said to have been the inventor of *tarén.*)

The Taulipáng belong to the Arekuna, or Pemón, group of Cariban tribes, which also includes the Camaracoto and the

Hunters: shooting a deer with a bow (upper right), a bird with a blowgun (center left), and a deer with a rifle (lower right).
Taulipáng drawings, about 1912.

Arekuna proper. According to the Cariban specialist David
Guss, myths as formulas are common to the entire Arekuna
group and have been observed among the Yekuana as well. Yet
another Cariban tribe, the Makushí, may also have had them,
since the Taulipáng say that their *tarén* come from "the region of
the Makushí."

   Although they have no doubt been underreported, narratives
used as incantations are surely rare in the Americas. Outside
Guiana they are known from the Ayoreo of the Gran Chaco.
They have also been reported from a cluster of tribes in
northern California and southern Oregon. While myth in general can be said to reinvigorate the spirit powers, these are
special cases where the telling serves as a direct message to the
other world.

CHAPTER
V

This World and
Its Beginnings

The Tree and the Flood

It is told that the Carib of Guyana, when they first arrived on earth from the sky world, could find no food. At that time, manioc, plantains, and all the other crops were growing on a single tree. But only the tapir knew its location. As the people watched the tapir getting fat, they wondered where he was eating.

To find out, they sent a woodpecker to spy on him. But the noisy woodpecker could not resist stopping to tap on trees. Aware that he was being followed, the tapir changed direction and slipped away.

Then the people sent a rat, who stealthily traced the tapir to the food tree. Once there, the two made a secret agreement to share the food, and when the rat returned, he claimed he had found nothing. While he was asleep, however, the people looked into his mouth and saw corn kernels.

They shook him to wake him up, then they made him show them the tree. Having found it at last, they picked up their stone axes and began to chop it down. The work was hard. It took many months. Finally, when the enormous tree had fallen, each man cut off a piece of it to start his own garden. At the same time, water began to flow from the stump.

According to the Arekuna, whose version of the myth is similar, the tree was chopped down by the culture hero *Makunaima* and his four brothers. Immediately water poured from the stump, and with the water came fish. One of the brothers made a basket to cover the stump, but *Makunaima* said, "Let a few more fish come out for these streams. Then we will close up the stump." His brother had already put down the basket. *Makunaima* lifted it just a little, and the water came out full strength, flooding the earth.

Widespread in Guyana and eastern Venezuela, The Tree and the Flood is occasionally replaced by a similar myth, which may be called The Gourd and the Flood. In this story, as told by the Kariña, the culture hero descended from the sky carrying a shaman's rattle filled with water and fish. He gave it to his brother to hold, warning him not to peek inside. Hungry, the brother unstoppered the gourd to get the fish, and as he poured out the water, it flooded the earth.

In addition to the Kariña version, The Gourd and the Flood has variants from the Camaracoto and from the Taino of Hispaniola.

In some of these Guiana flood myths the overflowing stump or gourd merely accounts for the origin of rivers. In cases where the entire earth is flooded, survivors are said to have held out in a canoe or climbed a tall palm until the waters subsided.

Warriors

The destruction of the so-called tree of life spoils the world in one way or another. It may bring on a flood or it may simply mean the origin of hard work, now that the ready supply of food has been lost. In an unusual myth of the Piaroa it is associated with the coming of war.

In the Piaroa story the tree in question is the chicle, or chewing gum, tree, the only tree left standing *after* the flood. A lone couple has survived the deluge, but they are childless. The man complains to his wife, "How can I populate the world? You have never given me any children. If I die, who will wash me? If I die, who will put me in the burial cave? How will I be able to live in the other world?"

The woman hid her grief and said nothing. But she prayed to Sun. In reply, Sun sent a bird to advise her that soon she would have as many children as there were chicle fruits lying under the tree. "How can this be?" she asked. "I have only two breasts to feed so many."

"Woman, never mind," said the bird. "The chicle tree will mother the children. It will have as many breasts as needed."

The next morning the woman woke up and saw a marvelous thing, a chicle tree filled with babies, each one hanging onto a teat. She ran to get her husband. "Look, my chief, so many children I can't feed them! My friend the chicle tree is suckling them all. What a miracle!"

But the bungling trickster, Sun's adversary, saw what had been created and was envious. He wanted to make people, too. So he fished up a pair of piranhas and set them to suck on teats that were not being used. Since he had neglected to pull out their teeth, these new children completely devoured the two teats that had been given to them, then moved on to eat all the other teats on the tree. The Caribs, it is said, are descended from these two voracious children; other tribes are descended from the normal babies, who were Sun's children.

In Guiana lore, when "Caribs" are mentioned, the speaker is referring to the Kariña of Venezuela, the Carib of Guyana, or the Caliña of Surinam. These groups are closely related and have a reputation throughout the region as merciless warriors and cannibals.

In its classic form The Origin of the Carib Warrior is the story not of a tree that bears teats but of the warrior's birth from the body of a slain serpent. According to a Sáliva version, it happened when the Creator's adversary, in a fit of jealousy over the race of humans that had been made following the flood, fashioned a serpent to eat them up. Although the spirit of lightning killed the monster, its body rotted and bred worms, which became the Caribs. It was to get away from the Caribs that the Sáliva moved to the west bank of the Orinoco.

The Warrau believe that the serpent was a young woman's lover, who caused her to bear a daughter. Her fearful tribesmen, when they learned what had happened, wanted to kill the little girl, but the mother pleaded with them to spare her. Impregnated again by the serpent, the woman gave birth to a son. This time the tribesmen were not to be dissuaded. They killed the serpent boy and cut his body into pieces.

But the grieving mother collected the pieces, covered them with red flowers, and so revived the corpse, which became the first Carib warrior. As a result the Warrau were driven from the mainland and forced to live in the swampy islands of the Orinoco delta.

Interestingly, the story is told not only by the Warrau but by the Carib themselves, who use it to explain their own origin.

A quite different myth, but one with the same intent, is proudly told—about themselves—by members of the warlike Yanomamo tribe. This story, too, takes place right after the flood. Naturally, at that time there were hardly any people left in the world. One of the few was Moon, who kept coming down from the sky to eat the soul parts of children. He would make them into sandwiches, putting them between two pieces of manioc bread.

Some say that Moon had a child bride who was always running and hiding from him. When he would find her, he would drag her over the ground and step on her head. Finally, having killed her with this treatment, he scooped out her intestines, cooked them into a broth, and drank it. Then he stretched out under the sun and went to sleep.

The hot sun caused his head to swell enormously. In the evening when he woke up, he began to turn somersaults, and, spinning like a whirlwind, he rose into the sky.

The little girl's father, seeking revenge, shot an arrow, hitting Moon in the leg. From the leg wound blood dripped to the earth, and from each drop a Yanomamo warrior was born. Since they have their origin in blood, it is said, the men today are fierce and warlike.

Yanomamo women do not share in this origin. Their birth was later, when one of the men became pregnant in the calf of his leg and delivered the women through an incision.

Whether Carib or Yanomamo, it seems clear that women are not born to be warriors.

Beyond the glimpse of ordinary mortals, however, the situation may be changed. According to a myth of the Kaxúyana, the women of today trace their origin to a single female child left behind by the ancient women, who rejected their husbands. Clasping hot peppers to their breasts, these women danced in a circle until they rose into the air and disappeared. Still alive on a remote mountaintop, they have become the legendary female warriors, or Amazons, widely known in Guiana, just as they are in Brazil.

The twins and the toad

Two major events in the development of the world as it exists today, the origin of fire and the origin of manioc, are often treated in Guiana as part of The Twin Myth. Unlike the usual Brazilian form of the story, there is no opossum seducer in the Guiana variants, and the jaguar's wife is here imagined as a frog or a toad.

In a Carib variant, told by a Warrau living in Guyana, the twins are the usual Carib culture heroes, *Makunaima* and *Pia,* and their irresponsible father is Sun. After impregnating his wife, Sun sets out on his westward journey, leaving the poor woman to follow after him as best she can. At first she is guided by one of the twins, whose voice she can hear from inside her womb. But when she slaps a wasp that has landed on her abdomen, the badly shaken child becomes angry and stops speaking. Before long the woman has taken the wrong path and is on her way to the house of Frog (Toad in most versions, said to be the wife of Jaguar).

Frog, "a very old and very big woman," greeted the traveler and asked her business. She was trying to find her husband, the Sun, she explained, but she had lost her way and was now very tired. Frog invited her in and gave her food and drink. Then she squatted next to her guest and asked to be loused.

"But don't put the lice in your mouth," she warned, "or they will poison you."

Overcome with fatigue, the woman forgot the warning. Picking a louse from the old woman's head, she placed it between her teeth to kill it, as was customary. But no sooner had she done so than she fell dead.

Frog immediately slashed open the mother and extracted the twins, a pair of beautiful boys, *Makunaima* and *Pia*. With loving care she brought them up, and soon they were shooting birds. Growing bigger, they began to shoot fish.

But every time they brought home fish a strange thing would happen. The old woman would send them out for firewood, and by the time they returned, the fish would be all cooked, ready to eat. In fact, while the twins were out, the old woman would vomit fire from her mouth, do her cooking, then swallow the fire before the boys returned.

To find out what she did, one of the twins changed himself into a lizard and ran up under the roof to spy on her. He saw her spit out the fire and lick it up again, and he also saw her draw something like milk from her neck, from which she prepared manioc flour.

Made uneasy by these discoveries, the twins decided to kill the

Animals and people: frog, woman lousing, woman grating manioc, surubim fish. Taulipáng drawings, about 1912.

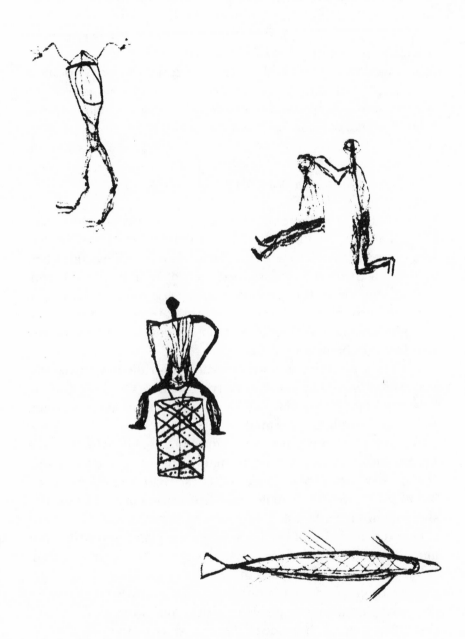

old woman. They cleared a large field, brought her to the middle of it, and lit kindling all around her. As her body burned, the fire inside her spread into the kindling, which happened to be of the kind called *hima-heru*. And so, today, whenever the people need fire they rub together two sticks of *hima-heru* wood.

A Kariña variant adds that the cleared field was a garden. In a version from the Waiwai the old woman freely enters the garden and allows herself to be cremated; manioc plants spring from her charred bones.

Expanding the story

In Guiana, as elsewhere in South America, myths are most often told separately. At times, however, an ambitious storyteller will string several myths together to make a more or less connected account of the events that shaped the world. The descent from the sky, the flood, the creation of the present race of humans, and the departure of the culture heroes are among the crucial themes as the story progresses from earliest times to a period that is felt to be more recent.

In some cases this "creation story," as it is called by folklorists, may be dominated by a single tale type, such as The Tree and the Flood or The Twin Myth. The various acts of creation then follow as a result or aftermath.

For example, in the Waiwai Twin Myth, at about the time the heroes incinerated the frog woman, causing manioc to come forth, they developed genitals. These had previously been lacking. Up until then male sex organs grew in the form of a small plant in the forest.

One day a bird told the boys about the plant, and they went and found it. Both brothers tasted it, then lay down to sleep. While they slept, the organs grew.

Next, desiring wives, the brothers went to a little creek, where they were accustomed to catching fish, and attempted to have sexual relations with an otter. Offended, the otter reproached the twins and told them that if they wanted wives they should go down to the river itself.

At the riverbank the older of the two boys began to fish. He thrust his arrow into the water and fished up a woman's bag. He tried again and pulled up a menstruation mat. The third time he got a basket containing dyestuffs, fish-egg beads, and a woman's apron. The fourth time, a spindle. The fifth time, he drew up the woman herself, who was one of the anaconda people, and he made her his wife.

Repeating the same five steps, he drew up a second woman, whom he gave to his brother. This woman and the younger brother, it is said, are the ancestors of the "civilized Brazilians." From the older brother and his wife are descended the Waiwai and all other Indian tribes—as well as the Europeans, who are admired by the Waiwai as bringers of superior knives and axes. (The story of the origin of tribes from the two women who were fished up is an important tale type of Guyana and adjacent Brazil, known from the Mapidian and the Taruma, as well as the Waiwai.)

When his work was finished, the older of the twins, whose name was *Mawari,* shot an arrow into the sky, then another and another until a long ladder had been formed, which swayed in the wind. On this ladder *Mawari* and his wife climbed to heaven. The younger of the twins, called *Washi,* is said to be still living "somewhere down in Brazil."

Thus The Twin Myth becomes a modest-sized epic of creation, accounting for the origin of hearth fires, manioc, sexual desire, and the various branches of humanity. Similarly, the Makushí use The Tree and the Flood as the nucleus of an expanded story explaining how certain features of the physical world came into being.

After the tree had been felled and the water had poured from the stump, causing the flood, the culture hero and his brother saved themselves by climbing Mauritia palms. From the tops of the palms they threw seeds into the water until the earth had been built up again. The younger brother established the alternation of night and day, then brought about the origin of fish. Their work accomplished, the brothers followed the sound of a conch horn and disappeared inside a rock. Their footprints, is it said, are still visible.

Obviously the expanded story holds more details than the basic plot of The Twin Myth or The Tree and the Flood. But it also extends the action into the present. The brothers whose footprints can still be seen and the hero who is "somewhere down in Brazil" cannot be long gone. Their closeness keeps people in touch with their beginnings, renewing the forces that were unleashed when the world was new.

PART THREE

Brazilian Highlands

―――――――

The Art of Myth

―――――――

Just so

Toward the east the broad floodplain of the Amazon shrinks to little more than two hundred miles wide, narrowly separating the highlands of Guiana, to the north, and, to the south, a vast, ill-defined area known as the Brazilian Highlands, reaching nearly to Uruguay. The term "Brazilian Highlands" as used in this book, however, refers only to the region of the Ge-speaking tribes, whose territory centers on the upper drainage of the Tocantins River.

More than with other large South American language families, the Ge group forms a mythological island. Here The Twin Myth is lacking; emergence myths, as in the case of Guiana, are virtually nonexistent; and the paired heroes Sun and Moon are put through a cycle of adventures quite different from those of the culture heroes of the surrounding region.

Traditionally the Ge themselves have been hunters and gatherers, spending part of the year in semipermanent villages, raising yams, corn, and other crops. The region is noted for fine mats, masks, and baskets woven from straw and palm fiber. Elaborate ceremonials and athletic games are characteristic. Shamanism is less well developed than in other parts of Brazil, and hallucinogenic drugs, much appreciated in regions to the north and west, are not used at all.

Among the Ge there is a tendency to take a worldly attitude toward ceremony and myth. The Apanyekra and the Canela, for example, regard masked dances more as theater than as ritual. And the same is true with the Shavante, who merely say that ceremonies are *we da* (to make beautiful). For the Shavante, myth itself has little or no religious value. In the words of David Maybury-Lewis, one of the foremost observers of the Ge, Shavante myths are simply "just so" stories.

In some of the shorter Ge myths an anecdotal quality is unmistakable:

The origin of laughter.   A friendly bat, unable to speak but wishing to communicate, caressed a man with its cold hands and long nails. Tickled, the man laughed, and this was the first laughter heard in the world.

Noisy vegetables.   From their hunting camp the people sent a messenger back to the village to see if the vegetables were ripe. As the messenger approached, he heard shouts. Potatoes, watermelons, squash, and yams were holding a festival. He stayed to watch and learned the games and songs.

Nighthawk's wings.   Dying of thirst, a woman held prisoner by her cruel husband magically detached her head from her body and flew off in search of water, using her hair as wings. Unable to find her body again, she became the nighthawk, whose wings

Tapajós R.

Tocantins R.

KRENYE
J Q

SHIKRI CAYAPO
C J W

APINAYE
C J
Q W

CANELA
J Q W
APANYEKRA
Q

Xingu R.

CAYAPO
C J Q
W

Araguaia R.

Tocantins R.

KRAHO
C J Q
W

Parnaiba R.

KREEN-AKARORE

TXUKAHAMAI

SUYA
J

SHERENTE
J Q W

Teles Pires R.

SHAVANTE
C J W

Grande R.

San Francisco R.

AREA OF
ENLARGEMENT

BRAZILIAN
HIGHLANDS

MILES

0   100   200

*All tribes shown on this map
speak Ge languages*

C Corn Tree
J Bird Nester
  and the
  Jaguar

Q Sun and Moon
  cycle (Ge type)
W Star Woman
  (Ge type)

flutter and tremble like hair ruffled by the wind.

Why didn't you come sooner?   Sun and Moon changed themselves into two large fish and tricked some fishermen into
shooting all their arrows at them. Later they brought the arrows
to the fishermen, who said, "Why didn't you come sooner with
your many arrows? You could have helped us catch two big fish."
"Ah," said Sun and Moon, "what a pity!"

Such stories are not in the mainstream of Ge myth. But even
the principal myths of the region—The Star Woman, The Corn
Tree, and the tale that will here be called The Bird Nester and
the Jaguar—are told for their own sake, functioning primarily as
entertainment. It is of interest to look closely at these three
myths, to see how they may be related to stories known from
elsewhere on the continent.

The Star Woman

A man had a beautiful young wife who became sick and died.
Feeling sad, he would go out into the village plaza at night and
lie down by himself on a leaf of the bacaba palm. One night a
brilliant star that he had been watching suddenly left the sky and
reappeared next to him. Asking him to move over a little so that
they could lie together on the leaf, the star began to talk. They
talked all night, and at dawn she returned to the heavens.

This happened for five nights. On the fifth night the star
woman agreed to marry the man. When dawn came, he put her
into a large gourd, which he hung up in the house, and after that
he would open the gourd whenever he wished, and they would
converse.

One day while the man was participating in the Feast of the
Racing Logs, his sister, who had become suspicious, looked into
the gourd and saw the woman. She immediately sent for her
brother and told him that instead of hiding a woman in his room
he would have to take her as his wife.

The marriage was arranged, and when the star woman had at
last become the man's wife she asked him to make a garden plot.

Since the people at that time ate only rotten wood, leaves, and wild coconuts, the man did not understand what his wife meant. By way of explanation the woman threw up a cotton thread and climbed it to the sky, soon returning with yams. A second time she brought down potatoes.

Fearful that these foods would make him sick, the man refused to try them. But his wife held his head and forced him. It was he who then persuaded the others that the foods were to be eaten.

When the garden plot was ready, the star wife went to the sky and brought back corn, rice, beans, peanuts—all the crops that are now planted. In addition she taught the people to make mats, bags, and the other straw articles in use today.

But the husband proved to be disloyal. Already he had fallen in love with another woman. Offended, the star rose into the sky and did not come back. If her husband had been true to her, she would have continued to bring gifts; it is because of his unfaithfulness that the people do not have all the things that exist in heaven.

This story, from the Apinayé, has been reported from Ge tribes throughout the Highlands. Yet no two tellings are exactly the same. Even among the Apinayé the story changes from mouth to mouth, producing the oral texts that tale collectors call versions or, more frequently, variants.

Since students of myth are often tempted to stray from agreed-upon principles, it is well to go back to the statements of Antti Aarne, the pioneering Finnish folklorist, whose idea of what a variant is, if unexciting, is perfectly clear. As viewed by Aarne, the variant may: (1) omit details through sheer forgetfulness on the part of the narrator; (2) add details, whether invented or borrowed, often at the beginning or end of the story; (3) multiply details by a favorite number, such as three; (4) reverse the roles of two major characters; (5) change a character from animal to human or vice versa; (6) add culturally specific or modern details; and (7) be forced into further changes to keep the story consistent.

With reference to point 1, it can be noted that the Apinayé

teller of The Star Woman, as given above, has apparently
forgotten that the woman first appears to the man as a frog.
Indeed, she does so in other Ge variants. Since the story calls for
her to be placed in a gourd, the teller is now forced into saying
that it is a "large" gourd (point 7).

On the side of invention, as opposed to forgetfulness, the
teller adds that the woman throws a cotton string to the heavens
(point 2). This seems to be new, since we do not find it in other
tellings. Notice also that the hero takes part in the Feast of the
Racing Logs, a culturally specific detail (point 6).

Numerous other observations of this sort could be made.
Eventually we might group the Ge variants into subtypes. This
would be difficult, since the changes from teller to teller are
continuous and overlapping. Among the Bororo, immediately to
the south of the Ge, the story is oddly missing. Still farther south,
in the Gran Chaco, it reappears, now as a clearly defined subtype
in which the woman takes the hero up to the sky, where he
nearly dies of the cold.

Different as they are, all these variants can be recognized as
the same story, with an obvious history of travel from one region
to another.

Not so with The Corn Tree, the second of the three Ge myths
under consideration here. This story resembles The Tree and
the Flood, the well-known Guiana myth that recurs in western
Amazonia and in the Gran Chaco. But not everyone would agree
that the two types are variants of each other.

The Corn Tree

While the men of the village were out hunting and the women
were in the forest collecting food, an old woman who had been
left behind with her grandson took him to the river to bathe him.
The boy was very dirty.

Next to the water a macaw, perched in a tree, was cutting off
ears of corn, which dropped down to an opossum. The opossum
offered some to the old woman, but she pushed him away. He

persisted, pointing to the corn tree, explaining that this was food.

Seizing the idea, the grandmother abandoned the little boy, gathered a gourdful of kernels, and brought them back to the village. There she prepared corn cakes. When her daughter returned from the forest, the old woman told about the good food the opossum had shown her. She proposed that they both grind corn the next day, putting on festive headdresses of resin and white vulture feathers, painting themselves with genipa.

Later the old woman gave cakes to some of the children in the village plaza and told them to bring these to the elders in the men's house. The elders approved of the food, finding it sweet, and sent the children for more. Finally they summoned the grandmother herself.

The old woman entered the men's house and spoke loudly (like a man who speaks in council). All were listening, the men inside as well as the women, who were outside, as the old woman explained how the opossum had shown her the new food.

The women picked up baskets and ran to the river. Before this, when people had bathed, they had always thrown away the kernels that had fallen into the water. Now they gathered them up carefully, leaving the place clean. When they returned to the village, they all ground corn and made cakes.

Afterward the men went to cut down the tree. But its kernels were falling on the ground as well as on the water. In fact, the tree was "as big as the village." So an elder sent two boys back to the houses to get a (better? bigger?) stone ax.

Along the way the boys saw an opossum running to hide in a hole in a coconut palm. They killed it and roasted it, and as soon as they had eaten it they turned into old men. Suddenly their ear ornaments were old and darkened, and their leg bands were slack. They wanted to hurry, but they could only walk slowly.

When the boys returned to the corn tree, they "were old men, and the corn was falling." The people then carried it off through the forest (after the tree was cut down?), and today, as a result, everyone has corn.

Told by a Shikrí Cayapó, this version fails to explain why the boys were sent home for a stone ax, making it seem as though the men at the river did not already have axes. Moreover, it does not tell us that the tree was finally cut down. These details are supplied by other versions, which make clear that the corn tree was so hard to cut that a better or at least an additional ax was needed.

Turning now to The Tree and the Flood, we can see a certain similarity between the two myths. In both, a miraculous tree is cut down and its benefits dispersed. But there are important differences. The greedy animals of the Guiana variants are here replaced by generous animals. There is never a flood, no fish-filled water gushing from the stump. Yet, curiously, the Ge stories always mention kernel-filled water flowing beneath the corn tree.

If we dig beneath the story line, imagining that the myth has an underlying structure, we may say that in both the Guiana and the Ge versions there is *food-filled water in a low position.* As for the animal characters, we may decide that the *greedy* neatly opposes the *generous,* revealing the Guiana and Ge types to be perfect opposites—hence symmetrical—in this regard.

The concept of underlying, or "deep," structure as applied to myth was introduced in the 1950s and 1960s by Claude Lévi-Strauss, who spoke of structurally similar myths as being "trans-formations," not variants, of one another. Evidently the term "variant" is not appropriate for this kind of relationship, which, in any case, remains theoretical.

The question whether transformations could develop natu-rally as myths travel from mouth to mouth must be left open. In short, it cannot be demonstrated that transformation actually takes place. But even if artificial, the concept has proved stimulating, awakening a new respect for the artistry and intel-lectual content of myth, especially South American myth, which formed the subject matter of Lévi-Strauss's best-known studies.

We are now ready to consider the surprising fact that The Twin Myth is absent from Ge collections and to take a careful look at The Bird Nester and the Jaguar, which is perhaps the most typical of all Ge stories.

The Bird Nester and the Jaguar

A boy was taken by his sister's husband to a cliff where macaws were nesting. So that the boy could get to the nestlings, the brother-in-law looked for a long pole, found one, and set it against the face of the rock.

The boy climbed up and saw the young birds. But instead of throwing them down, he lied and said there were only eggs. The brother-in-law asked for one. To taunt him, the boy threw down a white stone, hitting the brother-in-law's hand with such force that it made him dizzy. Angry, the brother-in-law threw the pole aside and returned home, leaving the boy stranded.

Night fell, and no one came. The next day the boy began to be thirsty. Three days passed. At last, hearing the roar of a jaguar, the boy called down, offering to throw the jaguar a young macaw. He explained that his brother-in-law had abandoned him, and he was now very thirsty.

The jaguar ate the macaw, and as the boy threw down the remaining birds, he asked the jaguar to save him one. But none were saved. When all the macaws had been eaten, the boy asked for the pole. Then the jaguar set it against the cliff, and the boy climbed down, even though he was fearful that he, too, would be eaten. But the jaguar was friendly and took him to a waterhole. The boy drank it dry.

Amazed, the jaguar led him to another pool, where again he drank all the water. Then he took him to a river, and he drained it completely. After that he rested. They talked, and the jaguar invited him to his house.

When they got there, the jaguar's wife was irritated because her husband had brought home only a "grandson" and no fresh game. There was roasted peccary on hand, which the boy ate while warming himself by the fire. This was a novelty, since the boy's own people did not have fire at that time.

The boy lived on with the jaguars. After many days the jaguar's wife called to him and said she would louse him. She picked a louse from his head, showed it to him, and at the same time opened her mouth. This terrified the boy, and he screamed.

The jaguar reprimanded her. Nevertheless she did it again. Finally he ordered her out of the house. Then he told the boy that he would prepare a stick of Mauritia palm for him to use against her the next time she frightened him.

The following day the old woman again called her "grandson" so that she could louse him. But when she opened her mouth, the boy, armed with the stick, shoved it into her throat as far as it would go. Howling with pain, she ran into the forest and became an anteater.

The boy now felt that he was ready to go home. He missed his family. To prepare him for his journey, the jaguar packed him a basket of grilled meat, warning him not to tell anyone about the fire or he would eat him. The boy was simply to say that the meat had been cooked on a warm stone.

When the boy got home, he pulled his brother-in-law away from his sister, threw his belongings outside, and sent him off to his own house. Then the meat was divided among all the people in the village. They marveled at how well cooked it was. Pressed to reveal the secret, the boy finally told them that the jaguar had fire.

While the jaguar was sleeping, they went to his house and stole the fire. He woke up cold, and his house was dark. Now the people had fire, and the jaguar said, "If that's how it is, then from now on I'm going to eat you!"

The story as given here in condensed form is from the Shavante teller called Jerônimo. It is of a type that is remarkably consistent from one Ge tribe to the next and apparently lacking elsewhere, even though some of the individual story elements are far-flung. A list of these would include the bird nester episode, the lousing incident, and the theft of fire.

Observe, however, that the structure of the story can be described in this manner: *the hero is abandoned by a male relative, then taken to the house of the jaguar and the jaguar's wife; menaced by one of these two, he takes his revenge and leaves to seek out the relative who had abandoned him.*

In The Twin Myth, by contrast, the hero is doubled; there are two of him. But otherwise the underlying plot is the same: the twin heroes are abandoned by their father, then carried (by their mother) to the house of the jaguar and his wife; threatened by the jaguar (who kills the mother and prepares to eat the twins), they eventually accomplish their revenge and set out to find the male relative (that is, the father) who had deserted them.

Looked at in this way, the story elements take on a detached, almost symbolic quality, like the images in a poem. At the same time there may be enough hard evidence here to show that The Bird Nester and the Jaguar is simply a remote variant, or perhaps a "transformation," of The Twin Myth. Readers can decide for themselves whether we have the germ of a scientific theory, connecting two very different stories, or a form of literary criticism that helps us appreciate the narrator's art more fully.

The dramatic monologue

It is well to keep in mind that the mythmaker is putting on a performance. Although he is customarily spoken of as the narrator, he may at times become a dramatist, stepping into the roles of the different characters with appropriate gestures and voice changes.

Here, for example, is the opening of The Bird Nester and the Jaguar, the Shavante version summarized above, as actually told by Jerônimo:

> "My brother-in law, let's go and catch some young macaws."
> "All right, let's." They went.
> "Listen, the macaw is taking food to its young; it seems they're already big. You'll be frightened! Quickly, climb up!"
> "What will I use to get up there? Go and fetch a pole for me to climb on."
> "Wait here while I go and cut one."

In print the text reads more like a play than a story, with the narrator himself taking both parts. In the following Suyá variant, told by the (male) narrator Bentugaruru, notice that the conversation between the two characters is supported by narrative fragments given in the present tense, like stage directions.:

> "There are some baby macaws a long way over there. They are already hard [have feathers but cannot fly]."
> "I want to look and see. Let's go." They leave and travel and travel. Finally they arrive.
> "I want a tree trunk [to place against the cliff]. See? It is way over there. I want a tree trunk. You knock one down."
> They knock one down. "Let's go."
> They travel and travel. The tree trunk gets caught. They free it and walk some more. At last they arrive.
> "Now, tell me, what are the fledgling macaws like?"
> "Wait a little. I will climb and look."

Although recent Shavante and Suyá collections may offer the best examples, the dramatic monologue is a technique used by narrators to a greater or lesser extent in all parts of South America. As texts that display this feature become increasingly available, mythmakers, who may have been thought of primarily as poets and thinkers, begin to emerge as lively performers as well.

CHAPTER VII

Myth and Society

The two halves

In the Brazilian Highlands, people within a village interact according to an elaborate set of rules. Nowhere else on the continent have men, women, and children structured their lives with such style or attracted so much outside attention on account of it.

Immediately noticeable is the twofold division of each village, as though an imaginary line had been drawn down the middle. Among the Apinayé and the Sherente the line is east-west, and the halves, or moieties, are assigned to the north and south. In other tribes the moieties lie east and west. Often it is said that each side belongs to one of the culture heroes, Sun and Moon, whose colors are red and black, respectively. Thus red is the color of Sun's people, black the color of Moon's people.

Some say that the halves were established by Sun and Moon in the ancient time, before the two heroes withdrew from the world. These two created humans, according to one version, by throwing gourds into a river. As each gourd hit the surface of the water, it changed into a man or a woman, who stepped ashore. The people from gourds thrown by Sun went and stood beside him, while Moon's people went toward Moon. Thus the world's first village took shape.

The villages themselves have a circular or horseshoe form, with a plaza at the center and houses around the rim. Among the Canela, paths connect the houses to the plaza like the spokes of a wheel, and a great ring-shaped walkway passes in front of each door.

The division into halves, rather than separating the community, helps to keep it together. Village activities are typically organized so that each side is represented. Even marriage rules may be affected. In many villages, women must take husbands from the other moiety. That way everyone has relatives on the opposite side.

The origin of names

The moieties create the overall design, but society is further divided into age grades that cut across the moieties.

Generally speaking, Ge communities grade each of the sexes according to four categories. Among males there are boys, bachelors, mature men, and elders. Females, similarly, are divided into girls, married girls, mature women, and women past childbearing. But subclasses are often recognized as well. Among mature men, for instance, some Cayapó villages distinguish men whose wives are pregnant for the first time, men whose wives are nursing their first child, and men who are heads of families.

Independent of these divisions, the people in some tribes

identify themselves as members of particular clans, or descent groups. In the most unusual case, that of the Apinayé, there were at one time four clans such that men of clan A married women of clan B, B married C, C married D, and D married A. Among the Canela, clans are replaced by fraternal organizations unrelated to the choice of marriage partners.

Understandably, each person's place in society carries with it a set of duties and privileges, and since each person has a particular role to play in village ceremonies, these events serve to dramatize the social order. Moreover, it is on such occasions that people receive the names that go with their station in life, names that are always changing as one passes to the next age class or is initiated into an organization.

Stories that account for the origins of ceremonies and personal names are among the most significant of Ge myths. Typically, the stories tell of a hero abducted by supernaturals, often from the underwater realm, who teach him a ceremony, give him a supply of names, and send him back to his village.

Such tales recall the Guiana myths of the shaman's visit to the other world. An essential difference is that the Guiana shaman returns with private knowledge, while in the ceremonial myths of the Ge the hero brings back lore that he shares with the community.

Among the Canela and the Krahó, ceremonial knowledge comes from water spirits called *kokrít,* who are impersonated by dancers wearing palm-fiber masks. In one of the Canela myths it is said that the youngest age class was returning from a hunt on the Tocantins River when the elder who had accompanied them remembered he had left his bow behind. Retracing his steps, he suddenly found himself surrounded by dangerous *kokrít.*

The old man asked for pity on account of his age, and the *kokrít* took him to their village so that he could observe their dances. After five days the elder returned to his own village, where he demonstrated the dances and showed people how to make palm-fiber costumes that looked just like the water spirits themselves.

In a similar story from the Shikrí Cayapó a shaman's nephew is accidentally burned. To show his sympathy, the shaman burns himself, then jumps into the river to cool off. He doesn't come back up until three winters and three summers have gone by, during which time the fish teach him dances and give him names for the naming ceremony. Virtually the same myth is told by the Txukahamai.

Somewhat different is the myth of the cannibal spirits told by the Suyá. In this story a man is mysteriously captured by the spirits, who take him to their underground village and eat him. Seeking revenge, his tribesmen slip quietly down the spirits' entry hole and set fire to their houses. Then they return to the earth's surface and cover the hole.

Breathing the smoke, the spirits sink weakly to the ground, turn white, and die. When the smoke has settled, the Suyá go back to the spirits' village to investigate. Under a large pot they find a small boy, still alive. They take him home with them, and in the Suyá village the spirit boy teaches the people a set of songs for a naming ceremony and gives them the names that they use from then on. It is said that this happened a long time ago in an "old, old village."

Thinking the unthinkable

Not all Ge myths emphasize social harmony. Nor is cooperation the only theme in Ge society itself. In many villages there are intense rivalries between clans and between particular lineages within the clans. There may also be bad feeling between in-laws. In fact, one of the most troubled relationships in Ge communities is between the husband and his wife's brothers.

When a man marries, he crosses to the other side of the village and takes up residence in his wife's house. He is therefore a stranger in his new quarters, and his wife's brothers resent the intrusion. At the same time he is a guest, who has to be treated with courtesy.

Kokrít body-mask with horns, palm fiber and wood, about four feet wide. Canela, before 1966.

In Shavante households, brothers-in-law must always address each other politely and pretend not to mind when one borrows the other's personal property. If someone offers a man a gift, he will say, "Oh, give it to my brother-in-law."

The myths, however, tell a different story. In The Bird Nester and the Jaguar, it will be recalled, the tension between the boy and his sister's husband breaks into open conflict, with the result that the brother-in-law knocks down the climbing pole, leaving the boy stranded in the nest. Yet it is the boy who starts the trouble by hitting his brother-in-law in the hand with a stone.

In a Suyá variant the abuse is no less flagrant for being strictly verbal. When the boy has climbed up to the nest, the brother-in-law shouts from below, "How are the baby macaws?" The boy replies, "They look like your wife's pubic hair." The brother-in-law puts on a formal manner and demands that the insult be retracted. But the boy merely repeats it, over and over. Finally the brother-in-law takes away the pole, leaving the boy with no way to get down.

In the Shavante version the story continues with further breaches of etiquette. It will be recalled that the jaguar eats up all the baby macaws, ignoring the boy's request that just one be saved. To even the score, the boy drinks all the water in the jaguar's water holes, including the river pool, which the jaguar and his wife must depend on for domestic use.

It is safe to assume that such details are calculated to amuse the people in the audience, who will recognize an allusion to real-life tensions in their own households.

Sun and Moon

Considered hilarious by Ge audiences, the antics of the culture heroes Sun and Moon go beyond bad manners. Calling each other "companion," these two torment one another in an endless struggle to get the upper hand. It may be true that they are creators, but their creations tend to be accidents resulting from their misdeeds, and although they are founders of society, their own behavior is self-centered.

If either has a trace of high-mindedness, it is Sun, the cleverer of the two. Moon is usually the dupe or the clumsy imitator. Good storytellers ring changes on the theme, but the standard set of adventures varies only slightly from one tribe to the next:

Hot meat.   One day when they had been hunting and were roasting meat, Moon complained that Sun had kept all the fat for himself. Annoyed, Sun picked up a piece of hot meat and threw it at Moon, burning his stomach. The burns show up today as Moon's spots. (The widespread story of Moon's sister, who caused his spots by staining his face with black dye, does not occur in Ge territory.)

Fiery headdress.   Sun got his red headdress from the plumed woodpecker, who threw it down to him from a tree. Moon begged for a headdress, too. But when the woodpecker had given him one, he found it too hot to hold and dropped it, setting the earth on fire. (The story is peculiar to the Ge, although the motif of the world fire recurs throughout South America.)

Palm fruits.   Sun has red feces caused by eating fruits of the Mauritia palm. Moon, who has black feces, is envious. Sun shows him the fruits, which are easy to reach, but Sun secretly spits on them, making them unripe on one side. Disgusted, Moon throws a fruit at the trunk of the palm, and the tree shoots to its present height. Since that time the fruits have been hard to collect.

Self-working tools.   Sun secretly clears and cultivates a garden plot with tools that work by themselves. Moon spies on him, and the moment he looks at the tools they stop working. Because of Moon's curiosity, gardening today is hard labor. (The story is found in scattered locations from Guiana to the Gran Chaco, but only the Ge tell it of Sun and Moon.)

Deaths and revivals.   Sun causes Moon to fall sick and die. Moon comes back to life and plays the same trick on Sun, hoping to get rid of him permanently by burying him in a deep grave. But Sun revives and climbs back into the light.

As a rule the cycle ends with the heroes' retirement from

earth, after having done as much harm as good. According to a
Krahó storyteller, the people did not even have anything to cook
with when the two heroes departed, because Sun and Moon took
their fire with them. It is for this reason that fire had to be stolen
from the jaguar.

Toward socialization

Despite their faults, Sun and Moon are not incapable of improve-
ment. It all depends on how the stories are told. If they are given
out singly, as they often are, there is no opportunity for growth.
But in the hands of a thoughtful storyteller the cycle can be
shaped into a sequence that begins with tales of pure ignorance
and self-gratification, progressing toward a state of awareness, if
not outright appreciation, of social values.

This trait was first recognized in the 1940s by Paul Radin, the
great student of American Indian trickster myths, who noted the
"gradual" development of the heroes Sun and Moon in the
Apinayé cycle that had been collected a few years earlier by Curt
Nimuendajú. In a narrative like this, in addition to the mere
retelling of standard tale types, there is undoubtedly a certain
amount of originality and what Radin called "literary remodel-
ing."

As reported by Nimuendajú, the cycle opens with an episode
in which Moon, alone in the woods, gets down on his hands and
knees like an animal and hides when he sees Sun coming.

It seems that Sun had descended to earth first. Moon followed
but landed in the wrong spot. The next morning when he went
hunting, he saw Sun approaching in the distance. At once he
stooped under a feather palm and crawled into the bush on all
fours to hide. Sun followed his tracks and called to him, asking,
"Are you afraid of me?"

"No," said Moon. Then he crawled out and said he had not
realized who it was. Sun told him he had already set up a house
by a stream and had stored some fruit there. He took Moon
along but made fun of him on the way for having hidden. Moon

begged him not to speak of it anymore, saying he had actually hidden because he was ashamed of having missed the spot they had agreed upon.

Sun went ahead. When he came to a wasp nest hanging over the path, he ran quickly by and called back to Moon, "Pick that bottle gourd and bring it along!" As soon as Moon touched the "gourd," the wasps attacked him and stung him all over his face. His eyes swelled shut. Then Sun had to lead him along like a blind man.

But when they came to a log lying across the path, Sun jumped over it neatly while Moon stumbled and fell. "Oh," said Sun, "I didn't even notice that log." He did the same thing three more times. When Moon refused to walk any farther, Sun carried him on his back, deliberately jostling him against branches. Moon wailed. Sun reached around and pinched his testicles, and when Moon screamed, Sun insisted it had been an accident.

When at last they got to the house, Sun pulled out the wasp stings with his fingernails and cured Moon with medicine. He took one side of the house for himself, gave the other side to Moon, and reserved a space in the middle for dancing.

The next day, Sun set out hunting on his own and came across a flock of plumed woodpeckers. Here, then, follows the familiar tale of the fiery headdress, which Sun acquired from the woodpeckers and which Moon coveted.

Later, when Moon had dropped the headdress and set the earth on fire, the two companions sought refuge from the flames. Sun slipped into a potter wasps' nest and was protected by the fireproof clay. Moon, less fortunate, got into a paper wasps' nest and came out all blackened and with his hair singed off.

Afterward they went out into the burned grassland to look for animals that had died in the fire. They found lots of game, and each set up a grate for roasting. All the meat on Sun's grate, when sliced, turned out to be nice and fat. But as Moon cut into his, Sun muttered under his breath, "Nothing but skin, nothing but skin," and all the meat turned out to be lean. Moon complained bitterly.

Here follows the episode of the hot meat, which Sun angrily threw at Moon, burning his stomach.

As usual, Sun excused himself by saying it had been an accident. Then the two brought home their meat and set up grates again in order to dry and smoke the roasted slices. But Moon failed to build a fire under his, and the slices became full of maggots. When he wasn't looking, Sun destroyed Moon's grate, then picked up a piece of peccary meat and threw it at the ground. Immediately the slices that had been on Moon's grate turned into the various species of furry game.

Moon took revenge by knocking down a piece of Sun's ostrich meat. At once the remaining slices became all the species of game birds.

Next, Sun's discovery of the Mauritia palm leads into the tale of the palm fruits. When Moon had had his tantrum and the tree had grown so high that the fruits were out of reach, Sun became disgusted. But Moon declared that it was all to the good, because now a thirsty person can discover water from a distance by climbing the tall palm.

Sun went hunting again and found a nest with two young parrots, which he brought home to raise. He kept the fluffier one for himself, giving the other to Moon. The two fed their birds, took them on their fingers, and taught them to speak.

One day when they returned from hunting together, they were amazed to find a meal already prepared and waiting for them. This continued for several days. Finally one morning they spied on the parrots and found that the birds turned into young women. Rushing toward them, Sun said, "Now you shall forever remain human!" Then Sun and Moon made platform beds for themselves and their wives and lived together with them. (Rare outside the Central Andes region, this story, The Parrot Brides, is not otherwise known from the Ge.)

Now that he was married, Sun thought he had better make a garden. The tale of the self-working agricultural tools here follows, with the predictable result that Moon spoils easy gardening for all time.

In their garden plots, Sun and Moon both planted bottle

gourds. When these were ripe, they took them to the creek and threw them in by pairs. As each pair rose back to the surface, it became a man and a woman.

When Moon had made four couples, Sun caused Moon's next couple to be blind and lame. Then Moon, too, uttered magic words, causing some of Sun's children to develop defects. Both continued until no gourds were left.

Then Sun said, "Let us lay out a village for our children." They looked for a piece of high ground and laid out a circle, which Sun divided by an east-west line, saying, "I put my children on the north side!"

"And I put mine on the south side!" answered Moon. Thus the two moieties arose, *Kol-ti* and *Kol-re*. Then Sun asked, "Who shall rule the village?"

Moon answered, "*Kol-re!*" But Sun said, "No, *Kol-ti!*" And so it was. That is why the Apinayé chiefs are of the *Kol-ti* moiety. Then they married off the people they had created and gave them good advice: "You must multiply. Let your wives smear their bodies with wasp larvae. That way you will have many children."

Then Sun said to Moon, "Now our children are all married. Come, let us go."

"Yes," Moon agreed, "let us go. You shall light up for them by day, and I by night." Then they assembled all the people in the plaza and Sun spoke: "My children, I am going off with my godchild." And Moon replied, "Well then, let us go, my godfather." Then together they rose to the sky.

PART FOUR

Gran Chaco

═══════

Tricksters of the Chaco

═══════

When people were animals

Called Chaco or Gran Chaco, the flat low-lying region centering on western Paraguay takes its name from the old Argentine Quechua word *chacu,* meaning "hunting ground." In fact deer, peccary, ostrich, and lesser game were once fairly common in the arid scrubland of the western Chaco. Toward the east, where rivers spread out and form swamps, ducks and other water birds are still plentiful. But the native people of the Chaco, unable to depend on hunting, must also engage in fishing, part-time gardening, and the gathering of wild fruits—all necessary to survival in an environment notorious for droughts alternating with disastrous floods.

Houses, which often had to be abandoned, were of the simplest construction, grass or palm leaves laid loosely over a frame of untrimmed poles, or even a few mats spread over the lowest branches of a tree. Except in bad weather, people slept outside.

Under the clear night skies, storytelling, now falling into disuse, was once a popular activity. Countless little tales, hardly deserving to be called myths, were and still are told to account for constellations and other features of the heavens. The Pleiades are said to be a band of hunters who climbed a tree to the sky and were stranded when a disgruntled old woman gnawed through the base of the trunk. The Southern Cross, in part, is formed by an ostrich that was chased to the sky by hunters and their dogs. The Pleiades are the ostrich's nest. Or, the Pleiades are a group of people gathered around a campfire.

Although star lore is a constant feature of South American mythology, usually in the form of an explanatory motif tacked to the end of a story, it is perhaps fair to say that folkloric astronomy is a special characteristic of the Gran Chaco.

Among major myths, The Tree and the Flood is well represented, but the region as here defined lies just beyond the southern limit of The Twin Myth. Echoes of Brazilian mythology are to be found in the various tales of the origin of women; and the recurrence of The Star Woman suggests a connection with the Ge tribes of the Brazilian Highlands.

Chaco lore is best known, however, for its trickster cycles. The culture heroes of Brazil are often tricksters; so are *Makunaima* and other heroes of Guiana, also, of course, Sun and Moon of the Brazilian Highlands. Yet nowhere else on the continent is the world-transforming scapegrace so immediately recognizable as in the Chaco. Those who are acquainted with North American lore will be reminded of Coyote.

As in many Indian mythologies, especially those in which tricksters predominate, the Chaco cycles describe a twilight world where human inhibitions are only starting to take shape.

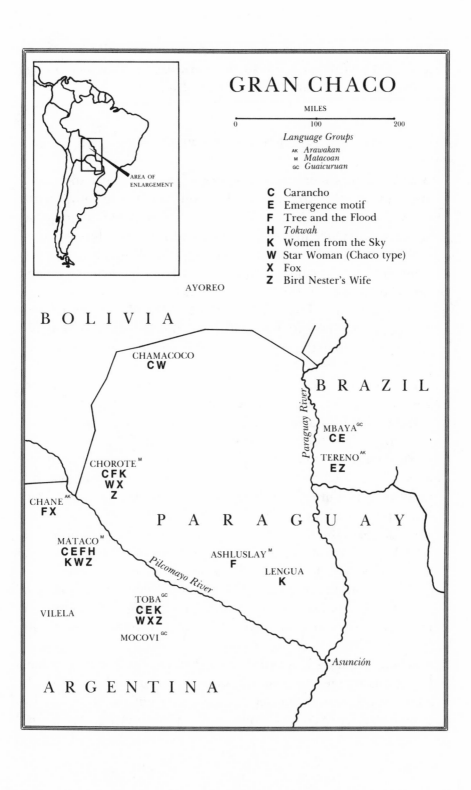

GRAN CHACO

MILES

0   100   200

Language Groups

AK   *Arawakan*
M   *Matacoan*
GC   *Guaicuruan*

C   Carancho
E   Emergence motif
F   Tree and the Flood
H   *Tokwah*
K   Women from the Sky
W   Star Woman (Chaco type)
X   Fox
Z   Bird Nester's Wife

AYOREO

B O L I V I A

CHAMACOCO
C W

Paraguay River

B R A Z I L

MBAYA GC
C E

TERENO AK
E Z

CHOROTE M
C F K
W X
Z

CHANE AK
F X

P A R A G U A Y

MATACO M
C E F H
K W Z

ASHLUSLAY M
F

LENGUA
K

Pilcomayo River

TOBA GC
C E K
W X Z

VILELA

MOCOVI GC

• *Asunción*

A R G E N T I N A

AREA OF
ENLARGEMENT

Like Coyote, the Chaco tricksters are shameless. In the words of a Mataco mythmaker, the stories hark back to "the beginning, when people were animals but were also men."

Thanks to Fox

A detailed treatment of fox stories would show that such tales are known in the Greater Brazil region (among the Chiriguano, the Mundurucú, and the Witoto), the Central Andes (among the Aymara, the Quechua, the Tacana, and the Uro-Chipaya), and in the Far South (especially among the Mapuche and the Tehuelche). Nevertheless, they reach their fullest development with the Chané, Chorote, and Toba tribes of the Chaco.

In Toba lore, Fox is a traveling schemer whose pranks backfire, usually resulting in his own death. Often as not, his corpse dries up in the sun, but with the first few drops of rain he revives and moves on again.

In one story he challenges a vulture to a tree-sitting contest to see who can last the night without freezing. In the dark the vulture slips into a hole, sheltered from the wind, and in the morning, Fox is the one who is frozen to death.

Another time he boasts of his ability to climb a tree. But in the attempt he catches his stomach on a thorn, ripping out his intestines. The innards are transformed into the creeper called fox tripes, which people henceforth use as food.

He admires the hunting methods of skunks, whose poisonous farts kill a herd of peccary. When he tries to imitate them, he merely defecates harmlessly, bagging no game.

Fed up with the tricks that have been played on him, Fox is so disgusted he vomits—and in that spot watermelons spring up. "I must be a shaman," he says. "Wherever I vomit, new plants grow."

When matching wits with Jaguar, Fox has little or no trouble. (Jaguar is dangerous, but his stupidity is proverbial in South American folklore.) On one occasion, Fox got rid of Jaguar by tying a bladder filled with stones to his tail and crying, "Wake up!

Hunters are coming!" When Jaguar had run off, Fox slept with Jaguar's wife.

Another time, while the men of the village were out gathering honey, Fox won the sympathy of the women, moaning that he was sick with a spider bite. He demanded that his sister-in-law nurse him, and when they were alone he tried, unsuccessfully, to seduce her.

Once he changed into a woman in order to marry a man. The newlyweds spent the night together, but the next morning the man was suspicious and placed an ant on his wife's thigh. Bitten by the ant, the "wife" howled with the voice of Fox. Then the man knew for certain that he had been deceived.

Fox offered his services as a baby-sitter. Alone with the baby, he placed his mouth against its buttocks and sucked out its insides, leaving only the skin.

He pretended to be a missionary with gifts for the people. When they asked him for maté (an herb tea), he gave them horse manure.

As can be seen, the Toba vision of Fox includes few benefits for humankind. Not so with Fox as he appears among the Chorote, who make him the dubious hero of The Tree and the Flood.

It seems that the bottle tree (*Chorisia insignis*) once contained all the water that there was and, naturally, all the fish. The tree had a door, which only the tree's owner could unlock. Fox stole the key. Without thinking, he opened the door wide and the water rushed out, causing the great deluge. Fox himself drowned, and his body floated on the surface. Meanwhile more and more water kept coming, bringing with it dorado, surubim, and all the other fish as well.

The Chorote also say that Fox planted the first algarroba, or carob, an important tree of the pea family whose pods are ground into flour or brewed into beer; and the same story has been reported from the Chané. Say the Chorote, "We give Fox thanks for what he did."

Tokwah, lord of the dead

Among the Mataco many of Fox's adventures are assigned to
Tokwah, a trickster not identified with a particular animal. Like
Fox, he is indiscriminately amorous and always hungry, traveling
from place to place. He wears clothes, though at times he
"thinks" he is an animal. Some say *Tokwah* is a little man.

In Mataco versions of The Tree and the Flood it is usually
Tokwah who releases the water from the bottle tree. At first the
entire ocean was enclosed in the tree, and when people needed
food, all they had to do was draw out a few fish. They were
careful to take only the small fish, but *Tokwah* was greedy and
hooked the enormous dorado. As it thrashed in the water, it
broke the tree, and the flood came forth.

Tokwah drowned and his body was swept to the sea. In one
version he tries to outrun the water. As the waves roll closer, he
becomes frightened and transforms himself into a palm tree.
The waves catch the tree; its leaves flutter and the tree falls.
Then he changes into a deer. Even so, he cannot run fast
enough. He becomes a gourd, but the waves smash it, and
Tokwah is killed.

In other versions he leads the water to the sea, carrying a staff
as he walks along. At night when he rests, he sticks the staff into
the ground, and it holds back the water until he is ready to set
out again the next morning. In this manner one or more rivers
are formed, and the fish are brought to the ocean. During their
annual upstream run, *Tokwah,* or at least his soul, comes with
them. It is said that *Tokwah* is the master of fish.

Tokwah is also the fire bringer. It was he who stole it from the
jaguar. He snatched a firebrand and ran with it, and as the
jaguar chased him, *Tokwah* hit the torch against particular trees,
which absorbed the flames. Later he showed the people which
trees these were, so that they could use them for kindling.

(In other Mataco stories, Jaguar's fire is stolen by either Rabbit
or Guinea Pig. Such myths are extremely variable in the Chaco;
for example, among the Toba, Rabbit owns fire, and Hummingbird is the one who steals it.)

Tokwah left many gifts, some of them less than welcome. He gave birds their colors. He taught the arts of dyeing and weaving. He made procreation possible by giving men their "milk." That is, he inserted a thorn into a toad's anus, causing it to exude a secretion all over its body, which he then dipped up with little meadow flowers, daubing it on the men's genitals— thus the origin of semen. Then he introduced adultery and, with adultery, murder.

Tokwah made death permanent by scaring away ghosts that tried to return. When the first man died, permanently, *Tokwah* taught burial customs. He is regarded by the Mataco as the lord of the dead.

Carancho

One of the familiar sights of the Chaco is the caracara or carancho, a long-legged vulturelike hawk that spends much of its time on the ground scavenging for whatever is foul or rotten. Imagined as human, the bird is equally familiar in the region's mythology. In stories told by the Mbayá, a tribe at the eastern edge of the Chaco, Carancho is the troublemaker. It was he who insisted that honey be placed inside of trees, so that it would be hard to get; and it was he who advised people to steal and murder.

The Chamacoco, the Toba, and the Chorote make Carancho the fire bringer. The Chorote say that he stole the fire from the anaconda. According to the Toba, he spoiled the easy hunting of ancient times by making animals wild. Formerly they were tame and would come when called.

These are all typical trickster roles, but Carancho is not a trickster in the full sense. He is never silly, never the dupe, and in many of the Toba myths about Fox he plays the part of the wiser, more level-headed companion.

In one of the stories it is said that the people of the old days were without fire, and because they had to eat their food raw, they were in constant danger of being transformed into animals. Some had already lost the power of speech. Unfortunately, their village was surrounded by water, and this water, which was armed with war clubs, would beat the people to death if they tried to cross over to look for fire.

Taking pity on the villagers, Fox and Carancho made plans to rescue them. But Fox, who went first, had the foolish idea of flying over the water with wings that he had made by gluing feathers to his fur.

When Fox had crashed to the ground and broken his neck, Carancho said, "I foresaw it. I am the only one who can help people, and nobody else."

Approaching the water, Carancho spoke to it sternly. It relented, and he crossed over without incident. When he reached the village, he threw heated arrowheads into the water, drying it all up. Then he showed the villagers how to use the fire drill, and from that time on, they were able to make fire on their own.

In the story of Fox pretending to be a missionary it is Carancho who unmasks him. In another tale the two companions instruct the people in the treatment of snakebite, but it is Carancho who takes the leading role.

In yet another kind of story, well developed among both the Toba and the Chorote, Carancho is the monster slayer. In tale after tale he kills ogres, ogresses, water monsters, killer birds, and man-eating beasts. Cycles of this sort, combined with the fire-bringer and doctoring myths, show Carancho, despite his trickster tendencies, to be a more well-rounded culture hero than either Fox or the death-dealing *Tokwah*.

———————

Dangerous Women

———————

The Bird Nester's Wife

The Gran Chaco appears to be just beyond reach of the story of the female warriors, or Amazon myth, which has not been reported farther south than Bolivia and southern Brazil. Yet the theme of conflict between the sexes persists, giving rise to a variety of myths that betray men's fear of women, including, among the Chamacoco at least, a ceremonial myth on the subject of male domination.

Some of the continent's fiercest ogresses are to be found in Chaco lore, monsters that masquerade as ordinary wives and mothers until their fury spills over, almost always without warning.

The story that will here be called The Bird Nester's Wife is both typical and widespread. It tells of a woman who takes her husband into the woods to capture parrot nestlings—a classic situation in American Indian myth and one that always bodes ill.

In a Chorote version the woman is supposed to have been pregnant. She has a craving for baby parrots, she says, and knows the whereabouts of a nest. Her husband readily agrees to go with her, since nestlings are a delicacy, grilled or roasted.

But when the husband hoists himself into the tree and throws down the first of the baby birds, the woman hides her head in her carrying bag and eats the bird raw, leaving only the wings.

"Here is another one!" he says, and the same thing happens. After four birds have been eaten, the husband begins to be suspicious. He calls to his wife, asking her if she is in fact eating the nestlings.

"Oh no," she says, and to deceive him she rattles the wings in the bag as though the birds were still alive and fluttering.

The next time, the husband watches her carefully and becomes even more suspicious. He asks himself whether he should climb down. "Now it is my turn to be eaten," he thinks.

In the Toba variants the husband hits on the idea of throwing down a nestling that is already able to fly. As the woman runs to catch it, the man quickly climbs out of the tree and tries to escape. But his wife overtakes him and kills him by breaking his neck with her teeth. She devours his body on the spot, saving the head for later.

The more unrestrained Chorote version has him armed with an ax, which he has taken into the tree in order to enlarge the nest hole. To save himself, he throws the ax at his wife, but it only grazes her head, leaving a shallow cut. As the blood trickles down, she begins to lick it, confirming the man's fears. Seeing that she is a cannibal, he refuses to come out of the tree. Finally, as the sun sets, he relents and descends into her arms. She bites his neck, breaking it, then devours him entirely, saving only his testicles, which she carries home. These she cooks with greens, and when the dish is ready she invites the neighbors in.

In both the Chorote and the Toba versions the people are soon alerted to the woman's true nature. With the help of Fox, the Chorote set a snare for the cannibal, capture her, and burn her alive. In one of the Toba variants, Carancho is called in, and again the woman is caught in a trap. Carancho kills her by cutting off her head and her "paws"; then the people set her on fire. From her ashes springs the first tobacco plant.

The Tereno, likewise, use the story to explain the origin of tobacco. At the same time, it is clear in most versions that the wife has been transformed into a jaguar. She is called jaguar woman by Toba storytellers, and among the Mataco the myth supposedly accounts for the origin of this species.

In the words of a Mataco narrator, "jaguars are women." Or, expressed a little differently by another teller, "in ancient times the jaguar was a woman."

Woman shaman

The practice of shamanism is generally reserved for men. Yet in many tribes there are at least a few women who are skilled in the art and who are able to attract clients. Such a shaman is the dreadful heroine of a Toba story in which the woman's services as a chanter, up to a point, are much appreciated by hunters.

While the men are out on the lagoon bird hunting, the woman recites incantations. Successful, the hunters return to the village, making sure to repay the woman with food. When a man brings her a bird, she says, "I give you power. You won't feel fatigue."

But there was a woman who became jealous and accused the shamaness of being a witch, saying the men gave her food only because they were afraid of her. "I am not a witch but a good shaman," she replied. "How dare you reproach me for the birds I receive?"

Offended, she made up her mind to take revenge. She said to herself, "Tomorrow people will get birds, but the day after tomorrow I shall destroy them."

That night she chanted continuously. The next day the men went to the lagoon and came home loaded with young birds. On the following day they again went to the lagoon, but as they were about to return, the wind started to blow.

They all cried, "Run for your life!" A whirlwind arose and pushed the water from all sides. They saw that there was no escape. They climbed trees, but the water kept rising, and the men were all drowned. The birds scattered. The shaman woman was chanting.

After that the woman left the village where she had been insulted and moved to a new village where people built her a house and, respectful of her power, used "nice words" whenever they spoke to her.

The mother of birds

The Chorote tell stories of the huge cannibal woman *Tséhmataki*, who used to come in the night, knocking down houses. When people heard her, they ran and hid in the bush. Some said she softened the ground so that her victims could not run away. With her large teeth she ate young and old alike. She even ate dogs.

It is said that on one occasion the people were forewarned and fled to a distant country, all except one old man, a shaman, who stayed behind and built a sturdy house of quebracho logs. No sooner had he finished the house than *Tséhmataki* was heard in the distance, causing earthquakes as she came.

When she reached the log house, she smelled fire and called out asking for a firebrand, saying she was cold and wanted to warm herself. For answer the old man let fly an arrow, the tip of which he had dipped in hot wax. It hit her in the eye, and she fell over dead with a terrible noise. All the people who had retreated to faraway places could hear the crash and feel the earth shaking. They suspected that the old man had killed the ogress, but they were not sure.

To let them know that the place was now safe, the old man cut off the cannibal woman's long red tail, tied it around his dog's neck, and sent the dog off as a messenger. The people had moved so far away that it took the dog many days to reach them all. Finally, when he had found the last one, he had so many blisters he could not walk home and had to be carried.

Meanwhile the old man burned the ogress. From her ashes came vampire bats and different kinds of birds, the rufous ovenbird, the burrowing owl, the striped cuckoo, and others. For this reason *Tséhmataki* is known as the mother of birds.

From the ogress's ashes still other creatures arose, including howler monkeys, which, like the birds, are shamanic helpers. The last thing to come out was a tobacco plant, which grew to the height of a person. When it had flowered, the people gathered the seeds, and from then on they planted tobacco.

The tobacco that grows today, however, is small. Only in the underworld does it grow as tall as a person. *Tséhmataki* herself, it is said, originated in the underworld.

Star Woman's husband

As told by the Ge tribes of the Brazilian Highlands, The Star Woman is usually an origin myth, explaining how corn and other crops were brought from the sky by a supernatural bride. In one version, as we have seen, the woman's husband betrays her. In the Gran Chaco variants, by contrast, it is the man who is persecuted, not only by his bride but by other women as well.

In a version given by a Mataco storyteller the hero is described as an "extremely ugly" young man who was "always dirty." He wanted a wife but could never get one; none of the women would have him. They spit in his face. They spit all over his clothes. (In a Toba variant the women are said to have wiped their noses on his hair.)

When the sky was clear, the young man would sleep outside under the stars. One star in particular, a large, very beautiful one, caught his attention. He called out to it, "Come down and sleep with me!"

The star was a woman. She descended from the sky and came to where the man was lying. She was beautiful, with hair to her waist. Although the man was ugly, she slept beside him, promising to come again the next night with clothes and other gifts.

In the morning the young man's mother asked him, "Son, what woman slept here last night?" He refused to give her an answer.

The following night the star woman came again, bringing "many things." (According to the Toba and the Chorote, she brought fruits and vegetables, appearing as a kind of corn mother, as in the Brazilian Highlands variants. In the Mataco stories her gifts are limited to toiletries and articles of apparel.) She had a comb in her hand, which she used to untangle his hair. In this way she made him handsome.

When the sun came up, she went to live with the man in his mother's house. At midday, when it was hot, they went to the water together. The women who had rejected him now followed him, gazing at his fine clothes. But when they tried to take him away from his bride, he scolded them. He and the star woman bathed together, then returned to his mother.

After four days the star rose into the sky again, taking her husband with her. He was not used to the intense cold, however, and complained that he was freezing. In the morning there was frost. To warm him, his wife covered him with mattresses, but it did no good. At night he nearly died of the cold.

When he was almost frozen to death, he got up to go look for fire. No one had any, it seems, except the Pleiades, a group of some ten women who lived together. He could see their fire in the distance. "I must go there," he said. "I can't stand this any longer."

"Very well," said his wife, "but you have to be careful. Their fire is not to be touched. When you get there, sit down next to it and be still. Don't poke it, or it will explode like a bomb and kill you."

When he arrived at the fire, he found the mistress of the Pleiades asleep beside it. He sat down very quietly. But he disregarded the warning his wife had given him and poked just one ember. With that the fire burst, and the flames enveloped his body, killing him.

The next morning his wife came and gathered up his bones and put them in a little sack. How could she tell his mother what had happened? She called to the owl *chustáh* that keeps its eyes open all night and cries *tah, tah, tah.* "You must go to the mother," she said. "Drag along the bones, and tell her her son is dead."

So the owl set out, dragging the sack. *Tah, tah, tah* went the bones as they bumped along. When the owl reached the mother, it gave her the news: "He has passed away." The mother wept. And to this day the owl, wherever it goes, makes the rattling sound of the bones.

The Women from the Sky

Myths of the origin of humans vary widely in the Chaco, not only from tribe to tribe but from teller to teller. According to a Chorote story, the first people were created by Moon's wife, Morning Star, who put earth into her vagina and conceived a son and a daughter. In a Lengua account the Creator is said to have been an enormous beetle, who first caused evil spirits to come out from under the ground, then produced a man and a woman from the grains of soil he had thrown away.

Stories in which people emerge from the earth have been reported from several groups, including the Mataco, Tereno, and Mbayá. In an Mbayá version not known from other tribes a keen-scented dog is said to have dug up the first humans after smelling their breath through the soil. A different report, also from the Mbayá, has it that the first man and woman emerged from a deep shaft. The opening of this shaft is in the center of a small grove of low, leafy trees at the summit of a hill somewhere to the north.

In all these stories, men and women originate in the same manner. But, as elsewhere in South America, many Chaco mythmakers favor the idea of separate origins for the sexes.

Perhaps the most typical stories explain how the first women came down from the sky after the men had already been created by other means. In such myths the prior origin of the males is simply taken for granted.

Or, as set forth in a Toba version, the men emerged from the earth; then, after the men had established a way of life, the women descended from above. Characteristic of the myths is the threatening, often destructive nature of the feminine intruders.

In one of the Toba variants the men, who are hunters, roast their extra game and store it on the roofs of their houses. While they are away, women climb down from the sky on ropes and steal all the meat. Returning in the evening, the men are puzzled. "Who has eaten our meat?" they ask one another. "No one but us is living here."

When the same thing had happened twice, the hunters decided to post a guard. Rabbit was chosen. But after the hunting party had left for the day, Rabbit went to sleep, and since he was hidden in the leaves, the sky women did not even see him when they climbed down to steal the roasted meat.

The next day Parrot stood watch. "Keep your eyes open!" they all said, and when they had left, Parrot climbed to the top of a quebracho tree and kept perfectly quiet to see what would happen. Soon the women descended and began taking the meat from the roofs amid cries of "This is my house! This is my house!"

Parrot could see that each of the women had two mouths, one above, in the usual position, and one "below" (the *vagina dentata*). They put all the meat in a pile and sat under the quebracho tree to eat in the shade.

Parrot plucked a fruit and let it fall on one of the women. "Look up in the tree!" exclaimed another woman. "There sits my future husband."

Others cried, "No, I am the one who will marry him. No, he is going to be mine." With these words they began to fight, scratching and biting. They hit one another with their fists. They threw sticks, and one of them struck Parrot in the mouth, breaking the bone under his tongue.

The women climbed back to the sky. That evening when the other men came home, Parrot was unable to tell them what had occurred. All he could do was point to the sky and move his hands as if he were climbing a rope.

On the following day, Hawk was the watchman. The women saw him, and when they had begun to fight over him, one of them said, "You may marry him, but I will kill him." Then they all started to pelt him with sticks, which he deflected with his wings. (In a variant the storyteller explains, "He was human, but he had wings. He could fly.")

Finally, tired of throwing sticks at Hawk without hurting him, they said, "Let's go." They started to climb back up the ropes and were already high in the air when Hawk threw a stick, cutting one of the ropes so that a bunch of women fell down and sank into the earth.

Hawk called to the other men, "Come back!" Iguana, who had keen hearing although his ears were very small, heard the cry, and the men ran toward the camp. When Hawk told what had happened, Armadillo dug up the women and gave one to each of his companions.

Hawk warned the men, "Take care! They have two mouths. Don't touch them until I tell you." But Fox could not wait. He attempted intercourse, and his wife bit off his penis, killing him instantly.

Then Hawk threw stones at the women, breaking the teeth in their vaginas. After that the hunters stayed with them, and all the women gave birth to children.

The *Anáposo* ceremony

Among the Chamacoco the myth of the origin of women takes a distinctive form. Instead of harking back to a time when only men existed, it recalls a dangerous moment in the mythic past when women became contaminated by too much knowledge and had to be put to death. Innocent women were then created to take their place, and the world got a fresh start.

The story is closely connected with the boys' initiation ceremony, in which the forest spirits called *Anáposo* are impersonated by masked men. As children the boys were deceived into thinking the impersonators were the spirits themselves. Now they learn the secret of the masks, which they must promise never to reveal. If the women, who innocently believe in the masks, were to share this knowledge, all humanity would be destroyed. The myth tells how an initiated boy once broke the promise and how the men exterminated the women in order to avert the indicated catastrophe.

Secret initiations similar to the *Anáposo* rites appear to have been conducted by the Vilela and may have been known to other Chaco tribes as well. By far the fullest reports come from the Chamacoco and date from the late nineteenth and early twentieth centuries, shortly before this lore fell into disuse.

The purpose of the rites was to make the boy a man. When the time came, two elders would arrive to fetch the candidate, and if his mother objected she was warned that the *Anáposo* would take the boy by force. Led to a forest clearing, the initiates witnessed the masked dances and learned for the first time that the spirits they had always feared were men like themselves. Later, when the spirits appeared in the village plaza, the women would hide behind a wall of mats, and some would press their faces against the ground, knowing that it would mean death to look.

According to the myth, which in part justifies the ritual, there was once a boy who was lying sick in his house when a gust of wind blew some thatch off the roof. His mother went up to repair the damage, and the boy caught sight of her genitals. Inflamed with desire, he seduced her, and in return she pressed him to reveal the secret of the *Anáposo*.

As soon as the men learned that their secret had been divulged, they decided to kill the women lest everyone die. This they did, though one woman escaped in the shape of a deer.

Men now stayed in the village performing women's work. But they were sad and depressed without female companionship. Meanwhile the escaped woman had climbed a tree, and when one of the men passed beneath it on his way to get water, she spit on him and asked him to join her. Hindered by an erection, he was unable to climb up and could only sprinkle the tree with his sperm.

All the men came and tried to climb the tree, but with the same result. Finally they reached the woman from another tree and raped her. At her suggestion they cut her body into small pieces, which fell in the sperm around the base of the tree. Each man then took a piece of flesh soaked in the sperm and brought it to the village.

Later, when they returned from a fishing trip, they were greeted by women, one for each man. Those who had brought home pieces from the woman's thighs had fat wives. Those who had taken fingers got lean ones. Thus the origin of a new race of women.

There can be little question that such a myth represents a male point of view. Indeed, the great majority of available Chaco stories, including all those that treat of dangerous females, have been obtained from male storytellers. In the case of myths such as The Bird Nester's Wife or The Women from the Sky, it is more than probable that women listeners appreciated the stories and offered comments that were calculated to improve the telling. But the *Anáposo* myth, necessarily, was told among men only.

Since the myth itself contained the secret of the masks, to share it with the opposite sex would have endangered the male-dominated society that men evidently felt to be always on the brink of collapse.

Cataclysms

The flight of the *yulo*

During the summer flood season in the Chaco an entire village can be swept away by a wall of water moving like a tidal wave. Yet often in the winter all water disappears, and even the riverbeds are dry. The highest temperatures in South America, rising to 115° F., have been recorded in the Chaco. Yet bitter cold with frost is not uncommon in the southern and eastern part of the region.

Natural disasters that interrupt or completely destroy the life of the world are a hallmark of Chaco mythology, but whether nature itself has inspired this lore would be hard to say. Freezes, blackouts, and especially floods and world fires are mentioned in the lore of many South American tribes. In the Chaco, nevertheless, stories of cataclysms are more noticeable than elsewhere.

Usually the disaster is blamed on a broken taboo or an offense committed against a spirit who controls one of the forces of nature. Such explanations suggest that the dire event, which occurred in mythic times, might be repeated, and in fact recurrences are feared. As a preventive, shamans make regular trance-journeys to the Master of Rain, the Master of Cold, or whatever spirit is to be controlled.

Among the Mataco the shaman induces a trance by inhaling snuff made from the seeds of the *hatah* tree (*Piptadenia macrocarpa*). His soul then leaves his body and flies to the other world in the form of a *yulo* (a large wading bird variously identified as a stork or a flamingo).

If, let us say, he flies to the fire spirits, they will ask him whether the earth has forests ripe for burning. He lies and says no, then returns and claims credit for having saved the world.

Fire

The fire spirits, or "masters of the fire," live either in the underworld or in the sky and are said to cook their food in huge pots, using only the heat from their own bodies. Believed to be made of flames, they are often imagined as a group of spirits but may also be spoken of as a single master of fire.

In the days when people were birds they visited this master because they were hungry and hoped to receive cooked food. Among them was Ovenbird, a man given to giggling fits. Any little thing, so the story goes, would start him laughing.

It made the people nervous to have Ovenbird along, since they knew the fire spirit was sensitive and would not tolerate being laughed at. When the spirit had taken out his enormous crock and had thrown in the beans and the water for cooking, the people looked at one another and said, "We had better be careful about brother Ovenbird."

Already he was beginning to titter. His stomach was bursting with laughter. Someone covered him with a rag so that he would escape notice as the fire master wrapped his arms around the crock and, holding it in a tight embrace, shot fire from his anus. The water came to a boil, and the food was soon cooked.

The spirit served everyone, including Ovenbird. When all had eaten, he began to cook again. The people said to each other, "If Ovenbird laughs this time, let's jump on our horses and get out of here."

As they spoke, Ovenbird was beginning to giggle. They again used the rag, but in their haste they left just a little of him uncovered. As they were all galloping away, Ovenbird included, the spirit heard the laughter and expelled a fire storm. The flames incinerated the riders and spread throughout the world, burning everything. The only one who escaped was Chunga (a long-legged terrestrial bird), who is said to have had an unusually swift horse.

Another story of the world fire, also from the Mataco, has it that the destruction occurred because women left their husbands and took up with other men. As punishment, a black cloud came from the south and covered the whole sky. Lightning struck, and thunder was heard. Yet the drops that fell were not like rain. They were like fire. The people tried to save themselves by jumping into the river, but the water was boiling. All but a few died.

A somewhat similar myth from the Toba tells how jaguars began to eat the moon in the middle of the night while people slept. It was pieces of the moon, falling to earth, that set the world on fire.

Man on horse. The rider, with his prominent navel, is completely encircled by the figure of the horse, whose tail is represented by the microbelike design at top left; the similar design at bottom center represents the horse's teeth.
Drawing by an Ashluslay boy, before 1912.

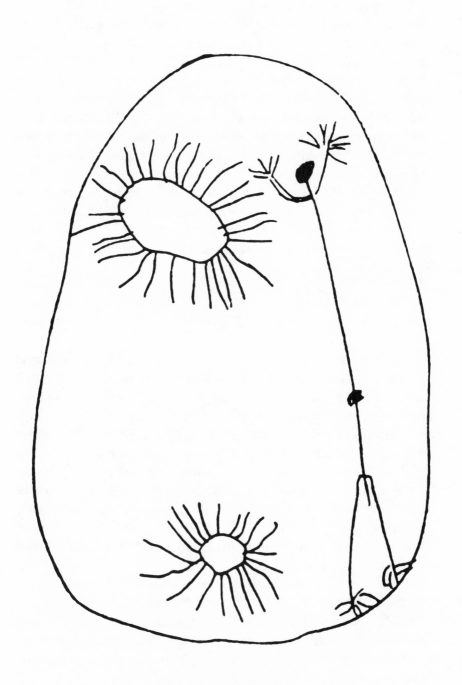

According to the Mocoví, it happened when the sun fell from the sky. Rivers of fire spread everywhere. When a man and his wife, who had tried to save themselves by climbing a tree, looked down at the earth, a flame leaped up and singed their faces, turning them into monkeys.

In one of the many Toba versions, people fled to the sky, becoming the various constellations. Among them were three old women, who may now be seen as the "old ones" (the bright stars of Orion's belt). Three children became the *piyolka* (probably the three small stars in Orion's sword). A group of boys became the Pleiades. At this time the Ostrich (the Southern Cross) ran to the sky, pursued by two dogs (the stars alpha and beta Centauri). Still other stars were formed in the same way, while survivors who stayed on earth, hiding in caves, were transformed into animals.

Flood

As we have seen, it was the trickster who caused the world flood by releasing the pent-up waters of the bottle tree. But although this is the principal flood myth of the Chaco region, it is not the only story of its kind.

A tradition among the Chorote says that at one time there were a great many people, "as many as in Buenos Aires." Suddenly the earth sank. Then, as in a dry riverbed, water began to seep out. It kept rising until it became a flood. A number of boys were saved by a white bird that fished them out, while all the other people drowned.

According to a rival tradition, also from the Chorote, the flood was caused by heavy rains.

Rains are again the cause in a well-known Toba and Mataco myth, which assigns ultimate responsibility to a menstruating woman. It is said that Rainbow does not like "women with blood" to enter the water. Even to go for a drink is not allowed. In former times the cataclysmic rains were unleashed when a thirsty young woman broke this taboo.

As was proper, the young woman stayed indoors while her mother and sisters went out into the bush. However, they had forgotten to leave her any drinking water. Driven by thirst, she went down to the lagoon. When she had returned to the house, Rainbow arrived, full of anger. A strong wind arose, accompanied by whirlwinds and heavy rain. In the ensuing flood, all were drowned. Thus "the word of Rainbow was accomplished."

Cold

Several myths of the great cold have been reported from the southern Chaco, especially from the Toba. In one of the stories the disaster is said to have been predicted by *Asin*, a minor hero of Toba mythology. The following version was collected by Alfred Métraux:

"*Asin* told a man to gather as much wood as he could and to cover his hut with a thick layer of thatch, because a time was coming when the weather would be extremely cold. As soon as the hut had been prepared, *Asin* and the man shut themselves inside and waited.

"When the cold weather set in, shivering people arrived to beg a firebrand from them. *Asin* was hard and gave embers only to those who had been his friends. The people were freezing, and they cried the whole night. At midnight they were all dead, young and old, men and women.

"The wind was blowing, making 'Sssss,' and tearing off the thatching of the huts. Therefore, people and animals were dying.

"This period of ice and sleet lasted for a long time and all the fires were put out. Frost was as thick as leather. When the people were all dead, *Asin* made them fly. He changed the old men into *yulo* birds. He transformed the adolescents into ducks and herons and the middle-aged people into vultures. There was an old man who had taken refuge in a well. *Asin* changed him into an alligator. Old women were turned into chaja birds [refers to one of the so-called screamers, large clumsy birds with trumpet-like voices]. And women with children were changed into anteaters.

"*Asin* performed all these things by blowing and clapping his hands."

Darkness

In relating a Toba tradition about the great darkness, a narrator once commented that the event had occurred "because when the earth is full of people it has to change. The population has to be thinned out to save the world." Evidently the same line of reasoning explains the Chorote tradition of the world flood, mentioned above, which occurred when the people had become "as many as in Buenos Aires."

In the case of the long darkness the sun simply disappeared, and the people starved. As they ran out of food, they began eating their children. Eventually all died—except those who had many children.

A more usual rationale, involving an offended spirit, is given in connection with a Vilela myth about the Master of Night. This spirit, who lived among the people as an ordinary man, had a wife and children. When his children complained to him that the boys in the neighborhood were bullying them, the man ordered his wife to make a long rope of caraguata (tough silky fibers of the *Bromelia argentina*), which he tied from his house to the lagoon. Then he caused night to cover the earth.

Enveloped in absolute darkness, the people were unable to get food or even draw water from the lagoon. Only the Master of Night and his children could get to the water, which they reached by following the rope of caraguata.

People were starved to the point of eating their dogs. Those who had no dogs kept praying for the return of daylight.

One day the Master of Night heard algarroba pods fall on the roof of his house, and he knew that a whole year had passed since he had caused night to settle over the earth. His wife begged him to restore daylight. In reply he summoned a strong wind, which blew away not only the darkness but the thatched houses as well. Then the Master of Night went to take a look at the people and found them so weak that they crawled on all fours. This was their punishment.

Apparently the crime of bullying children, though serious enough, does not deserve death. As we have seen, however, darkness and the other cataclysms generally result in the total or near-total destruction of humanity.

The restoration of life

In place of creation myths, Chaco narrators tell stories about the reestablishment of the world after one of the cataclysms. For instance, the Chorote say that after the flood there appeared a man, who gave birth to a girl from his hand. He married her, and from these two are descended the people of today.

A completely different story, again from the Chorote, tells how the earth was reborn after the great fire. It is said that Moon, who had previously made the earth, the plants, and the trees, escaped to the sky by climbing a fire-scarred quebracho tree, the only thing that had been left standing. From above he sent a heavy rain, and the burned tree began to sprout buds.

More elaborate tree-of-life myths are told by the Mataco, who assign the creative role to the algarroba tree. It will be recalled that the only "person" to survive the fire was the bird Chunga, whose horse outran the flames. It was Chunga who discovered the little sparrow who in turn planted the algarroba that saved the world.

Known as *tus* in the Mataco language, the chunga is imagined as standing alone after the fire, like a creator contemplating the primal void:

"There was a bird called *Tus*. He went on until he reached the top of a hill where the fire spared him and he was saved. When the fire had passed, *Tus* wanted to go back, but there was nothing, not even brush. Nothing. All was bare. Burned-up trees. There was no grass. There was no one but him. When he looked up, he saw only the sky. *Tus* looked for the other people, but no one was there. He was alone. Everywhere there was silence."

Looking more carefully, *Tus* at last saw Sparrow, and the two of them traveled together until they found a place where people had been able to save themselves by digging into the earth. They walked back and forth, trying to break through a hole so that the people could emerge. But it was no use; *Tus* and sparrow, even together, were too light.

It occurred to them that they needed a tapir, and when they had found one and brought him to the spot, he stamped the earth, it caved in, and the people came out. But the sun at this time was very hot, and there were no trees to give shade.

The people appealed to Sparrow, who found a little piece of charcoal left over from the fire and planted it. Or, according to another version, he beat the piece of charcoal as though it were a drum and began to dance. All day he danced, and when he looked at the charcoal the next morning, he saw that a shoot was coming out.

As Sparrow danced, the shoot grew larger, becoming a tree with the trunk of an algarroba. Yet each of its branches was a different tree, and the whole plant become known as the *ayavu ute* (test tree, or tree of trials).

Then Sparrow threw rocks, breaking off the branches. Wherever a branch fell, a tree shot up (which accounts for the different trees found today).

As for the tree of trials itself, also called the firstborn tree, this has become the mystic destination of shamans making their first trance-journey. When their souls have left their bodies, the apprentice shamans fly toward the tree in the form of *yulo* birds. The "trial" begins as the birds perch in the tree's branches. The whole tree then shakes, causing the birds to fall to the ground, where they must elude a pack of alligators before returning to the world of ordinary reality. Having passed the test, the initiate becomes a full-fledged shaman, capable of whatever duties he may be called upon to perform.

The shaman's power is thus connected to the first tree that sprang up after the cataclysmic fire, providing yet another example of the ways in which myth, though it belongs to an ancient time, continues to operate in the world of today.

PART FIVE

Far South

CHAPTER
XI

═══════════

Providers and Deliverers

═══════════

Remote authority

South of the Gran Chaco, the native populations rapidly thin out. No more than a few scattered remnants of the old Puelche and Tehuelche tribes are to be found in the lush grasslands, or pampas, of central Argentina and in the arid prairie lands farther south, known as Patagonia. In Tierra del Fuego, at the bottom of the continent, virtually all Indian life had been extinguished by the mid-twentieth century.

From historical records we know that these people lived a simple, fragile existence dependent on fishing, hunting, and gathering. Many were nomadic, settling briefly and in small groups, with lean-tos or wigwamlike structures called toldos providing the barest protection against the cold.

Hats and cloaks made of animal skins were worn. Yet the Yamana, who roamed the southernmost reaches of Tierra del Fuego, often wore no clothing at all, even in subfreezing weather.

An exception must be made for a relatively small territory in Chile and western Argentina, where an extension of the sophisticated Central Andean culture still survives among the Araucanian Mapuche and Pehuenche tribes. The mythology of these groups, were it better preserved, might show a closer relationship to the Central Andes than to the region here called Far South. As matters stand, there is very little from which to draw conclusions. The most persistent myth, a Mapuche story that is still widely told, is the little tale of the serpent (some say bird) called *Kai Kai* who caused a world flood, from which the people saved themselves by climbing the mountain *Tren Tren*.

Most other stories from the Araucanians are strictly fictional, including adventure stories, horror tales, and humorous anecdotes. In fact, a preference for the art of fiction, as opposed to myth, may be tentatively cited as a characteristic of the Far South.

Moreover, storytellers throughout the region exhibited a rare degree of originality, with the result that we find few standard tale types passing from tribe to tribe. Nevertheless, myths of culture heroes who either provided the structure of daily life or delivered the people from dangers were reasonably common— at least among the non-Araucanians. These figures include *Elal*, the hero of the Tehuelche, and the various pairs of brothers reported from the Yamana, the Selknam, and the Alacaluf.

As a rule, the heroes are not deities. They are simply extraordinary men who lived in early times among the first inhabitants of the land. They do not receive prayers, and they are creators only in a very limited sense.

Standing behind them is a remote power, a figure more of religion than of mythology, which closely parallels the Old

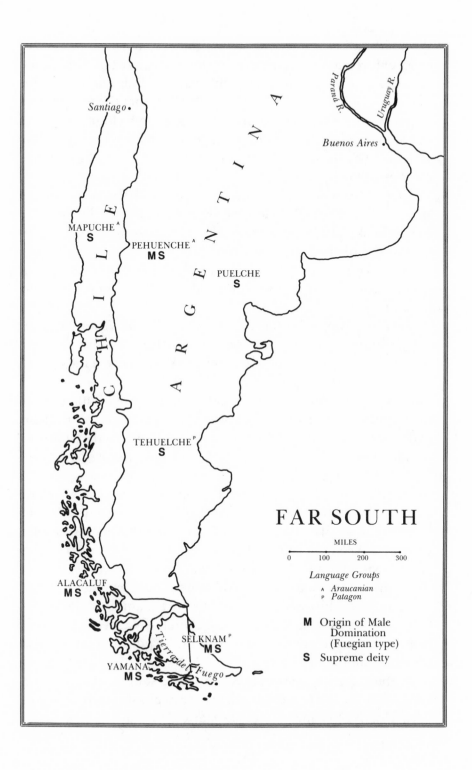

Santiago •

MAPUCHE ^A
S

PEHUENCHE ^A
MS

PUELCHE
S

Buenos Aires •

Paraná R.

Uruguay R.

C
H
I
L
E

A
R
G
E
N
T
I
N
A

TEHUELCHE ^P
S

FAR SOUTH

MILES

0   100   200   300

Language Groups

^A *Araucanian*
^P *Patagon*

M Origin of Male
Domination
(Fuegian type)

S Supreme deity

ALACALUF
MS

SELKNAM ^P
MS

Tierra del Fuego

YAMANA
MS

World idea of God. Varying only slightly from tribe to tribe, the concept is remarkably uniform throughout the region. Occasionally the question of Christian influence has been raised, but the prevailing opinion among anthropologists is that the high god of southern South America is an independent development.

The names and attributes of the deity, as understood by the several tribes from which it has been reported, may be summarized as follows:

Kólas (Alacaluf). A pure, bodiless spirit, *Kólas* is said to be "like a soul after death." He never eats, never sleeps. The stars of the night sky are his eyes, with which he sees everything. He is the creator of the world and of all life.

Kóoch (Tehuelche). His name means "sky." He dwells along at the eastern end of the world. Although recognized as the Creator, he is not worshipped.

Nyenéchen (Mapuche and Pehuenche). Unlike *Kólas*, he has a wife; and unlike *Kóoch*, he is not all-powerful. He is merely the most important of many gods and in this respect stands apart from the other deistic conceptions of the region.

Soychu (Puelche). Vague, conflicting accounts dating from the eighteenth and nineteenth centuries state that the Puelche had a "great spirit" or "God," who gave them all they desired without their praying for it. *Soychu* is only one of the names recorded for this deity.

Temáukel (Selknam). One of the remotest of the high gods, *Temáukel* lives above the stars and takes little or no interest in the affairs of men. He ordered the Creation but did not participate in it. Like *Kólas*, he is a bodiless spirit who is all-powerful, who always existed, and who has no wife.

Watawinéwa (Yamana). The all-seeing, supreme deity of the Yamana was addressed in prayer by such names as "Powerful One" and "My Father." Bodiless and wifeless, he lived above the heavens but intervened in human affairs by punishing those who broke his moral code.

Of these lofty deities only *Kóoch* is the subject of myths. As Creator, he is said to have existed at the beginning, enveloped in dark clouds. Feeling alone, he started to sob, and his tears formed the ocean. When at last he stopped crying, he heaved a sigh, which blew away the darkness, allowing a dim twilight to shine through.

In order to see more clearly, *Kóoch* raised his hand and scratched at the shadows. He thus struck a bright spark, which became the sun. Then he raised an island from the sea and filled it with birds and animals.

As mentioned above, myths of this sort have not been recorded for the other deities of the region. Yet the high gods are felt to exert an influence on the culture heroes even if they are not named in the stories.

The Selknam in particular believed that the acts of the hero *Kenós* were in response to orders given by *Temáukel*. Similarly, the Yamana held that the one who had taught them how to live was *Watawinéwa,* issuing commands to the *Yoáloh* brothers, who in turn passed them along to the people. Even among the Tehuelche the god *Kóoch* is described as simply getting things started; the Creation was finished by the hero *Elal,* who worked out the details.

The *Yoáloh* brothers

The older of the two *Yoáloh* discovered fire by accident. He had collected a number of small rocks and was having fun hitting them against each other. One of them happened to be a firestone. When he struck it, a spark came out.

He used the spark to light a handful of dry down, adding kindling and firewood. "Let's keep it burning all the time, so it will never go out," he said. But his younger brother objected, insisting that people must work to keep the fire burning. He scattered the coals, and the flames died.

The older brother then instructed the people in the use of the firestone. But they had to tend the fire constantly, and if they let it go out, they had trouble starting it again.

In another story the older *Yoáloh* decides that people will hunt birds just by looking at them. He tries out the idea, and when he stares at a bird it drops dead. Again the ill-tempered younger brother objects, decreeing that hunters will have to use weapons and work hard to catch game.

It must be kept in mind that these and other events involving the hero brothers occurred in the ancient time before the origin of male domination. We are not surprised to learn, therefore, that the *Yoáloh* got some of their best ideas from *Yoáloh-tárnuhipa,* their older sister. This woman far surpassed her brothers in cleverness.

When the two men were ready to hunt large game, they invented the arrow. But their arrowhead, though sharp-sided and well pointed, had a rounded base, which prevented it from being securely fastened to the shaft. The sister corrected their mistake by reworking the base to give it a plug shape with a shallow notch on either side. Thanks to her, arrowheads became usable.

Another time, she showed the brothers how to fashion a harpoon with barbs and how to throw and retrieve it using a harpoon line made of hide. When the two reported back to her, they were able to tell her that they had caught sea lions, providing themselves with much blubber.

In further episodes the brothers discover sexual intercourse and, by accident, establish menstruation. It seems that in the early days (but evidently after the time of female domination) Wren had too many wives, while the *Yoáloh* had none. In hopes of reducing their numbers, Wren painted them prettily and sent them around to the brothers. The *Yoáloh* rejected all but the single most beautiful woman, who promptly decided she preferred the younger of the two men. The older, in a jealous rage, raped the woman, causing her to bleed, and this was the origin of female periodicity.

As she wished, the woman became the wife of the younger *Yoáloh.* When she gave birth, it was to a boy who split in two, forming the first "real" human beings; that is, the first people to be born from the womb of a woman.

Permanent death was introduced by the younger brother when his aged mother fell into her "deep sleep." By staring at her fixedly the older *Yoáloh* tried to revive her. When she moved a little, he cried for joy. But his brother rebuked him: "Our mother is asleep because she is very old and feeble. She must sleep now forever!" And so it happened.

Finally the brothers themselves grew old, and when they had given names to all the objects, places, plants, and animals, they went to the sky with their sister, *Yoáloh-tárnuhipa,* and became stars.

Among the Selknam similar stories were told of the hero *Kenós,* who created the first humans, saved people temporarily from the "sleep" of death, then went to the sky as a star; and of the two *Kwányip* brothers, who, like the *Yoáloh* of the Yamana, were accompanied by an older sister. Among the Alacaluf the two brothers were known as the *Yáloh*; they taught the people how to hunt and gather wild plants, and when their deeds were done they rose to the sky.

Elal of the Tehuelche

At first only the armadillo had fire, which he shared with his two friends, the skunk and the pampas cat (a small wildcat of Argentina). To conceal the flames from others, Armadillo sat on them. People began to question Skunk. "You must have fire," they said. "You smell like smoke."

Skunk denied it. But the hero *Elal* sought out Armadillo, kicked him off the hot coals, and lighted a firebrand, which he brought to the people. A simpler story has it that *Elal* merely struck stones together, lighting the first fire in order to keep himself and his companions from freezing.

Such myths cast the Tehuelche hero in the role of the typical provider. He is also said to have invented the bow and arrow and to have taught the use of houses and leather cloaks. By far the greater number of *Elal* stories, however, show him not as the provider but as the intrepid deliverer, who saves the world from monsters.

Elal, it is said, was the son of the man-eating giant *Nóshteh* and the woman called Cloud. Before the child could be born, the impatient *Nóshteh* tore him from his mother's body and devoured the woman, laying the wet infant on a meat drying rack, to be eaten later. His grandmother, Fieldmouse, stole him from the rack and brought him to her burrow, where she secretly raised him. In the manner of heroes everywhere, he matured rapidly.

Before long, Fieldmouse was warning the boy of assorted monsters—including the boy's own father—who would kill and eat him if he strayed from the burrow. Naturally, as with all heroes, he disobeyed her and took her warnings as a guide to adventure.

In one of the most popular tales he slays a swallowing monster from the inside, after entering its body in the form of a fly. In another he subdues the condor that had been carrying off little children and plucks the feathers from its head—which explains why the condor is bald. In the inevitable encounter with his father, the giant pursues him, but the hero stamps his foot, causing a thicket to spring up. The giant then tears his belly on the thorny branches and falls dead.

In bare outline, the story of the hero's birth and early years suggests The Twin Myth of Greater Brazil and neighboring regions to the north. The similarities are not close enough, however, to place it within the same family of variants. Moreover, the hero's later deeds are entirely different.

A noteworthy feature of the *Elal* cycle, included by most tellers, is the story of his courtship. His intended bride, they say, was the daughter of the sun, and in order to win her, he was subjected to a series of tests. The fairy-tale quality of these episodes is established at once: traveling through the air on the back of a swan, *Elal* arrives at Sun's house, described as a splendid toldo, shining with light.

Once there, he is commanded to kill a certain guanaco who is a looking monster (people are literally petrified by its gaze). Then he must fetch a ring hidden inside an ostrich egg so poisonous that a single drop of its yolk kills at a touch. In some versions he is forced to cross a barrier of upturned spikes, made to fetch rocks from an exploding mountain, or told he must bring home the horns of a bull said to be very wild.

Eventually the young woman in question becomes *Elal*'s bride, and, some say, their children are the ancestors of all the Tehuelche.

Cónkel and *Pedíu*

The ordeals of *Elal* have a parallel, if not a variant, in the Pehuenche tale of the brothers *Cónkel* and *Pedíu*, who attempted to win the two daughters of the old shaman *Tatrapai*. In the first of three tests the suitors are given a seat of upturned spikes; they are next required to chop down an oak so hard that it breaks every ax; and finally they are sent to hunt the wild bull (or the cannibal guanaco, according to a different version).

Having gotten through all these trials with perfect success, the heroes claim their brides. Here, however, the story diverges from the Tehuelche model, as old *Tatrapai*, in a fit of rage, kills his daughters rather than give them away in marriage.

To punish the old man, the brothers declare four years of darkness and put their revenge into effect by imprisoning the sun in a pot. Unable to feed himself in the dark, old *Tatrapai* dies. But the world's animals are suffering, too. In hopes of appeasing the brothers, all the birds get together and offer them brides.

One by one the bird women are rejected: the vulture is too smelly, the dove too small, and so on. (Perhaps here we have a remote variant of the myth in which the *Yoáloh* brothers reject the bird brides sent by Wren.)

At last the partridge, inspired by necessity, flies between the legs of the brothers' mule. The startled mule kicks over the pot, and "the dawn comes out."

And there is more. An ostrich, taking pity on the wifeless brothers, now performs a mystery dance that causes human brides to appear. Already, however, we have left the realm of myth and entered the province of the wonder tale, evidently influenced in this case by European folklore.

Unlike the *Yoáloh* brothers or even *Elal,* the Pehuenche heroes provide nothing for the benefit of humanity; nor do they deliver the world from evils. They are merely adventurers, however engaging, who set out in quest of their own fortunes.

Men's Liberation

"Never let them know"

Upon their initiation into the men's lodge, Selknam boys were advised, "Be affectionate with your wives, but never let them know your intimate thoughts, for if you do they might regain the power they had in the past." When each of the boys, in an actual trial by fire, had demonstrated that he could handle live coals without flinching, he was told the secret that gives men the ability to control women.

Although it was recognized that men possessed superior physical strength, this was not thought to be the crucial factor. It was through a clever deception that one sex intimidated the other. Women could do it as well as men. Indeed, in the distant past the secret had been theirs. Men had wrested it from them in a great revolution and since that time had been able to dominate women only by keeping them in ignorance.

Originally it was the women who owned the ceremonial lodge, and it was they who terrorized the opposite sex by impersonating murderous spirits. In a regularly recurring drama, these spirits threatened any husband who did not obey his wife's commands. When the men discovered it was all a trick, done with masks, they revolted, killing the women and sparing only uninitiated girls.

After their revolution the men controlled the ceremonies, and the girls grew to womanhood without becoming aware of the secret. Should they ever learn it, the spell would be broken and the tables could be turned once again.

Among the Selknam the ceremony was known as the *hain*. The Yamana called it the *kina,* and in Alacaluf usage it was the *yincháwa*. The accompanying myth, though not the ceremony itself, has also been reported from the Pehuenche, who are thought to have received it from the Selknam by way of the Tehuelche.

The story is most fully developed among the two tribes of Tierra del Fuego, the Selknam and the Yamana, and is best regarded as a Fuegian myth. Obviously it has points of similarity with the myth of male domination known from Brazil and the Gran Chaco. It is distinctive, however, in its insistence on female power both human and supernatural.

The headwoman and the ogress

The two *Yoáloh,* who were the culture heroes in Yamana mythology, were not the only ones who received instructions from

---

Kina mask. Painted bark. Yamana, collected 1924. Courtesy of the Museum of the American Indian, Heye Foundation, New York.

Yoáloh-tárnuhipa, their older sister. As we know, she was cleverer than her brothers. But she was cleverer than all the other women as well. She directed them, and they in turn told their husbands what to do.

Among the Selknam and the Alacaluf, however, it was Moon who was said to have been the headwoman during the days of the women's *hain,* or *yincháwa,* as the case might be. The woman Moon had not yet become the heavenly body. She and her husband, Sun, still lived on earth as ordinary human beings.

Moon, according to the Selknam, assigned each of the men his daily chores by giving orders to the women, who passed them along. While the men were cooking and taking care of the children, Moon and the other wives spent almost all their time in the ceremonial lodge, even sleeping there at night. Only rarely did a woman sleep with her husband. (The Yamana described the situation in severer terms: "We do not know how children came into being in those days. Since women played the leading role, they would not lie under the men. So we do not know how children originated.")

Notwithstanding their household chores, the men had to hunt and bring home game. When the women were hungry, which was nearly always, they would send to the men for meat, saying they needed it not for themselves but for the ogress *Hálpen,* who was visiting their lodge.

The men dared not offend *Hálpen.* Though huge and sluggish, she had been known to move quickly when aroused, whisking her victims up to her home in the sky. In short order their bones, picked clean of flesh, would be seen dropping from the clouds.

Hálpen had an equally terrible sister, *Tanu* or *Tánuwa,* whose home was in the earth. Seldom mentioned by the Selknam, she was preeminent in the lore of the Yamana *kina.* In the early days, when the women ruled the men, they kept saying to them, "We are looking for *Tánuwa!* We are trying to see whether she will let herself be found, whether she will come out of the earth and enter the great lodge."

But at first they could not seem to find her. So they traveled to another place, and then another, moving east to west through

Tierra del Fuego. Wherever they set up their lodge and performed the *kina*, the surface of the ground changed, and the
country became level and open. Woods and mountains are the
places they missed. Thus the quest for *Tánuwa* shaped the land.

Despite their continued search, they did not find the ogress.
Finally they said to one another, "We shall now fool the men and
call out to them, 'We found *Tánuwa*! She has just come out of the
earth and is with us in the great lodge!' " Then they rolled up
some dried skins, beat the earth with them so that it shook, and
roared and howled as though they were terrified. When the men
heard this, they ran and hid.

Such accounts, though mythic, accurately describe certain
features of the Fuegian masked dramas. The men (not the
women) did in fact invoke *Hálpen* and *Tánuwa*, as well as other
spirits, and when the maskers came close, the women would run
and hide, afraid to look at them.

Flood, fire, and darkness

In Fuegian mythology the men's revolt against the women
assumes the significance of a great turning point in the history of
the world. Accordingly, narrators associated it with one of the
mythic cataclysms that paved the way for a new beginning.

In Yamana lore the world flood is most often mentioned. As
explained by one informant, "The moon woman caused the
great flood. This was at the time of the general upheaval [i.e., the
men's war against the women]. Moon was filled with hatred
toward human beings, most of all toward the men who had
gained control of the women's *kina*. At that time everybody
drowned with the exception of those few who were able to
escape to the five mountain peaks that the water did not cover.
As soon as the flood subsided, they came down from the
mountains to the shores of our channels, and our country
became populated anew."

Another similar account adds the information that Moon
caused the flood by falling into the sea. Later, when she rose to

the sky, the waters receded, and the survivors came down from the mountaintops.

According to the Alacaluf, the event was associated with the great fire. "The men themselves were the ones who kindled the flames and stirred the fire, and everything burned. The men were stronger and overcame the women. They took the women's places, and since that time they have done what they had observed the women doing.

"After the great fire the moon woman ran to the sky with the rainbow. The sun man chased them but could not catch up to them. To this day they have remained in the heavens. And to this day the women are not allowed to know that they themselves were once in possession of the *yincháwa* and that the personages that appear are their own husbands in masks."

The only surviving Pehuenche account is unusual in several respects. It associates the upheaval with darkness, rather than flood or fire. It clearly implies that women, not men, did the hunting in prerevolutionary days, and it puts both Sun and Moon on the side of the women.

"There was a time," so the story goes, "when the men turned against the women. They got together and complained, 'They treat us badly. We have to work while they go hunting. Whatever they catch, fish or game, we have to prepare it for them, and when they're not tracking game, all they do is give orders. We must kill them all. Their existence is hateful, they know no law. We refuse to be *nillan-ché* [slaves]. Let's kill them.'

"So the women were killed, all of them, all of them. But the sun, the righteous *Antu,* had seen everything and said, 'My wife will not light up the night for the men, and I will give them no light during the day. Thus they will have perpetual night. I am ashamed of the men.'

"Then he put on a fur cap and hid under the *koken* [the large hide upon which the grinding stone is placed]. Moon, his wife, looked for him and found him, for a slight vapor was rising up from the skin covering. Then they both hid.

"The world stayed that way for a while, without light, until finally two giant condors carried both the sun and the moon back up to the sky."

The origin of birds and animals

The myth evidently requires that the men get rid of the women, so that none will be left to communicate the secret to girls just growing up. But it is not necessary that the women be killed. They need only be banished from human society. In fact many narrators connected the story of the men's revolt with yet another of the turning points in mythic history: the transformation of the people of the ancient time into the birds and animals of today.

Some said that when the men attacked them, the women, having just finished one of their masked dramas, were wearing body paint in different designs and colors—and this accounts for the colors of the animals we see now.

As the women turned to run, the men threw spears, which lodged in their backsides, explaining why animals today have tails.

True to the nature of mythic thought, these ancient women were perhaps not fully human to begin with. Thus we hear that the man who chased "fox woman" had no spear and threw the next best thing, a winter pepper tree with its twigs and leaves. For this reason the fox has a bushy tail.

"Squid woman," it is said, ran into the sea without taking off her mask. She has remained there to the present time, still wearing the conical mask, or hood, of the *kina* dancer.

According to several versions of the story, Sun was the man who first discovered the women's deception. Walking near a lagoon one day, he observed his own two daughters washing off their body paint and heard them laughing about the tricks they had played on the men. Revealing his presence to them, Sun warned them to stay in the lagoon—where they became ducks. Then he angrily returned to camp and informed the other men. It was Sun, by most accounts, who led the men's revolt.

At the time of the great attack, there was a fat woman who waddled down to the beach as fast as she could, sheltering her daughters with her robes, which she spread over them as she ran. They all escaped into the sea and were changed into the flapping loggerhead ducks, which are not quite able to fly.

"I shouldn't speak of these things"

It may be noticed that The Origin of Male Domination as set forth in this chapter has been given in bits and pieces, picking up the thread of the story near the middle, then jumping back and forth to fill in the details. As it happens, this is the manner in which most Fuegian myths were collected from male narrators.

The men had little interest in telling the tale straight through from beginning to end. Rather, they used it in conversation, piecemeal, to reinforce personal statements or to draw comparisons between current happenings and the mythic past. Therefore the great collections of Selknam and Yamana narratives made by Father Martin Gusinde—around 1920—consist largely of stories reconstructed from fragments.

Women narrators, on the other hand, would tell a story without interruption, introducing the characters in orderly fashion and bringing the tale to a satisfying conclusion. But of course women could not tell The Origin of Male Domination. In theory at least, they did not even know the story. "Maybe they suspected," wrote E. Lucas Bridges, who collected Selknam lore around the turn of the twentieth century. But if they did, "they kept their suspicions to themselves."

Although Fuegian culture became virtually extinct in the 1920s, anyone interested in the subject should be aware of the valuable fieldwork of the anthropologist Anne Chapman, who interviewed the last surviving Selknam people in the 1960s. Her informants included Angela Loij, who died in 1974, and Federico Echeuline, who lived until 1980.

Chapman writes: "On one occasion, when Angela was participating in a ceremony, she whispered to a woman friend that one of the spirits looked human. A man overheard her comment and later repeated it to the men in the *hain* hut. After telling me this,

Angela commented in earnest, 'In old times a shaman would have killed me.'

"One day while Angela and Federico were telling me about the *hain*, Angela left the room for a minute and Federico said to me, 'Even though everything is finished, Angela is a Selknam woman and I shouldn't speak of these things in her presence.' This was forty years after the last *hain* had been held."

PART SIX

Northwest

CHAPTER
XIII

─────────────

Mothers and Their Children

─────────────

Early reports

Long before the conquest of Peru, and even before Cortés
entered Mexico, exploration had begun in the northwest corner
of South America. In 1510, less than twenty years after Columbus' landfall in the outer Antilles, the first mainland colony in
the New World was established at Darién, near the present
border of Colombia and Panama.

Over the next hundred years, while most of native America
remained unaware of the European presence, literally dozens of
chiefdoms east and south of Darién, each with its own culture,

were being exterminated in the rush for land and gold. A few
groups, such as the Kogi and the Yupa, not to mention the
still-numerous Cuna and Chocó, whose lands were less desirable
or who fled to inaccessible retreats, have survived into the
twentieth century.

But most of the tribes of Colombia and eastern Venezuela
persist only as names in old chronicles—Calamari, Tolú,
Patángoro, Dabaiba. And only in rare cases do we have even a
scrap of oral tradition from these cultures. It is therefore
difficult, perhaps impossible, to characterize the mythology of
the region as a whole.

The two great myths of South America, The Tree and the
Flood and The Twin Myth, are minimally represented. Emergence myths, though not lacking, are less prevalent than might
be expected among cultures that practice agriculture. A curious
myth that will here be called The Food-Inhaler Bride may once
have been typical of the region. But perhaps the most interesting
feature of Northwest lore is the great goddess, or mother spirit,
that dominates the mythologies of at least several of these tribes.

Among the earliest reports are those written between 1514
and 1524 by Peter Martyr, who preserved a sketchy account of
the myths from the district he called Dabaiba. Its people, he
claimed, worshipped a goddess of the same name, *Dabaiba,* said
to have been warlike and cunning.

This *Dabaiba* was "the general deity" of the community. But
she was not the Creator. That role was reserved for her son,
"who made the skies, the sun, the moon, and all that is invisible
and from whom all blessings proceeded." *Dabaiba* herself, if
people were careless with her ceremonies, threw temper tan-
trums "like a child" and hurled thunderbolts that destroyed the
cultivated fields. Once, in the ancient past, she had dried up all
the rivers and springs.

Beyond these few details, the deeds of the mother and her son
the Creator are not described by Peter Martyr. He does tell us,
however, that the people had a variant of Moon and His Sister,
the myth that accounts for the moon's spots. Also, they had a
story of "certain heroes" who rescued the world from a pair of
giant man-eating birds.

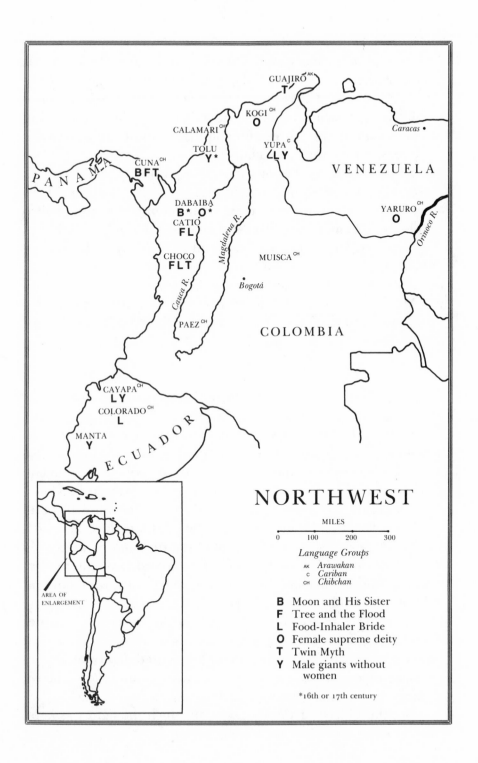

GUAJIRO ^{AK}
T

KOGI ^{CH}
O

CALAMARI ^{CH}

TOLU
Y *

CUNA ^{CH}
BFT

P A N A M A

YUPA ^C
LY

Caracas •

V E N E Z U E L A

DABAIBA
B * **O** *

CATIÓ
FL

CHOCO
FLT

Magdalena R.

Cauca R.

MUISCA ^{CH}

YARURO ^{CH}
O

Orinoco R.

• *Bogotá*

PAEZ ^{CH}

C O L O M B I A

CAYAPA ^{CH}
LY

COLORADO ^{CH}
L

MANTA
Y

E C U A D O R

AREA OF
ENLARGEMENT

NORTHWEST

MILES

0   100   200   300

Language Groups

AK *Arawakan*
C   *Cariban*
CH *Chibchan*

B Moon and His Sister
F Tree and the Flood
L Food-Inhaler Bride
O Female supreme deity
T Twin Myth
Y Male giants without
     women

*16th or 17th century

Briefer still is the glimpse of Tolú mythology given by the Franciscan missionary Pedro Simón in the early 1600s. Of the Tolú, Father Simón writes: "They said that their origin had been from a man called *Mechión* and a woman called *Maneca*, who had only one teat, which collected the milk of both breasts and thus gave it with greater force and abundance to her sons, which is the reason they were so valiant."

This powerful mother of warriors has evidently been forgotten over the course of three centuries. Yet the modern Chocó preserve an echo of her in their tradition of the monster called Tolú Old Woman, who lives in caves and has only one teat. If anyone approaches her waving a club, she squirts milk, making the club so slippery that it becomes impossible to hold.

Considerably fuller and much better known is Simón's account of Muisca mythology with its great mother *Bachué*, who emerged from the waters of a mountain lake and gave birth to the tribal ancestors.

Myths of the Muisca

Conquered by Spaniards in 1538, the thriving city-states of the Muisca, also called Chibcha, quickly faded away, and within two hundred years even their language, once spoken by a million persons, had ceased to exist. Though less advanced and on a smaller scale, their society resembled that of the Incas of Peru.

Moreover, their traditional lore includes a culture hero, *Bochica*, whose deeds are reminiscent of the Inca god *Wirakocha*. As the stories unfold, however, *Bochica* is preceded by the mother *Bachué*, and she herself comes after a primal spirit who stands as Creator.

"They have an account of how the world was created," writes Simón, "and they explain it by saying that when there was darkness, by which they mean nothing existed, light was kept in a large object far away, and to give this a name they called it *Chiminigagua*, and from there it flowed out.

"So, this object, or *Chiminigagua*, in which the light was kept, started to dawn, showing the light inside it—for by this they mean what we call God—and from this first light it began to create things.

"The first were two large black birds, which it sent out from the place where they had come to life, telling them to spread wind, or breath, from their beaks. This wind was all bright and shining, and when they had done what they had been told, the world was lit the way it is now."

After the light had appeared "and all the other things had been created," a woman called *Bachué* came out of a lake high in the mountains, leading a little boy by the hand. When the child had matured, she took him as her husband and began giving birth to children, "four or six" at a time. She traveled all over, leaving people behind her wherever she went.

When the world had been populated, and *Bachué* and her husband had grown old, they returned to the lake from which they had emerged, accompanied by many of their children. Bidding these people farewell, *Bachué* ordered them to keep peace among themselves and to remember the laws and teachings she had given them. Religious ceremonies in particular were not to be neglected. Then she and her husband changed themselves into great serpents and disappeared in the waters.

We are not told what ceremonies the goddess, or female culture hero, had in mind. But at least one spectacular ritual is described by Simón, who says that it was observed several times a year at a certain lake in Muisca territory. On these occasions gold and jewels were thrown into the water, and a chieftain, his body coated with gold dust, rode out in a splendid canoe and was bathed in the lake until all the gold had been washed away.

This, or so many writers have presumed, is the source of the Spanish legend of El Dorado (the golden man), which lured generations of explorers into the jungles in search of kingdoms ripe for plunder.

The story that begins with the spirit *Chiminigagua* and the mother *Bachué* now continues with the account of a second culture hero, said by Simón and other chroniclers to have been an old, bearded man, who passed through the Muisca country, traveling east to west. This was the famous *Bochica,* who established customs, preached righteousness, and taught weaving, spinning, and cloth painting. Disappearing into the west, he left footprints and various landscape features as reminders of his presence.

Shortly thereafter, *Bachué* reappeared, now as a beautiful young temptress who preached vice, pleasure, and drunkenness. To punish her, *Chiminigagua* changed her into an owl, and from then on she came out only at night.

As hinted by the anthropologist Alfred Kroeber, the tale of the mother *Bachué* may represent an earlier Muisca mythology, to which the stories of *Chiminigagua, Bochica,* and the temptress *Bachué* were added in order to reduce the influence of an old female-centered religion.

Myths of the Kogi

Well north of Muisca country, in the Colombian highlands that overlook the Caribbean, the modern Kogi, also known as the Cágaba, have continued to practice an ancient religion based on a female Creator. Usually referred to as *Gaulchováng,* this deity has many other names as well. She is Song Woman, in allusion to the songs and dances that are essential to Kogi worship. She is also Sun Woman, because it was she who created the sun.

In the words of a native priest, "The mother Song Woman, mother of all our seed, gave birth to us in the beginning. She is the mother of all peoples, all tribes, the mother of all.

"She is the mother of thunder, the mother of rivers, the mother of trees and everything. She is the mother of songs and dances. She is the mother of the world."

But the myths themselves are rich in overlapping ideas. The Kogi, it seems, consider themselves to be descended from the jaguar, at least in a spiritual sense. More directly they trace their origin to four "fathers of the world" (some say nine), among whom the most prominent is *Sintána,* the culture hero. Yet these ancestors are regarded as offspring of *Gaulchováng.*

According to the basic myth of creation, the great mother gave birth to the first people, separated the land from the water, and allowed the fertile black earth to be deposited so that crops could be grown. In the most elaborate of the several versions that have been recorded, life as we know it today was built in a succession of nine evolutionary stages, or "worlds," said to have been superimposed on each other.

Gaulchováng herself, fat, beautiful, and naked, and with long black hair, sits on a stone in the first, or lowest, of these worlds. She is imagined in a variety of other ways, too, however, as the myth will show.

As the story opens there is nothing but water: "The sea existed first. Everything was dark. There was no sun, no moon, no people, no animals, no plants, only the sea, everywhere. The sea was the Mother. She was water, water everywhere. She was river, lake, stream, and sea, existing in all places. And so, in the beginning there was only the Mother. She was called *Gaulchováng*.

"The Mother was not a person, not anything, nothing at all. She was *alúna* [soul, life, or desire]. She was the spirit of what would come, and she was thought and memory. The Mother existed only as *alúna* in the lowest world, the lowest depth, alone.

"When the Mother existed in this manner, the earths, the worlds, were formed above her, up to where our world exists today." These were the nine preliminary worlds, containing:

1. The Mother, accompanied by a father spirit and a child spirit;
2. A father jaguar spirit;
3. The beginnings of human life, as yet boneless and without strength, "like grubs and worms," born from the Mother;
4. A father spirit who understood that humans would have a body, legs, arms, and a head;
5. The idea, or plan, for the first house, also the feet of the first human;
6. Legs, trunk, arms, and head;
7. Blood within the body;
8. The fully formed culture hero *Sintána* and the other ancestors;

9. A great tree, also the first temple, hanging in the sky over the water.

Since the earth had still not been created, *Gaulchováng* gave birth to nine daughters, Black Earth and eight other earths. She swallowed half the sea, and mountains appeared. Then *Sintána* said, "Mother, give me a woman."

One by one, the Mother gave him the eight useless daughters, White Earth, Red Earth, and so on, pretending she had only eight to give. Finally *Sintána* took matters into his own hands and eloped with Black Earth, and wherever they ran, the dark, rich soil was scattered.

The tricksterlike personality of *Sintána,* merely suggested in the elopement, comes out more strongly in the myth of the origin of the sun. *Gaulchováng* was the one who created it—or him—and *Sintána* was to put him in the sky. But first he played an elaborate prank in which the Sun was tricked into seducing his own son, whom *Sintána* had changed into a woman. When the truth came out and the Sun was properly angry, *Sintána* made a road for him high over the mountaintops and carried him up to run his course.

Another time the trickster asked the Mother for fire, so that there would be a way to cook food. "No," she replied, "I won't give you fire because it is dangerous." But he kept on asking until at last, worn down by his teasing persistence, she gave birth to a child, whom she named Fire.

Though reluctant to give, the Mother always relents. At the time of Black Earth's elopement she is said to have ordered a lizard to pursue the fleeing lovers, and they barely escaped with their lives. Afterward *Sintána* said, "Mother, I was very afraid. I was nearly caught."

But she replied, "Do not be frightened, my son. I will always save you. You must never be afraid." As he heard her answer, *Sintána* began to cry, and his were the world's first tears.

———

Sun mask. Kogi, collected 1914–15. Museum für Völkerkunde, Berlin.

Kuma of the Yaruro

The mythological pattern of the reluctant female deity and the tricksterlike culture hero is repeated by the Yaruro, a small, much diminished tribe of western Venezuela. *Kuma* is the name given to the deity, believed to be the creator of everything and the ruler of the world. "Everybody sprang from *Kuma*," so it is said, including the little boy *Hatchawa*, the culture hero, regarded as *Kuma*'s grandson.

A conflicting tradition has it that the original ancestors were a snake and a jaguar, both females, from whom the two Yaruro clans are descended. The clan guardians, however, are male spirits, also called Snake and Jaguar, and these two also figure prominently in the myths of Creation.

Some say that Snake was the first to appear and that he created the earth. The water in the rivers was made by Jaguar. Others say *Kuma* came first, accompanied by Snake and Jaguar.

It was Snake who made the first bow and arrow, which he gave to *Hatchawa*, showing him how to hunt and fish.

One day *Hatchawa* found a hole in the ground and looked into it. He saw many people. But when he asked to have them released, *Kuma* was unwilling. She would not let them go. The little boy insisted, and at last Snake made a thin rope with a hook and dropped it into the hole. The people began to emerge, as many men as women. When a pregnant woman tried to come out, she broke the thin rope, and the emergence ceased. This, they say, is why the Yaruro today are so few.

At first the world was dark and cold, because the people had no fire. At this time fire was carried in the breast of *Kibero*, an evil woman who had appeared in the beginning with *Kuma*. At *Kuma*'s request *Kibero* gave the fire to *Hatchawa*. But when the boy wanted to give it to the people, *Kuma* refused. Cleverly he threw a live fish on the fire, which scattered the coals. Then the people seized them and ran off in all directions.

Kuma, it is believed, lives with *Hatchawa* and other spirits in the far west beyond the horizon. In their trance-journeys, shamans visit this Land of *Kuma* and return with song-messages for the people. Typically, the songs begin with the word "Greetings!" and in the stylized scenes etched on the shamans' rattles *Kuma* is shown with her hands raised in greeting to her people.

The Cuna earth mother

A culture hero named *Ibelele* (sun shaman) has been reported for the Cuna of eastern Panama, another of the several Northwest groups, along with the Kogi and the Yaruro, who speak Chibchan languages. In at least one version of the most significant myth involving this hero, he is said to have been inspired by a deity known as Butterfly, Salt Tree, or Golden Salt Tree Woman.

The story in question is a variant of The Tree and the Flood, which, as we have seen, is one of the widespread myths of South America, serving many tribes as the principal Creation story. *Ibelele,* so it appears, descended to earth and made war, sending all the "big men" (giants?) underground. Afterward he caught sight of a woman dressed in blue, singing:

> *salt tree*
> *woman tree*
> *drinking*
> *salt tree*
> *woman tree*
> *drinking*

She was intoxicated and came carrying a fish. To find out her meaning, *Ibelele* built a *surba* (a special enclosure used in the girls' puberty ceremony, which is marked by repeated drinking of the alcoholic beverage *chicha*). The next day he announced to his people, "Yesterday a woman came to me singing. She is the Salt Tree, and in the top of the Salt Tree there is earth planted with crops. There is salt water, sweet water, fish, all kinds of animals, birds, and vegetables."

Ibelele ordered the tree to be chopped down. However, the

trunk was so hard that only a small cut could be made in a day's work. At night, jaguars and an enormous frog would come lick the wound, causing it to heal. In an act of heroism a brother of *Ibelele* killed the beasts, and at last the trunk was cut completely through.

When the tree was about to fall, nets of gold and silver were spread beneath it to catch the foods. As it hit the earth, water poured out, forming the ocean, and all the people came running to the nets and divided its contents among themselves.

"You see," explains the storyteller, "Salt Tree means our great mother who gives us life, our land where we now live, here talked about only in secret words."

The Guajiro animal mother

The Guajiro, who live at the northernmost tip of the continent, preserve a fully developed mythology based on a variant of The Twin Myth, in which the hero *Maléiwa,* after driving off the jaguar that had killed his mother, goes on to drill fire, save the world from the great flood, and establish human reproduction. But this mythology, at least today, is largely rejected.

Instead, the Guajiro pay close attention to the lore of *Pulówi,* who is the underground mother of game animals.

A rich woman, *Pulówi* is known to be stingy with her animal children. She hates to part with them, and hunters who kill regularly are doomed to feel her vengeance. Irresistibly seductive, she lures men into her embrace and holds them prisoner.

It is told that there was once a man who hunted all the time, bringing home deer, goats, and other game to feed his wife and children. One day the game disappeared. Looking everywhere, the hunter was at last able to shoot a large white deer, which slipped under a rock and entered the earth.

Following the wounded deer, the man found himself in an

Shaman's rattles. Yaruro, before 1939.

underground country, surrounded by women. These were the animal children of *Pulówi*. Then, to quote from the text,

Late in the evening Pulówi *appeared,*
The man saw a rich woman coming,
A woman of great riches, immense riches,
Wearing jewels on her ankles,
Chains of gold around her wrists.

It's Pulówi*! It's she!*
What will become of me?
Alas, I'll do what I must!
I don't want my children to suffer!

To demonstrate his own power, the hunter chewed tobacco and spit the juice on the women around him. Immediately they turned into game animals. Impressed, *Pulówi* asked him if he could remove the arrow from the white deer. He did so. And as a reward, so it seemed, she allowed him to return home.

In the days that followed, the man hunted successfully. But one day, without warning, he, his wife, and their children disappeared, never to be seen again. Presumably the vengeance of *Pulówi* had only been delayed.

In another story *Pulówi* is shown as a voracious monster, whose consort, the rain spirit, carries bottles in order to bring back human blood for her to drink.

Yet other tales are told of the game mother's offshore counterpart, *Pulówi* of the sea. A mother of fish and sea turtles, this *Pulówi* is even richer than *Pulówi* of the land. But whoever "steals" from her must outrun the surf, which she hurls after the thief with a terrifying sound: Oú! Ouuuuuuu! Ou! Ouúuuuúuuú. . . .

Reading and hearing

The lore of *Pulówi* was published in 1976 by the Guajiro specialist Michel Perrin, who had tape-recorded the stories before attempting to translate them. His idea was to put the words down on paper in such a way that the reader would have some sense of the listening experience. As can be seen in the nine-line passage quoted above, the narrative does not flow like prose. It comes in bursts.

This is not the same as chanting. But it does display a kind of rhythm we would associate with singing or with poetry. To read the story in this form, broken into short lines, is to become attuned to the live performance. (Cuna narratives with a similarly interrupted flow were also being recorded in the 1970s, following the trend toward greater accuracy in the study of native American spoken arts.)

In appreciation of Perrin's work, one of his Guajiro acquaintances commented, "You have written well what we have narrated. This is good. And so our name will be in a book, and it will never be lost. Later our young men wearing trousers, who have no ears today, may come find out what the old men used to know."

CHAPTER XIV

When Myths Die

Keeping the plausible

Indian tribes are not equally rich in myths. Some, such as the Yamana of southern Tierra del Fuego, may have been so far from the mainstream that few myths reached them. Others, such as the Cayapa and the Colorado in the well-connected Northwest region of the continent, evidently have forgotten the myths they once had.

In the case of the ancient Muisca, whose culture is suprisingly well documented in sixteenth- and seventeenth-century writings, we may feel that the myths are rather few and less than exuberant. Yet the Muisca were one of the great societies of South America.

As a general rule, myths die as a fully formed society becomes either stronger or weaker.

As the society grows more powerful—to take the former case first—it becomes more interested in its own history than in the timeless "history" of an ideal world. Thus we know more about the state-building chieftains of the Muisca and their political alliances than we do about their goddesses and culture heroes. The myths, or at least some of them, are still there, but they have been pushed aside by real persons and remembered events.

On the other hand, a society that is shrinking or in the process of losing its culture tends to simplify its traditional lore, including its mythology. The Cayapa and the Colorado are examples, to which may be added the interesting case of the Guajiro, mentioned in the preceding chapter.

Either way, there is a category of spirits that die hard. These are the giants, witches, gnomes, and assorted demons whose existence is always felt to be plausible.

To speak only of giants, we need remember that these spirits continue to be cherished by Europeans on both sides of the Atlantic; and if the locale is South America, still envisioned as a limitless wilderness, Europeans are all the more susceptible.

In the early 1970s, shortly after the discovery of the Kreen-Akarore, the westernmost of the Ge tribes of Brazil, vivid newspaper accounts in the United States and Europe reported the people as "giants" or "naked giants, whose bodies were painted black." By the middle of the decade the Kreen-Akarore had become better known, and the reports ceased.

As if to take up the slack, a United Press International news story of February 1976 told of a band of red-haired, hunch-backed giants in the jungles of Peru—olive-skinned, barefoot, and with feet twice normal size. According to the dispatch, "one scientist said he *doubted their existence,* but a well-known amateur anthropologist claimed it was *well within scientific possibility.*" I have added italics to emphasize that both the "scientist" and the "amateur" were leaving the door open.

But let us turn to what Indian people themselves have to say about giants, concentrating on the Northwest region, where the theme is particularly well developed.

Males without females

When an attempt was made in the early twentieth century to collect the myths of the Cayapa of northwestern Ecuador, nothing could be obtained except a fragmentary account of human creation, evidently inspired by the Book of Genesis. But if the myths had died, folk beliefs were very much alive, including a tradition that male giants still roamed in the hills.

More numerous in former times, when they would come down to the camps along the river, these creatures took flight after the Cayapa acquired firearms. Between eight and twelve feet in height, they have very long fingers without nails, enormous eyes, and no teeth. They eat no food whatever, although they carry long whips studded with thorns, with which they strike and kill hunters who stray too far into the jungle.

In its various details the belief echoes a well-known tradition of the sixteenth-century Manta Indians, also of western Ecuador. Preserved in old Spanish chronicles, the accounts tell of a race of male giants that had once invaded the Manta settlements. The creatures were four times the height of an ordinary man, and their eyes were as large as small platters. Since they had no women, and the Manta were too small for them, they practiced "the abominable crime of sodomy among themselves."

Eventually the Manta were saved by "a young man bright as the sun," who came down from the sky and drove off the giants with thunderbolts.

Farther north, among the now extinct Tolú, Father Pedro Simón obtained strikingly similar information about male monsters: "There were giants in that province, people three times the size of ordinary men and with corresponding excess of strength and appetite, and also of ruinous customs, for they committed the sin of abomination, to which they gave themselves one to another with much bestiality, for they hated women to death, with whom they coupled only for reproduction, and if females were born, they suffocated them, so it is told, in the arms of the midwife. But these abominations did not go without punishment, heaven being their executioner, which threw them down with lightning, and finished them off to the last one."

Such traditions provide a male counterpart to the Amazon myth, which seems to be lacking in the Northwest region.

The Food-Inhaler Bride

Another class of supernaturals recognized by the Cayapa is the *pehuru pútyu,* a race of beings that have neither buttocks nor anus. These almost human creatures live underground, where they are said to cook ocean fish. However, they merely inhale the aromas that rise from the cauldrons, since it is impossible for food to pass through their bodies.

In the ancient days, before they were buried by a tremendous earthquake, they lived aboveground. At some future time the earth will turn again, burying the human race and bringing the *pehuru pútyu* back to the surface. Meanwhile they pose no threat to the Cayapa.

The Colorado, who are neighbors of the Cayapa, also know of the underground food inhalers, whom they call *fimiyo.* The mythology of the Colorado, though not quite as destroyed as that of the Cayapa, has largely been replaced by simple folktales. Yet the Colorado have preserved a significant myth about the *fimiyo,* which tells of a man who became the husband of one of these creatures.

Accompanied by his brother, the man fell into a hole and landed in the top of a palm tree. The two men, it seems, had reached the country of the *fimiyo,* who at that moment were preparing peccary head with manioc, served on a bed of leaves. But the *fimiyo* did not actually eat. They simply inhaled the vapors.

By contrast, the two men in the tree began to gorge themselves on palm fruits and were soon defecating. Filled with admiration, the food inhalers set poles against the tree, climbed up, and carried the brothers down.

They asked them if they would take brides, so that children capable of complete digestion could be born among them. The men agreed, and the brides were brought forth. One of the brothers was given an old woman, whose vagina pinched off his penis, killing him. The other brother, more fortunate, received a young woman, and all went well.

A fuller variant of this story, The Food-Inhaler Bride, has been collected from the mountain-dwelling Yupa of northwestern Venezuela, whose myths, though apparently declining, are better preserved than those of the Colorado. Among the Yupa the food inhalers are called *pipintu,* meaning little people, or pygmies.

One day, so the story goes, a funeral party had entered a burial cave in order to deposit the corpse of the deceased. While the mourners were inside, an avalanche blocked the entrance, and several of the people were killed by falling boulders. Trapped, the others died one by one, until a single survivor made his way to the back of the cave and squeezed through a crack.

The man at first thought he had found his way to freedom, but soon he realized he was in the underground world of the *pipintu.* He heard voices and saw a bonfire, around which the little people were dancing. With their hands raised they bent forward from the waist and inhaled, nourishing themselves with the smoke. They had long beards but no hair on their heads, having lost it on account of the human waste that continually fell down from the world above.

As the man took up residence among the *pipintu,* the little people became increasingly envious watching him eat. Finally they asked him to operate on one of their children, promising him that they would remain friendly toward him even if the experiment failed. Reluctantly the man took an arrowhead and punctured the child's backside to provide an anus.

When the child died, the operation was tried on a second child and then a third, all with the same result. Resigned to their fate, the *pipintu* gave up the project, yet remained friendly to the visitor who had caused their children's deaths—so friendly that they gave him a bride and showed him the way back to the earth's surface.

The man's *pipintu* wife bore him many children, who were normal in every way except that they were of small stature. From these children are descended the pygmies who today inhabit the mountains on the Colombia-Venezuela border.

Noticeably smaller than their masters, the pygmies exist as a servant class among the ordinary-sized Yupa, whose language and customs they seem to share. Although they have their own houses, where they sleep at night, they spend their days with the big people, cooking, weaving, making pottery, and performing other chores. Since they are reticent, little is known of their folklore. It is perhaps significant that a variant of the tale about male giants was collected from these diminutive people.

In a chapter devoted to folkloric giants and little people, it is worth emphasizing that the Yupa pygmies are real.

Kurupira

Apart from the tale of the underground bride, the notion of anusless creatures is widely distributed as a free-floating motif. Known also from the Catío and the Chocó of Colombia, it is more sparsely scattered in the continent's other regions. In Greater Brazil it is found among the Shipaya, the Trumaí, the Tukuna, and the Urubú; in Guiana, among the Carib, the Taulipáng, the Warrau, and the Yanomamo; in the Far South, among the Tehuelche; and in the Central Andes, among the Tacana.

Other Northwest folk beliefs, many of them preserved only as traditions, not as fully developed myths, include a few of particular interest that may be singled out:

Palámbele (Cayapa). The tiny *palámbele* live around the hole where the sun comes up. It is the sun's intense heat that stunts their growth. Yet they never travel. Content to remain where they are, at the eastern edge of the world, they pose no threat to humanity.

Blood drinkers (Chocó, Páez).   In the lore of the Chocó these little monsters are twin boys who suck blood from women's bodies, draining it out through the foot. The Páez envision them as the thunder spirit's numerous children, each of whom kills a series of wet nurses in the process of growing up; once grown, they offer themselves as shaman's helpers.

Ulili (Colorado).   Tiny in the extreme, the *ulili* are described as a miniature man accompanied by a miniature woman who carries an infant. When the moon is out and people are asleep, they enter the camp to steal cooked food. As they come, they cry *ulili ulili*. Small as they are, they eat everything in sight.

Mashíramu (Yupa).   Hairy all over and with feet turned backward, *Mashíramu* once attacked the Yupa with a pack of jaguars, killing nearly everybody. Since that time, men and jaguars, whenever they meet, have fought to the death.

The hairy little gnome with backward feet is by no means typical of the Northwest. Though the Yupa call him *Mashíramu*, he is much better known as *Kurupira*, one of the principal forest spirits of Brazil. Usually a master of animals, *Kurupira* is perhaps a personification of the anteater, whose exceedingly long claws turn backward under its feet as it walks.

Known from Tupian sources as early as the sixteenth century, *Kurupira* evidently traveled up the Amazon with the Tupian trade language called lingua geral. Over the centuries the tradition escaped from Indian mythology and entered the folklore of rural Brazil, where it remains firmly entrenched— even as tribal Indians have forgotten it.

Indeed, not many Indian groups today preserve stories of *Kurupira*. The Yupa of Venezuela, far removed from the presumed source, are one of the few.

PART SEVEN

Central Andes

Highland Gods

Myth and empire

Homeland of the most powerful of native American societies, the Central Andes is one of the poorer regions from the standpoint of pure mythology. The fascination of Inca civilization itself, nevertheless, lends weight to the bits and pieces of Inca myth that have survived.

Conquered by Spaniards in 1533, the Inca empire had patched together dozens of highland tribes, stretching from northern Argentina and Chile through Bolivia, Peru, and Ecuador. It had subdued the towns of the central desert to the west and, to a

limited extent, had penetrated the forest lands, or montaña, to
the east. Today its legacy persists among the nearly ten million
highland people who still speak the imperial language, Quechua,
and have their own versions of the old lore.

From the writings of sixteenth- and seventeenth-century
chroniclers it appears that the Incas had pushed mythology in
two directions: upward to the topmost level of state religion and
backward to the beginning of official history.

At the very top stood the Creator, *Wirakocha,* who was also
"world instructor," or culture hero. Lofty prayers were addressed to him, and the lesser gods were regarded as his servants
or his children.

Inti (sun) was the most important of the secondary deities,
having evidently served as the supreme spirit of the Inca tribe
before the days of empire. The others included *Ilyapa* (thunder),
Mamakilya (mother moon), *Pachamama* (earth mother), *Mamako-
cha* (mother sea), and *Kolka* (the Pleiades). Beneath these were
innumerable local spirits known collectively as the *waka.*

But if there were myths about *Pachamama,* for example, they
were not recorded. Inca mythology by and large concerned the
deeds of *Wirakocha,* which, naturally, formed the prelude to Inca
history.

Wirakocha

The Spaniards arrived in 1532 during the reign of Atahuallpa,
the eleventh of the Inca rulers in a succession going back to the
legendary Manco Capac, whose reign may be dated about A.D.
1200. The Incas did not have written records, but the life of each
of the rulers was painted in pictures, and these were kept in a
kind of museum near Cuzco, the capital of the empire. In the
painted document pertaining to Manco Capac was a flood myth
and the story of the origin of nations.

Since the flood had risen above the highest mountains, so it
was told in the pictures, all life had been destroyed. But as soon
as the water receded, the Creator began to mold new people out

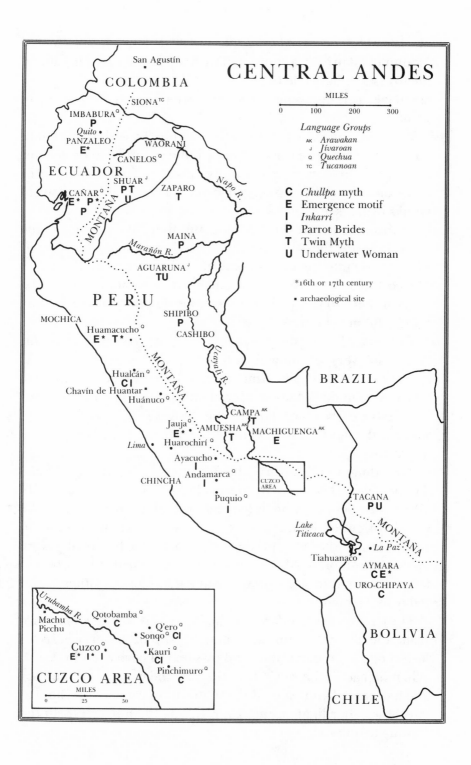

CENTRAL ANDES

MILES

0   100   200   300

Language Groups

AK   *Arawakan*
J   *Jívaroan*
Q   *Quechua*
TC   *Tucanoan*

C   *Chullpa* myth
E   Emergence motif
I   *Inkarrí*
P   Parrot Brides
T   Twin Myth
U   Underwater Woman

*16th or 17th century

• archaeological site

San Agustín

COLOMBIA

SIONA ᵀᶜ

IMBABURA ᵠ
P
Quito •
PANZALEO
E*

ECUADOR

WAORANI

CANELOS ᵠ

SHUAR ᴶ
P T
CAÑAR ᵠ   **U**
E* **P***
P

ZAPARO
T

Napo R.

MONTAÑA

MAINA
P

Marañón R.

AGUARUNA ᴶ
T U

PERU

MOCHICA

SHIPIBO
P

Huamacucho ᵠ •
E* **T*** •

CASHIBO

MONTAÑA

BRAZIL

Hualcán ᵠ
C I
Chavín de Huantar ▪
Huánuco ᵠ

Ucayali R.

Jauja ᵠ
E*
AMUESHA ᴬᴷ
T

CAMPA ᴬᴷ
T

MACHIGUENGA ᴬᴷ
E

Lima •
Huarochirí •

Ayacucho •

Andamarca ᵠ
I
CHINCHA
•

CUZCO
AREA

Puquio ᵠ
I

TACANA
P U

*Lake
Titicaca*

MONTAÑA

• *La Paz*

Tiahuanaco ▪

AYMARA
C E*

URO-CHIPAYA
C

BOLIVIA

CHILE

Urubamba R.
Machu
Picchu ▪

Qotobamba ᵠ
• **C**

Cuzco ᵠ
E* **I*** • **I**

Q'ero ᵠ
• **C I**
Sonqo ᵠ
• **I**
•Kauri ᵠ
C I

Pinchimuro ᵠ
• **C**

CUZCO AREA

MILES

0   25   50

of clay. This occurred at a place called Tiahuanaco (site of monumental pre-Inca ruins). On each figure the Creator painted the dress and hairstyle to be worn, and to each nation he gave a language, certain songs, and the various seeds they were to plant.

When he had brought the people to life, he ordered them to go into the earth and travel underground in different directions, so that each nation emerged in its own way. Some came out of caves or hills. Others emerged from springs, still others from trunks of trees.

At this time the world was dark. But there at Tiahuanaco the Creator made the sun, the moon, and the stars and ordered them to rise into the sky. As *Inti* (sun) was ascending, it called to Manco Capac and said, "You and your descendants are to be lords and are to conquer many nations. Look upon me as your father. Be my children. Worship me."

Variants of the story, while not quite contradicting this "museum" version, show differences in the sequence of events and add missing details. Among these fuller accounts is the one given by Juan de Betanzos, official interpreter for the viceroy of Peru in the early 1550s. His version derives from narrative song, which is the most frequently mentioned Inca method of preserving history.

According to Betanzos, the Creator emerged from Lake Titicaca, near Tiahuanaco, and made the sky and the earth. He also made people, who inhabited the land. But because the people offended him, he emerged again and changed them to stone. (From other variants it appears that these first beings were giants, whose only offense was that they turned out to be too large. Changed to stone, they became the colossal statues found today at Tiahuanaco.)

The Creator, or *Wirakocha,* at the time of his second emergence from the lake brought with him a host of lesser *wirakocha,* including two in particular (said by some to have been his sons). When he had lit the world with the sun, the moon, and the stars and had carved and painted the "pattern" of each nation, he sent out these subordinate *wirakocha,* ordering them to call forth the various peoples.

As they traveled along, they cried, "So-and-so! Emerge and populate this empty country by command of *Kon Tiksi Wirakocha* [thunderclap origin *wirakocha*], who made the world!" The main body of the Creator's assistants traveled south or southeast, while the two sons proceeded northeast and northwest, calling forth the people and, according to some, teaching the names and uses of all the different plants along the way.

Wirakocha himself traveled due north toward Cuzco, calling forth other tribes, or nations, as he went. A little south of Cuzco he brought forth the Cana nation, which emerged fully armed. Not recognizing their Creator, the Cana attacked him with intent to kill. To demonstrate his power, *Wirakocha* made fire fall from the sky, causing a mountain to burn—which left a scar that can still be seen. In response, the Cana threw away their weapons and prostrated themselves at the Creator's feet.

Moving on, *Wirakocha* established Cuzco, then kept traveling north until he reached the seacoast in what is now Ecuador. There he was joined by his assistant creators, and together they walked over the water "just as they had walked on land."

Since he was last seen among the waves, some said that his name, *Wirakocha* (ocean grease or sea-foam), referred to his departure. When the Spaniards arrived with their firearms and their oceangoing vessels, it was thought that the god had returned. Spaniards were therefore called *wirakocha,* a usage that is still found in some parts of Peru.

The god in disguise

Aside from the creation story, two further tales of *Wirakocha* have been preserved in the old chronicles. One is the legend of *Tonapa Wirakocha Nipacachan,* or simply *Tonapa,* in which the deity appears as a wandering preacher. In the other story he has the personality of a trickster and takes the name *Koniraya Wirakocha.*

Tonapa, according to an early-seventeenth-century source, traveled through the highlands as an old man with a staff. He was thin, long-haired, and bearded and wore a long tunic. As he went from place to place, he preached virtue and worked miracles that cured the sick. In one place he erected a large cross that he had carried to the top of a mountain on his shoulder. Often he slept in the fields with nothing to cover him but his tunic.

Contemptuous of him, people drove him away. Once he was thrown into prison for attempting to baptize the daughter of a chief. Those who offended him, however, were turned into stones, and their false idols were broken or burned. At last, after more failures than triumphs, he departed from the high country, turning his steps toward the sea.

Before the introduction of Christianity, tales of a wandering hero called *Tonapa* might well have been imported from the southern provinces, since the geography of this lore strongly indicates the territory of the Aymara. After the Conquest, as suggested by the episode of the cross and the mountain, the old legend seems to have absorbed at least a few details from the life of Christ.

The myth of *Koniraya Wirakocha* also comes from the provinces, in this case from the community of Huarochirí in the mountains east of Lima. The story was recorded not only in Spanish but in Quechua, along with other lore of Huarochirí— the first important body of native traditions to be written down in the language of the Incas.

Koniraya, we learn, affected a humble style, much as did *Tonapa.* In fact the tunic worn by *Koniraya* was all in rags. Nobody knew who he was. When he passed by, people cried, "Louse-ridden wretch!"

Yet *Koniraya* was creating as he traveled. He was calling fields and terraced hillsides into existence simply by speaking a word. Dropping a reed blossom, he made water flow.

In the country through which he passed there was said to have been a beautiful young woman named *Kawilyaka.* All the local spirits, or *waka,* desired her. But she would give herself to none of them.

Changing into a bird, *Koniraya* perched in an eggfruit tree, then placed his semen inside a ripe eggfruit, letting it fall next to

Kawilyaka. She ate the fruit and nine months later gave birth.

When her child was a year old, she summoned all the *waka* to find out which of them might be the father. Arriving in their finest clothes, they sat down in a row, with *Koniraya* at the end, dressed in tatters as usual. "Go find your father yourself!" she said to the little boy, and he crawled on all fours to the foul-looking *Koniraya.*

Horrified, the young woman picked up her child and ran to the seashore, where she and the boy were both changed to stone.

In a sequel *Koniraya* runs after *Kawilyaka,* asking directions of various animals along the way. Those that encourage him are rewarded; those, like the skunk, that tell him he will never catch her are cursed with undesirable characteristics. Reaching the seacoast, he seduces one of *Kawilyaka*'s sisters, then eludes her irate mother by saying, "I'll be back in a moment, I have to urinate." Returning to the highlands, he continues to "play tricks," making fun of "many towns and many men."

Comparisons with other lore reveal a couple of significant characteristics of Central Andean myth: its surprisingly strong relationship with other South American mythologies and its susceptibility to European influence even at an early date.

Variants of the main part of the *Koniraya* story, excluding the sequel, have been reported not only from the Uro-Chipaya of the Central Andes but from the Chiriguano and the Tupinamba of the Greater Brazil region. This is no doubt a very old South American myth. The sequence involving the helpful and un-helpful animals, however, appears to have been inspired by the medieval European legend of how Christ was chased by his enemies. In that story, Jesus blessed the animals who helped him and cursed those who hindered him as he fled from his perse-cutors.

And as we have seen, the legend of *Tonapa,* though it may be accepted as basically Indian, owes much to the Gospel accounts of Christ's life. The *Tonapa* tale dates from 1613; the myth of *Koniraya,* from 1608.

New gods

Among the old gods destroyed by *Tonapa* was a certain idol in the form of a woman, which filled him with such hatred that he burned not only the statue but the hill on which it stood. It was an "awful miracle," says the teller of the tale, "the most fearful that was ever heard of in the world."

Without attaching too much significance to this fragment of a story, it may be mentioned that female deities, if they ever played a leading role in the old mythologies of highland Peru, must have done so in the very distant past. Surviving myths on the subject of religious change tell mostly of male gods replacing older ones of the same sex.

In Huarochirí it was told that the country had formerly been tyrannized by the cannibal god *Walyalyo,* who had created people in such a way that each couple could have only two children. One child was for the mother and father to raise, the other for the god to eat.

But then, five large eggs appeared on a nearby mountaintop, and one of these eggs contained the hero *Pariakaka*. When the eggs hatched, the hero-god and his four brothers raised a storm that drove out the false *waka*. Then *Pariakaka* himself became the *waka* of Huarochirí.

A somewhat similar story, associated with the Chincha of the coastal lowland, tells of the harsh deity *Kon,* who created the world and its first inhabitants but made deserts when the people annoyed him. *Kon* was driven out by the famous *waka* called *Pachacamah,* who created a new race of humans and gave them everything they needed.

A further myth, supposedly from the Chincha but probably contrived by Inca invaders, related that *Pachacamah* starved his subjects and led them to commit murder. Eventually the evil god threw himself into the sea, and order was restored by Sun, who brought forth a new race of people from gold, silver, and copper eggs. From the gold came chiefs; from the silver, their wives. Commoners were born from the copper eggs.

The egg-birth motif, familiar in the region, is another of the features that link the Central Andean cultures with other parts of the continent, specifically the Greater Brazil, Guiana, and Gran Chaco regions.

World ages

Whether told of *Wirakocha* or of one of the local gods like *Pachacamah,* the old highland myths stressed the theme of re-creation and the establishment of a new age. For the Incas this fresh start meant the beginning of imperial history, which could be neatly divided into the lifetimes of the eleven rulers, ending with Atahuallpa and the arrival of the Spaniards.

For the Quechua-speaking people who survived the Conquest, Inca traditions began to recede and the details became blurred. Nevertheless, the tendency to divide the world's history into distinct eras has continued to the present day.

Thus the Hualcán Quechua recognize two ages, a time of ancient people and a time of Christian people. Similarly, the Cañar Quechua speak of an age of God the father and the present age of God the son.

In the community of Pinchimuro the time of God the father is itself divided into two periods, an era of Creation and an era of giants. Next comes the time of God the son, which also has two divisions, the age of the Incas and the present age. Finally, a future era is envisioned, and it is said that this will be the time of the Holy Ghost.

In Qotobamba there are three ages: the time of creative spirits, the time of the first beings, and the time of man.

Within these varying frameworks a single tale, which may be called the *chullpa* myth, provides a thread of continuity, not only from community to community but between the present and the distant past. The story tells how the people of the ancient time were put to death and how their influence, nevertheless, may be felt today.

In the Quechua language, *chullpa* is either a preserved corpse or a small stone structure in which the corpses, or mummies, were laid to rest. In the cold dry highlands, not to mention the coastal desert, these bundled and usually blackened remains have kept remarkably well since Inca times and earlier. Modern Quechua believe that they represent the first beings.

The *chullpa* myth

In the communities of Qotobamba and Q'ero the first beings, called ancient ones, are said to have lived when the world was still dark. Although they were not giants, they possessed extraordinary powers. They caused stones to become buildings automatically, and they could level a mountain with a single shot from their slings.

Annoyed by their arrogance, the Creator ordered the sun to rise for the first time, and the ancient ones, almost blinded by the light, took refuge in their "small houses." Since their doorways were facing east, the heat of the sun as it rose each morning gradually dried them out. Some say they were finished off by a rain of fire and were trapped in attitudes of terror, doubled up clutching their knees or with their hands covering their faces.

Today the ancient ones survive as spirits that come out at night to harm people, especially at the time of the new moon. According to the Aymara, they are the cause of *"chullpa* sickness," which results from being stabbed by a bone fragment. The supposed weapon must be extracted by a native doctor, who removes it magically.

Christ in the Andes

In one version of the *chullpa* myth, Christ replaces the sun as the angry destroyer of the ancient people, burning them to a crisp. In another version, more in keeping with Christian tradition, God's son is victimized by the ancients, who imprison him, then kill him. In revenge, God sends the rain of fire that turns the people into blackened mummies.

A view of Christ as culture hero comes from the Quechua of Imbabura, who say that all the foods were once gathered together in a kind of trough. *Jesucristo* then came along and gave each person his proper portion: potatoes for the man, corn for the woman, and the little cereal called quinoa for the children.

Afterward a mouse stepped up and said, "I will open the sepulcher so you may get out when your enemies kill you and bury you." In exchange for this promise, *Jesucristo* made Mouse the master of grain and allowed him to remain hidden in people's houses.

A similar view, calculated to remind his readers of Christ, was expressed in the late 1500s by the native historian Waman Puma of Huánuco, who wrote that the ancients had believed in a sacred trinity. There had been God the father, who meted out justice, and his two sons, the older of which showed compassion to the people, while the younger gave them food and sent them rain from the sky. Far from being the evil *chullpa* people of modern myth, the ancients, according to Waman Puma, were the industrious builders of Andean society and true believers in God the father.

In Waman Puma's "trinity" may be recognized the outlines of the old *Wirakocha* myth, in which the Creator is assisted by his two sons.

The deity as trickster is another of the traditional figures that survives in latter-day Quechua lore. In a tale from twentieth-century Imbabura, to take one example, the Christ child gets even with two bullies by changing them into pigs. The story itself, however, may stem from European sources, since it strongly resembles the trickster episodes found in the so-called Infancy gospels of the New Testament Apocrypha.

European elements—but derived more from folklore than from scripture—are predominant in a version of Christ's life collected among the Cañar Quechua in 1976. The story begins with the immaculate conception, proceeds to the nativity and the infancy, then skips to the crucifixion.

The child is conceived when Joseph throws a lily that touches the Virgin's abdomen. But Joseph does not realize what he has done, and when he sees Mary pregnant he runs away in anger. As Mary follows after him, the child, still in the womb, appears to Joseph in a dream, reminding him of the lily. By the time Mary catches up to him, he has been convinced of her innocence, and together they "return to paradise," which is called Bethlehem.

When the child is born, the news is spread rapidly by trees, rocks, and animals, which in those days had the power of speech. Soon the cow arrives and warms the infant Jesus with her breath. But the selfish mule comes only to eat the hay that had been gathered to protect the child against the cold. For this the Virgin curses the mule, which has been unable to bear offspring since that day.

Later, when the child Jesus is about four years old, he plays tricks on his parents. He hides from them, he turns Joseph's mortar into mud, he kills and revives a flock of chicks, and he chops up Joseph's carefully prepared lumber.

When he is a little older, soldiers come to Bethlehem to capture him. He flees, and as his pursuers follow his trail, he changes into a silk-cotton tree. Deceived, they pass him by. When they are about to catch him again, he changes into a rooster and again eludes them.

Farther along, he comes to some people who are sowing a field. He tells them that their crops will be ripe the next day and that they must say to the soldiers who come along that Christ passed when the seeds were being planted. They do so, and the soldiers, concluding that Christ went by months earlier, relax their pursuit.

In another place, Christ comes to a farmer who is planting wheat and asks him what he is doing. Annoyed, the ill-tempered farmer replies, "I'm planting stones." Then Jesus says, "So be it," and the next day the field is all stones.

Continuing his "way of the cross," having now reached the age of thirty-three, he is abruptly taken by the soldiers who have been pursuing him all along. They bring him to the house of Pontius Pilate, and after being tied and whipped, he is made to carry the cross to Calvary. At last he is crucified, and the tale ends.

Looking back over the story, one may identify at least three well-defined European tale types: The Cow and the Mule, The Sown Field, and Christ and the Farmer. Of these, Christ and the Farmer is the most important for South American folklore, not only because it is scattered from one side of the continent to the other, but because it is sometimes fully integrated into the native mythology.

Reappearing among the Siona, a montaña tribe just east of the highlands, Christ and the Farmer is given as a myth of the "beginning of life," when those who answered rudely found themselves with stony fields and poor crops. Since the hero is not identified as Christ, the collector of the myth, apparently unaware of its origin, published it as native American lore. And yet, there is no harm in having done so, since the story already has a long history in the New World and is surely more alive today in South America than it is in Europe.

═══════════

CHAPTER XVI

In the Montaña

═══════════

Highland connections

Amazonia begins along the continental divide in the highlands of Bolivia, Peru, and Ecuador. Within a few miles of this line the scrubby Andean vegetation gives way to rain forest, and east-bound travelers suddenly find themselves in a different world. Known as the "eyebrow," this upland jungle leads toward the low hills and increasingly level valleys of the montaña itself (also called yunga), where the native cultures, of necessity, more closely resemble those of Brazil than of western Peru.

The contrast is sharp between the picturesque towns and

villages of the highlands and the riverside camps of the montaña. Clothing, often made of wool in the highlands, is here reduced to a minimum. Corn and beans are grown, but the essential potato of the high country is replaced by either manioc or the bananalike plantain, known as the "potato of the forest."

Among most tribes of the montaña, mythology is not strongly organized. The idea of a culture hero or a single creative spirit is weakly developed or sometimes absent. Several groups, however, recognize a distinct class of supernaturals reminiscent of the old Quechua concept of *waka*. Among the Shuar these powers are called *arútam*. The Campa and the Machiguenga know them as *tasórintsi*, and for the Tacana they are *edutzi*. Myths, to a large extent, are concerned with the doings of these personages.

Within the spirit classes are at least a few beings that take their names from highland or even coastal mythology. The Campa, for instance, have a hero who created landscape features, transformed "people" of the old time into the animals of today, established the night by playing night music, and molded humans out of earth. His name, *Avíreri,* is possibly related to the word *wirakocha.*

More obvious is the connection between *wirakocha* and *Varinkoshi,* the Shipibo deity who came down from the sky, established the important crop mani, then reascended to become the sun. Among the Machiguenga the hero who corresponds to the Campa *Avíreri* is *Pachacamah,* the old *waka* of coastal Peru. The Campa, too, are acquainted with a supernatural called *Pachacamah.* For them, however, he is not a major deity but merely the spirit who holds up the earth.

In at least some cases these recurrences of familiar old names from western Peru have more to do with the spread of the Quechua language than with the borrowing of mythological ideas. In other cases the concept itself has been taken over but with a shift in emphasis or a new interpretation.

The garden mother

The Inca earth mother, *Pachamama,* recurs in the lore of the modern Tacana, who regard her as an old woman of the forest. She taught people to make corn beer and created the spirit responsible for the alternation of night and day.

Modern Quechua in the Cuzco area also recall *Pachamama,* who they say lives inside the earth and has charge of agriculture. She is the special deity of women, who pray to her, calling her "companion."

The Tacana, however, make a distinction between the earth mother and the crop mother, calling the latter Manioc Mistress. This lesser spirit is small, white, and very fat and is believed to have many children. The Shuar, likewise, say that she is very fat and about three feet tall. But for the Shuar she is a major deity. The Aguaruna also regard her as a spirit of first importance, as do the Canelos Quechua, who call her *Chagra Mama* (garden mother).

Known to the Aguaruna as *Nunkwi,* the garden mother is all-important in the eyes of Aguaruna women, for whom she is the chief supernatural in what may be called a women's mythology. Women identify with *Nunkwi,* believing that she enables them to make pottery and care for domestic animals, helps them in time of pregnancy, and, especially, makes them good gardeners.

In the beginning, so it is said, the Aguaruna had no proper food. From their miserable gardens they harvested leaves, vines, and balsa wood, which they warmed in their armpits, because they did not yet have fire for cooking. These inferior foods, the only sustenance available at that time, had been discovered by a certain woman's husband.

One day the woman saw manioc peelings floating down the river. Hungry, she traveled upstream and saw for the first time the garden of *Nunkwi,* filled with manioc. *Nunkwi* herself was peeling the white tubers and dropping the skins into the water. "How would you like to give me a little manioc?" asked the woman.

"I would not," replied *Nunkwi*. But finally she said, "All right, I will give you my little daughter. Take good care of her. In this way I myself will be living with the Aguaruna. While I am with them, there will be no death, and the people will not have to work their gardens."

When she had returned to her home, the woman said, "*Nunkwi*! Say that there are ripe ones!" And the little girl said, "Let there be plantains, ha ha!" Immediately the walls were hung with ripe plantains already picked.

Then the woman said, "*Nunkwi*! Say that there's manioc beverage! *Nunkwi*! Say that there's smoked meat!" And all was done.

Later, when the woman had left the house, a curious little boy cried, "*Nunkwi*! Say that there are ghosts!" And immediately the ghosts arrived. When he saw them, the boy was terrified and demanded that they be taken away. But it was too late. In a fit of rage the boy threw ashes into the little girl's face. Taking offense, she slipped into a bamboo stem and returned unseen to her mother.

When the woman came back to the house and discovered what had happened, she cut open the bamboo stem, hoping to retrieve the loss. But the daughter of *Nunkwi* had left nothing behind but the tiny person called *Iki* (fart). *Iki* jumped into the woman's anus. And this, incidentally, was the origin of intestinal gas.

That night the woman cried herself to sleep. In a dream, however, *Nunkwi*, came to her and told her where to find the seeds of all the crops. The next morning, just as her dream had foretold, the woman found the seeds, and from that time on, the people have had good food, although they have had to work hard in the garden.

It is said that if the little boy had been older and had known better, *Nunkwi* would not have been so generous.

Twins hatched from eggs

Just as women look to *Nunkwi,* men identify with *Etsa* (sun). For both the Aguaruna and their neighbors the Shuar, *Etsa* stands for competence in such male tasks as hunting and housebuilding. Following his example men avoid sweets and toughen themselves by eating hot peppers.

In the principal story of *Etsa* the hero is pitted against the ogre *Iwia,* who, after testing *Etsa*'s hunting skills by demanding to be fed constantly, is ultimately conquered by *Etsa* with the aid of resourceful animals. The tale in question is a variant of The Twin Myth.

According to a recent Shuar version, *Iwia* had taken a member of the Shuar tribe as his wife. But when the woman went to the riverbank to wash manioc tubers, she would meet a duck, who would bring her gifts of fresh fish. Enraged upon discovering these secret meetings, *Iwia* beat the woman to death and was in the process of eating her when he noticed two large eggs in her abdomen. From these eggs were hatched *Etsa* and his twin brother, *Nantu* (moon).

In an Aguaruna variant a dove eventually tells *Etsa* how his mother had been killed, and the hero, predictably, takes his revenge.

Known to several tribes of the montaña, The Twin Myth has a variant from the highlands as well, recorded in the community of Huamacucho in the mid-sixteenth century. Here again the woman has a bird lover—named *Wamansiri,* from *waman* (falcon)—and the twins are hatched from eggs. Outraged, the townspeople kill the bird-man, and the woman dies giving birth. In time the principal twin learns the truth, revives his mother, and avenges his father's death.

The Parrot Brides

Another story known from both the highlands and the lowland forest is the tale of two parrots that nourish the survivors of the world flood. In view of the Maina version recorded by a Jesuit father in the seventeenth century, The Parrot Brides is perhaps the earliest fully reported myth of the montaña.

As received from the Maina, the story opens with the predicament of a solitary hunter whose people have all perished in the deluge. The man has no wife to prepare the fish and game he catches. Yet, every evening when he returns to his hut, he finds meat freshly grilled.

One day he hides in the woods close by and sees two parrots fly into the hut. Transforming themselves into beautiful young women, they light the fire and prepare cooked food. The hunter, filled with desire, steps forward and seizes one of the women. He takes her as his bride, and their children become the ancestors of the present-day Maina tribe.

Presumably obtained from a male informant, the text concludes with the observation that the hunter in his haste chose the less industrious of the two parrots—which explains why women to this day are susceptible to laziness.

In the unusual Tacana variant the birds are not brides but *edutzi,* or spirit powers, that aid two children who have survived the flood. Taking the form of parrots, they build a new earth for the little boy and the little girl by making countless flights to the frog who owns mud, bringing the stuff back in their claws. With a final trip they bring home a roasted ear of corn and a live ember as well, saying, "We have provided for you. Now you will go out into your world."

Underwater power

An important myth of the montaña not shared by the highlands is the story of the water spirit known to the Shuar and neighboring tribes as *Tsunki.* With its familiar plot involving the daughter of the spirit and a man caught in a conflict of loyalties, the tale may be regarded as a distant variant of The Underwater Woman, typical of the Guiana region, a thousand miles to the east.

A Shuar variant recorded in 1978 begins with a hunter at the riverbank who hears a strange whistling sound. Wondering if it could be a signal from the spirit world, he returns home and induces a "dream" by means of tobacco smoke. In this dream the daughter of *Tsunki* appears to him, telling him to go back to the river. He does so, meets the woman, and follows her underwater to her father's house.

The woman's mother provides the man with an aphrodisiac, and he becomes the son-in-law of *Tsunki*. When he brings his new bride to his home on earth, she takes the form of a snake.

With time the snake bride becomes pregnant, and the man is forced to leave her at home while he goes off to hunt. During his absence, his two earthly wives discover the snake and torment her, causing her to return to her father. In a fury, *Tsunki* cries, "Now they shall see me!" and he floods the earth, drowning everyone but the hunter and one of the hunter's own little daughters, who escape to a mountaintop. When the water subsides, these two repopulate the world.

The conversational style

The teller of the Shuar myth of *Tsunki*, given above in outline form, refers to his sources by saying, "Thus our old people relate in their conversations," implying that he has heard the tale in segments, interspersed with commentary. His own performance, recorded on magnetic tape by the missionary-ethnographer Siro Pellizzaro, takes the same approach. As the storyteller goes along, he links the myth to his own experiences and clarifies it in conversational asides.

Unlike Martin Gusinde, who suppressed the conversational style of his Fuegian informants, Father Pellizzaro, the great modern collector of Shuar mythology, has allowed the performance to stand as recorded. The storyteller-conversationalist in this case is a married man named Pítiur, fifty years old.

When the underwater woman has invited the hero of the tale to come meet *Tsunki*, Pítiur comments: "And what do fathers customarily say to their daughters when they marry? They, too, always demand that they bring the sons-in-law home to meet them."

Ushered into the underwater house, the hunter finds *Tsunki* seated on a throne, and the narrator remarks: "Indeed, isn't that the way it is with important people? And do we not sit facing our visitors when they enter our houses? And when the visitor comes close, do we not say, 'Who is this *shuar* [person] that comes here?' "

Later, the bride's mother gathers the herb *pirípri*. Chewing it, she blows the vapor on the man's genitals in order to produce an erection. "Nowadays," remarks the narrator, "we do not have this kind of *pirípri*.

"We only have the *pirípri* that causes swelling in children. Yes, we have other kinds of *pirípri* that parents chew and blow on the bodies of babies when they are sick—because the parents have failed to observe the tabu of not eating the tripe of animals, or other tabus that prevent children from becoming sick. I myself am very observant of these. So that my children will grow up well, I abstain from meats that are forbidden."

Finally, when the flood has abated and the world has been repeopled, Pítiur explains the significance of the whole myth, which in his view establishes the essential link between humans and the underwater power that controls food animals: "In spite of everything, the *shuar* are related to the *tsunki*, since that woman who was made pregnant by the man gave birth yonder beneath the water in the house of *Tsunki*.

"We are related to the *tsunki* because it was a man of our people who caused that child to be born.

"That is all."

═══════════

CHAPTER XVII

Myth and Archaeology

═══════════

Interpreting the past

Without regard to time layers or differing pottery types, the Quechua of Hualcán in the Peruvian highlands attribute ancient artifacts to the people of the dark, who were burned to death when the sun first rose. Some say these *chullpa* people buried their belongings when they saw that they were going to be killed, and this is why farmers today find pots and carvings as they dig their fields. Architectural remains are explained on the theory that in the dark time, stones responded to verbal commands or fell into place of their own accord.

Providing a somewhat fuller view of the "ancient people," modern archaeology divides pre-Inca civilization into a range of styles, progressing gradually from a simple agricultural stage beginning about 4000 B.C. By A.D. 500 a classic period has developed, marked by impressive architecture, notably at Tiahuanaco in the Bolivian highlands; by textiles, especially in the Lima area and southward along the coast; and by the pictorial pottery of the north-coast Mochica.

Although it is impossible to know what stories were told among the early people, it is reasonable to assume that a rich mythology had developed, perhaps richer than that of the Inca period with its emphasis on semihistorical legend. The many artworks depicting gods, monsters, and unearthly scenes cry out for interpretation. It is well to take a look at a few noteworthy specimens. Yet it must be kept in mind that efforts to explain them are purely conjectural and that the ancients themselves remain silent.

The feline god

One of the most striking subjects of Mochica art is a human figure, evidently male, with a pair of overlapping fangs protruding from either side of the mouth. Appearing in various roles, he is sometimes a hunter, rarely a warrior, more often a monster slayer who confronts a dragon or a manlike vampire. Among his animal helpers are a dog, a falcon, an eagle, and a lizard.

On the ceramic picture-vase shown in the accompanying illustration, the god assumes a dignified pose among high mountains, wearing a sunburst headdress with the face of a jaguar or puma at its center. Apparently sacrifices are being performed in his honor. Near the middle of the group a man carries a young animal, perhaps as an offering. Above, another man has been thrown over a precipice, his hair hanging downward, ending in a broad stream (of blood?) flowing into the valley.

On other Mochica vases the feline god takes the role of a

doctor, a musician, or an agriculturist shelling grain. A favorite type of pot shows just his head, peeking out from a mound of corn ears.

Having studied a number of these ceramics, the pre-Columbian specialist Elizabeth Benson suggests that the god is not one but two, a dignified Creator and his more active son, a kind of culture hero. From the evidence it is possible to imagine a cycle of myths built around the two supernaturals.

Rarely, a scene may be connected, at least tentatively, with a myth known from the modern period. For example, on one vase the feline god holds up the rainbow in the form of a double-headed serpent. This recalls a Tacana story in which Grandfather Lightning lifts the sky to its proper position with the help of the rainbow—which has the form of a two-headed serpent.

Archaeological specimens similar to the Mochica feline god have been found throughout the Andean region, especially at San Agustín in southern Colombia, known for its squat statues of ferocious-looking fanged deities, and at Chavín de Huantar, where the fanged feline has a dragonlike appearance. The bulging eyes and protruding fangs of the "devil" masks worn in modern Aymara dance-dramas also suggest the old feline god. Here, however, the inspiration seems to come from Spanish sources, and the resemblance to the ancient Andean figure may be sheer coincidence.

The Revolt of the Utensils

Another of the Tacana myths, recorded in the mid-twentieth century, tells of a time before the great flood when "pots, grating boards, weapons, and other utensils rebelled against the people and devoured them." Some say it happened during an eclipse of the sun. According to others, the utensils began to knock about

---

Mountain scene with feline god and worshippers. Mochica vase, about A.D. 500. Museum für Völkerkunde, Berlin.

when the moon was eclipsed; when it reappeared, they again fell lifeless.

Virtually the same story was current among the Quechua of Huarochirí over four hundred years ago. In the ancient time the sun had disappeared for five days, it was said, and in the darkness, stones knocked against one another and the mortars and the grinding stones began to devour people.

Just east of the Central Andean region several modern tribes, including the Barasana, the Tukuna, and the Chiriguano, also have the myth of the rebellious utensils.

And going back more than a thousand years, it would appear that a similar story was known to the ancient Mochica. In a vase painting, from which two details are reproduced on the opposite page, personified weapons and articles of apparel are shown bringing human prisoners to a sinister owl deity and his hench-man.

The owl can be seen in the lower detail, standing on a stepped platform with the henchman to his rear, wearing a headband. Each is receiving a prisoner brought in by a personified war club. On the left, a rope with a snake head at either end is delivering a third captive.

But in the upper detail a warrior deity surrounded by solar or lunar rays stands victorious as he receives utensil-people being brought in as captives by animal warriors. At the left, a puma soldier brings in a belt-person, while a dog soldier at the right delivers a personified nose ornament and, in his other hand, the owl deity's henchman (whom we have already seen in the lower detail).

In the opinion of the late German scholar Gerdt Kutscher, who made a careful study of this vase, the central warrior is the moon, and the vase as a whole represents the moon's victory over the hostile utensils.

Revolt of the utensils? Two details from a painted vase. Mochica, about A.D. 500. Redrawn by Gerdt Kutscher.

The fish-filled serpent

Among the Shipibo, a tribe of the Peruvian montaña, it is said that the first people used to make river crossings on the back of a huge boa, which formed a bridge from shore to shore. Regarded as a "mother" of species, the boa is believed to have at one time contained all water creatures in its stomach.

One day a menstruating woman crossed the boa bridge, and some of her blood fell on the boa's back. In its writhings, as it attempted to wash away the blood, the serpent threw off all the people who were crossing, and since that time it no longer forms a bridge for humans.

The Shipibo myth is modern, but there is reason to believe that at least a portion of it has a long history in the Central Andean region. Two ceramics from the Mochica culture, illustrated here, show water crossings on the backs of aquatic monsters. At left, a boatman rides on a giant fish. At right, he crosses on the arched body of a serpent, whose insides are filled with fish.

Not far to the east of the montaña, similar ideas have been recorded in the myths of the modern Toba of the Gran Chaco and the Ufaina of the Northwest Amazon. It was Claude Lévi-Strauss who first called attention to the Toba connection, citing a myth collected by Alfred Métraux in which the fabulous serpent *Lik*, filled with fish, becomes the friend of man.

Once in the winter season, when water disappears from many lagoons, *Lik* found himself stranded on dry ground. A kindly passerby agreed to carry him to water and in exchange was given all the fish he needed, whenever he needed them. Later, however, the man told Carancho, the culture hero, about his good fortune, and Carancho, disapproving of such an easy way of life, decreed that all food animals would henceforth be hard to catch.

Water monsters with boatmen. Two Mochica vases, about A.D. 500. The vase at right represents a fish-filled serpent.

Like both the Shipibo and Toba stories, the Ufaina myth is also a tale of paradise lost. Here it is said that the fish-filled boa stood upright in the form of a tree trunk, or post ("It was not just a post, it was a boa"), whose contents could be tapped at will by an old woman who knew the secret. In an act of mischief the culture heroes' little brother cut down the tree, and it formed a river in which the fish swam freely.

The Ufaina story is a typical Northwest Amazon variant of The Tree and the Flood, a myth that is curiously missing from the Central Andes. However, applying Lévi-Strauss's concept of transformation—by which a familiar story reappears in a totally new guise—we may say that the Shipibo motif of the lost bridge corresponds to the lost tree, each symbolized by the fish-filled serpent; and thus The Tree and the Flood has a faint echo, though not a variant, in the Central Andean region, an echo that resonates in the Mochica art of a thousand to fifteen hundred years ago.

Staff god

Of particular interest to archaeologists is an authoritative-looking personage who stares out from tapestries, vases, and architectural carvings of both the coast and the highlands, spanning a period of two thousand years. Fully erect, the presumed deity faces front and holds a long staff in each hand. Sometimes referred to as Staff God, he is best known as the central figure on the great stone gateway at Tiahuanaco.

Tourists have come to know this monument as the Gate of the Sun and its chief figure as *Wirakocha*. But the evidence for such identifications is not strong.

It is true that Tiahuanaco is the scene of the Inca creation myth, the place where *Wirakocha* made the sun. Moreover, the story tells that this site had been *Wirakocha*'s principal residence,

---

Staff God. Stone carving on the Gate of the Sun,
Tiahuanaco, Bolivia. About A.D. 500.

which would account for its imposing architecture.

To put the myth in perspective, it helps to recall that Tiahua-naco, built about A.D. 500, was already in ruins by the time Inca civilization reached its peak a thousand years later. In a sense, the Incas who contemplated the ruins were themselves archae-ologists, looking for clues. Neither they nor we could know for sure what the Tiahuanaco people had in mind when they made the carvings on their gate.

Nevertheless, the idea of a Creator by whatever name must have been important in the Central Andes long before the Incas, and it is not unlikely that Staff God was at least a spiritual ancestor if not the immediate forerunner of *Wirakocha*.

Fox in the Andes

In the Indiana University Art Museum in Bloomington, Indiana, is a Mochica fox head crafted of sheet copper with a silver wash, its tongue hanging out as if it were panting, and danglers attached to its ears and under its chin. A similar, almost identical piece is preserved in the Linden Museum in Stuttgart, West Germany.

Open at the back, these objects are evidently sheaths of the type mentioned by early Spanish chroniclers as having fitted over the ends of a dignitary's litter poles. Carried on the shoulders of official litter bearers, the two poles had a small platform between them to support the stool and cushion on which the royal person sat while being transported.

As part of the entourage, Fox can be imagined with his tongue and whiskers vibrating slightly and his danglers tinkling as he jogs along.

To see one of these pieces today is to be reminded of Fox the

Fox head. Copper with silver wash. Mochica, about A.D. 500. Courtesy of the Indiana University Art Museum, Bloomington, Indiana. Photograph by Michael Cavanagh and Kevin Montague.

traveler and trickster of Gran Chaco myth and to wonder about the history of the Andean Fox, who still makes regular appearances in the Indian folklore of Ecuador, Peru, and Bolivia. In the Chaco, Fox is a strong mythological character with overtones of the culture hero. Not so in the Central Andes.

Yet the modern Quechua tell at least a few stories about Fox that are unquestionably related to the Fox tales collected farther south and east:

Endurance contest. Fox brags to Condor that cold doesn't bother him. To put it to a test, the two agree to sleep out in the open on a cold stormy night. Whoever lasts longer gets to eat the other. Outwitted by Condor, Fox loses. (The very similar Chaco variant, as we have seen, is told of Fox and Vulture.)

Big mouth.   Formerly Fox had a small, dainty mouth. One day he heard Wren singing and asked to borrow his flutelike bill. Wren gave it to him and sewed up his mouth to make it even smaller, so that the "flute" would fit. To the sound of Fox's music, dancing skunks suddenly appeared, causing him to laugh so hard that the stitches broke and his mouth tore open to its present size. (In the Chaco variant, Wren is replaced by Crested Screamer.)

Disguised suitor.   Dressing up as a man, Fox stuffs his tail into his trousers and goes to a dance. The young women find him charming until the trousers, stretched tight, rip open, revealing Fox's bushy tail. (In the similar Chaco story, Fox is about to marry a young woman when his true identity is revealed by the hero Carancho.)

Could such lighthearted stories have been told by the Mochica of A.D. 500? There is no way of knowing. In fact, South American tales of this sort do not show up in Spanish and Portuguese writings until the nineteenth century. Yet students of mythology are convinced that the trickster is an ancient concept in the Americas, and given the playfulness of Mochica art it is reasonable to assume that tricksters of one kind or another, perhaps including Fox, were not unknown to their storytellers.

From Myth to
Politics

The rod of gold

In the official Creation myth of the Incas, the god *Wirakocha* emerged from Lake Titicaca, made men and women, caused the sun to rise, then proceeded north to the site of Cuzco, the future capital; and while the sun was ascending, it spoke to the man named Manco Capac, charging him to rule the empire. As founder of the royal dynasty, the chosen one became known as "Manco Capac Inca," with the term "Inca" used in the sense of chief, or ruler.

The Creation myth makes no further mention of Manco,

whose tale is told in a separate legend. His is the story of the rod of gold and of the founding of Cuzco. Perhaps the single most important piece of propaganda ever issued in the central Andes, the legend is still very much alive today.

Most influential of the many variants is the one given by the chronicler Garcilaso de la Vega in his *Royal Commentaries of the Incas,* published in 1609. The son of a Spanish soldier and an Inca princess, Garcilaso wrote toward the end of his life, drawing upon traditional lore that he claimed to have heard as a child from an uncle on his mother's side.

Garcilaso's version of the Manco Capac tale evidently owes much to the *Wirakocha* myth, borrowing the northward trek and even the Lake Titicaca setting. Here, however, the first Inca is sent down from the sky together with his sister, who will become his *koya,* or queen.

It seems that the Sun in that early time took pity on the world, which as yet had no knowledge of farming or weaving, and sent his two children, the Inca and the *koya,* to teach the arts of civilization. Bringing them to earth, he put them in Lake Titicaca and ordered them to proceed from there in any direction they chose. But wherever they stopped to eat or sleep they were to push in the ground a rod of gold, half the length of a man's arm and two fingers thick, which the Sun had given them as a sign. They were to found their city in whatever place the rod could be made to disappear with a single thrust.

The Sun's parting words were these:

"When all the people have become your subjects, you must rule them wisely and justly, with pity, with mercy, and with tenderness. I want you to treat them as a compassionate father would his beloved children, and in this you must imitate and resemble me, for it is I who take care of the world and give it light and warmth. . . .

"As you are my son and daughter, you must be like me. You must go into the world and provide for these people who have lived like animals. I therefore establish and name you rulers over all those races whom you will lift up with your good instruction, good works, and lawful government."

When the Sun Father had left them, the two children came out of the lake—note once again the Central Andean emergence motif—and began traveling northward. After many stops, the Inca and his *koya* reached the Valley of Cuzco, where they drove in the rod with just one stroke. They then summoned all the people from the countryside, who came and learned women's work from the *koya* and men's work from the Inca, worshipping these two as children of the Sun.

Inkarrí

In a remarkable act of cynicism the foregoing legend, or some variant of it, was served up to the common people in the tribes the Incas had conquered. The Incas themselves did not believe it.

This at least was the finding of Father Miguel Cabello de Balboa, whose report on the ancient Peruvians is dated 1586. According to Cabello, the ruling elite had its own private legend, which told how the Incas had tricked the tribesmen of the southern highlands into believing that their ruler was a child of the sun. They had simply brought him forth at some distance, wearing a gold mantle that caught the light, and the dazzled onlookers thought they were seeing an embodiment of the sun itself.

As for the official legend, the one put out for public consumption, it would be difficult to say how widely this was believed. The story does not appear in the sixteenth-century collections of legends from such provincial centers as Huamacucho and Huarochirí, where local traditions continued to take precedence over the lore of Cuzco.

During the period that followed, however, whatever indifference or even resentment there may have been toward the Incas became transferred to the Spaniards, and Quechua people in many parts of the highlands began to think of *themselves* as Incas. Looking back, they counted among their heroes Atahuallpa, the last true emperor; Manco Inca, the puppet ruler set up by the Spaniards after Atahuallpa had been murdered (not to be confused with Manco Capac Inca); Tupac Amaru, last of the royal dynasty, who led a rump empire in the montaña until he was caught and murdered in 1572; and, especially, Tupac Amaru II, whose rebellion against Spanish rule was crushed in 1781.

In latter-day adaptations of the old Manco Capac legend one or another of these leaders becomes the hero who inaugurates the Inca period (after the sun's victory over the *chullpa* people), founding a city by throwing or implanting a rod of gold. In some versions the hero is beheaded by the envious Spaniards, but it is believed that his head will eventually grow a new body, and when it is complete, the Inca will return.

Sometimes called by such names as "Manco" or "Amaru," the hero of the story is more often presented simply as *Inka* or *Inkarrí* (from "Inca" and the Spanish word *rey,* meaning "king").

In a modern variant from the small community of Q'ero, the hero *Inkarrí,* who carried the rod of gold, is accompanied by his consort, *Kolyari,* carrying a spindle. First he establishes Q'ero by throwing the instrument and having it land a little crooked. Then, with a perfect throw that plants the rod upright, he founds Cuzco and lives there for a while. After sharing his knowledge with the people, he departs for the montaña, leaving footprints that can still be seen.

Presumably this version from Q'ero derives strictly from oral tradition. But the possibility of Garcilaso's influence should not be ruled out. Over the centuries his *Royal Commentaries* have been repeatedly studied by bilingual Indians and part-Indians—the work had to be banned after the rebellion of 1781—and it may well have enriched later folklore.

More fully typical of the modern *Inkarrí* legend is a variant from Puquio, in which the hero ties up the sun, "so that the day will last, so that *Inkarrí* can do what he has to do." Throwing the rod of gold, he establishes Cuzco. But then, "the king of the Spaniards captured *Inkarrí,* who was his equal. We do not know where. They say that only the head of *Inkarrí* exists. From the head it is growing downward. They say it is growing toward the feet. Then he will return . . . if God wills it."

Thus the traditional story of the rod of gold has become a

millenarian legend, or myth of prophecy, in which the lost native leader will be returned to his people in the hour of their need.

The *pachakuti*

In the community of Sonqo and elsewhere in the highlands it is said that the Incas will return to power during a *pachakuti*, or cataclysm, which may refer to floods, storms, or earthquakes. The idea comes from the old mythology, where the *pachakuti* marked the transition between world ages, often with the idea of punishing the creatures that had ruled the land up to that time.

Bringing the myth into the modern era, native people in southern Peru interpreted the great earthquake of May 1950, which all but destroyed Cuzco, as a kind of *pachakuti*. Specifically, they regarded it as divine punishment for the cruelty of non-Indian landowners. And in fact the Cuzco earthquake ushered in a period of political ferment in southern Peru, which saw the strengthening of trade unions and farmers' organizations.

According to the story that circulated later, an old bearded man dressed in rags had gone into a bake shop in Cuzco asking for food. But the owners merely threw dirty water on him. As he backed out the door, he warned them that something would happen. Shortly afterward he boarded a bus for one of the outlying villages. At the edge of the city he asked the driver to stop while he urinated. When he did not return, the driver went looking for him. Meanwhile the earthquake struck, destroying all the shops on the main square in Cuzco.

To the folklorist acquainted with Andean traditions the old bearded man can be none other than *Tonapa* or *Koniraya Wirakocha*, the loathly god unrecognized until it is too late. If the tale of *Koniraya* is recalled, even the trickery of disappearing while supposedly answering a call of nature can be seen as a folkloric motif.

"Inkarrí is here!"

By the 1960s the Indian people of the highlands had come to be appreciated by the government of Peru as a force that might shape the future of the nation. Their sheer numbers were impressive. Out of every hundred Peruvians nearly fifty were Quechua speakers.

To win Indian support, politicians in Lima announced a new program of land reform in the late 1960s. Addressing crowds of Indian farmers, President Juan Velasco Alvarado and his representatives made stirring promises: *"Campesino!* The *patrón* will no longer eat off your poverty!" "The time of Tupac Amaru II has dawned!" *"Inkarrí* is here!"

By 1970 the engraved portrait of Tupac Amaru was appearing on the paper money of Peru, and a decree of 1975 made Quechua an official language, together with Spanish.

But land was still the key issue, and it soon became clear that the transfer of title from landlords to Indian peasants, mandated as early as 1962, would not be completed under the new government. The officials in Lima had promised more than they could deliver.

Although there were lasting accomplishments, efforts toward reform were often frustrated by the Indians' long-standing distrust of the authorities. Here again folklore played a role.

Widespread in the highlands, as well as the montaña, is the belief in a kind of human monster known as *pishtaco*. It kills at night, choosing only Indian victims, whose bodies are melted down for grease to lubricate airplane engines and other machinery used in the cities. Aware of the tradition, landowners expecting reform officers from Lima would convince their Indian farmers that *pishtacos* were coming. When the officers arrived, they would be met with hostility.

The sporadic violence that erupted during these years intensified after 1980. Guerrilla groups, in some cases using the name Tupac Amaru, began making armed attacks on banks and police stations. By 1983 worldwide attention had been focused on one band in particular, called Shining Path, which had seized control of the countryside around the city of Ayacucho. At first reluctant to use its army, the Peruvian government by the mid-1980s was engaged in open conflict with the "Path."

Some scholars believe that this highly secretive movement represents yet another in the long series of attempts to restore Inca rule. It is by no means certain, however, that Shining Path has broad Indian support or that its leaders envision other than a centralized revolutionary government in which the new world of *Inkarrí* would remain elusive.

The future of myth

As the twentieth century draws to a close, it is difficult to imagine a time when the legend of the returning Inca will no longer be heard in the highlands, even though it would seem to have outlived its life span. One does not expect Indian lore to withstand the pressures of Western civilization. And yet it can.

Inevitably, the moment of contact between the two cultures represents a turning point, the definitive break between past and future, of which there have been instances in various parts of the New World in every decade since Columbus' first voyage. To consider the case of the Quechua is illuminating, since the future of Quechua mythology really began 450 years ago.

As we now know, the lore of the Quechua-speaking provinces would become increasingly subordinate to the remembered lore of Cuzco. Christian legends would become important, and even as early as 1600 European folktales would begin to elbow the native traditions. By the twentieth century the Br'er Rabbit cycle and the European tale of John the Bear would be firmly established from Bolivia to Ecuador.

At the same time, traces of the past, including the names of *Inti* and *Pachamama*, would endure, along with the concept of world ages and the class of spirits, or *waka*, now often referred to as *auki* (fathers) or *apu* (lords). Ancient tale types such as The Parrot Brides would not be entirely forgotten, and behind the widespread story of the Inca and the rod of gold, perhaps still worthy of being regarded as a myth, the spirit of *Wirakocha* would continue to haunt the highlands.

In the montaña the future began late—or so it might appear. Actually Spanish missions were established in the forested areas as early as the mid-1500s. Yet with rare exceptions local mythology was not recorded and, perhaps, remained free of outside influence. In the case of the Shuar, an early attempt was made to impose Spanish control, but the native people drove out the invaders in 1599 and have remained independent ever since.

When the Shuar began receiving anthropologists in the early twentieth century, very few myths were given out, and in the 1940s the *Handbook of South American Indians* could record that Shuar mythology "is being forgotten." No one would have predicted that in the 1960s and 1970s the Shuar themselves would be helping to make important collections of their own myths, including the twelve-volume *Mitología shuar* (1976–83), published in Shuar and Spanish.

For the Shuar the publication of tribal lore is part of a program of heightened cultural and political awareness, which began with the founding in 1964 of the Federation of Shuar Centers. Dedicated to the continued independence of the Jívaroan peoples of eastern Ecuador, the Federation has been called the most powerful native organization in South America. At home and in school, children are taught the lore of *Nunkwi, Etsa,* and *Tsunki,* and it is recognized among native leaders that the preservation of myth will help keep the people vital.

In the Peruvian montaña, where Indian politics are less forceful than they are in Ecuador, programs similar to those of the Shuar are being made available through the Centro Amazónico of Lima. Sponsored by the Catholic Church, this group has helped the Aguaruna publish two large volumes of their myths in a bilingual edition. Here, too, the myths are considered important to native self-esteem and, ultimately, to the survival of the tribe.

Like the lowland forests of Brazil, the montaña has its little-known and newly discovered tribes, notably the Waorani of extreme eastern Ecuador, who rejected outsiders until after

1950. For the Waorani the future is just beginning, and it remains to be seen whether a significant myth collection will be forthcoming.

Evidently the Central Andean region has not exhausted its sources of traditional lore. This is true even of the highlands, where reports from out-of-the-way communities keep revealing unsuspected connections with the past. In the montaña, just as in parts of Brazil and Guiana, the future remains young. Valuable and possibly great collections are yet to be made, holding out the promise that of the earth's inhabited continents South America will continue to rank as the foremost producer of living myth.

Notes on Sources

Intended primarily as an accompaniment to the text, these notes may also be used to verify the myth distribution patterns shown in the maps. In each case the appropriate references are collected in the note that corresponds to the text location where the myth is discussed. Such notes are marked with an asterisk (*).

Most sources are identified only by author, date, volume number (if needed), and page number. Full bibliographic entries can be traced in the References that come after the Notes.

The abbreviation FLSAI stands for Wilbert and Simoneau's The Folk Literature of South American Indians; HSAI stands for Steward's *Handbook of South American Indians.*

Introduction

Page 5/"Tall and substantial-looking": Brown 1985, 41.

Page 5/"Wore black clothing": Perrin 1976, 73.

Page 5/Erland Nordenskiöld: Wassén 1933, 106–7.

Page 6/Lévi-Strauss had argued: Lévi-Strauss 1967, 206.

Page 8/Kogi myths: Preuss 1921–22, 46off.; Reichel-Dolmatoff 1951, 9.

Page 8/Quechua stories: Allen 1983, 41.

Page 8/Shuar stories of creation: Stirling 1938, 123.

Page 8/Suyá narratives: Seeger 1981, 206.

Page 8/Yekuana stories: David Guss, personal communication 1986; cf. Civrieux 1980, vii.

Page 8/Mataco stories: FLSAI 5, 29 & 30.

Page 10/"Stem of the story": Hildebrand 1975, 325.

Page 10/"While striving to maintain": Brett 1868, quoted in Alexander 1964, 269.

Page 10/Myth of the origin of tobacco: Reichel-Dolmatoff 1951, 60.

Page 10/Janet Siskind: Siskind 1975, 48.

Page 11/Cubeo myth of *Kúwai*: Goldman 1963, 182.

Page 11/Mataco storytelling: FLSAI 5, 17–18.

Page 13/"A long time ago": Farabee 1967, 113.

Page 14/Thompson motifs: Stith Thompson 1970, 280–84.

Page 15/As far as Belize: J. Eric S. Thompson 1930, 134–35.

Page 15/Lodge Boy and Thrown Away: Bierhorst 1985, 157–58 & 247; Stith Thompson 1929, 319.

Page 16/Story of Moon's incest: Bierhorst 1985, 59 & 60 & 239; Stith Thompson 1929, 4–5 & 273.

Page 16/Bird Nester in North America: Bierhorst 1985, 10 & 69 & 86–91 & 135 & 145.

Part One : Greater Brazil

Page 26/Culture hero identified with jaguar: HSAI 3, 241 (Shipaya); Reichel-Dolmatoff 1971, 28 (Desana).

* Page 28/Twin Myth: Nimuendajú 1914, 393–400 (Apapocúva); Steinen 1894, 372–86 (Bakairí); Hugh-Jones 1979, 274–83 (Barasana); FLSAI 7, 180–85 (Bororo); Balzano 1984, 29–32 (Chacobo); Métraux 1931, 154–65 (Chiriguano); Koch-Grünberg 1967 2, 159–60 (Cubeo); Métraux 1931, 147 (Kaingang); Basso 1973, 10–12 (Kalapalo); Villas Boas and Villas Boas 1973, 57–70 (Kamayurá); ibid., 72–88 (Kuikuru); Trupp 1977, 64–69 (Makuna); Cadogan 1959, 69–88 (Mbyá); Steinen 1894, 438–39 (Paressí); Nimuendajú 1919–20, 1016 (Shipaya); Wagley 1983, 179–80 (Tapirapé); Wagley and Galvão 1949, 137–40 (Tenetehara); Nimuendajú 1952, 122–23 (Tukuna); Métraux 1928, 235–36 (Tupinamba); Huxley 1957, 217–20 (Urubú); Chaumeil and Chaumeil 1978, 162–68 (Yagua); Orbigny 1844, 210–15 (Yuracaré); Preuss 1921–23 1, 330–43 (Witoto). See also Guiana, Northwest, and Central Andes.

* Page 31/Tree and the Flood: Chaumeil and Chaumeil 1978, 169–70 (Yagua). Similar variants but without the twins: Hugh-Jones 1979, 269 (Tatuyo); Hildebrand 1975, 337–39 & 343–45 (Ufaina). Guiana-type variant: Preuss 1921–23 1, 170–206 (Witoto). See also Guiana, Gran Chaco, and Northwest.

Page 31/Story of Hummingbird: Nimuendajú 1946, 111 (Botocudo); ibid., 111n (Kaingang).

Page 31/Plant from the Grave: Orbigny 1844, 213 (Yuracaré).

* Page 32/Theft of Fire from the Vulture: Nimuendajú 1914, 396–97 (Apapocúva). Variants without the twins: Nimuendajú 1946, 11–12 (Botocudo); Villas Boas and Villas Boas 1973, 25 (Carayá); Métraux 1931, 171 (Chiriguano); Wassén 1934a, 644 (Guarayú); Villas Boas and Villas Boas 1973, 105 (Kuikuru); Cadogan 1959, 64–66 (Mbyá); HSAI 3, 294 (Parintintin); Nimuendajú 1919–20, 1015 (Shipaya); Wagley 1983, 177 (Tapirapé); Wagley and Galvão 1949, 133 (Tenetehara); Villas Boas and Villas Boas 1973, 25 (Trumaí).

Page 32/Origin of peccaries: Nimuendajú 1919–20, 1013–14 (Shipaya); Murphy 1958, 70–73 (Mundurucú); Wagley and Galvão 1949, 134 (Tenetehara).

* Page 32/Moon and His Sister: Hugh-Jones 1979, 274–75 (Barasana); Crocker 1985, 135 (Bororo); HSAI 3, 438 (Guarayú); Trupp 1977, 50–56 (Makuna); Siskind 1975, 47–48 (Sharanahua); Nimuendajú 1919–20, 1010–11 (Shipaya); Wagley and Galvão 1983, 179 (Tapirapé); Nimuendajú 1952, 143 (Tukuna); Hildebrand 1975, 345–46 (Ufaina); Huxley 1957, 164–66 (Urubú); Preuss 1921–23 1, 330–31 (Witoto). In Guiana: Roth 1915, 256 (Arawak); Koch-Grünberg 1916, 54 (Arekuna); Fock 1963, 54–55 (Waiwai); FLSAI 1, 63–66 (Warrau); Armellada and Bentivenga 1975, 217 (Yabarana); Civrieux 1980, 47 (Yekuana). In the Central Andes: Whitten 1978, 844 (Canelos); Cháves 1958, 144–45 (Siona); HSAI 3, 649 (Záparo). See also Northwest.

Page 33/*Karusakaibe* and Armadillo: Murphy 1958, 70–79; Kruse 1951–52.

* Page 34/Origin of Night: Couto de Magalhães 1876, 162–74 (Anambé); HSAI 3, 379 (Arua); Crocker 1985, 135 (Bororo); Koch-Grünberg 1920, 231 (Cashinawa); Reichel-Dolmatoff 1971, 26 (Desana); Cadogan 1962, 51–52 (Guayakí); Hugh-Jones 1979, 267–68 (Tatuyo); Wagley and Galvão 1949, 142 (Tenetehara); Hildebrand 1975, 333–36 (Ufaina). In Guiana: Roth 1915, 212 (Arawak); FLSAI 1, 377–79 (Warrau). In the Brazilian Highlands: FLSAI 4, 88–93 (Cayapó).

* Pages 34–36/Emergence stories: Reichel-Dolmatoff 1978, 62 (Barasana); Ehrenreich 1891, 39 (Carayá); Goldman 1963, 93–112 (Cubeo); Reichel-Dolmatoff 1971, 25–26 & 30 (Desana); Cadogan 1962, 46 (Guayakí); Murphy 1958, 77–78 (Mundurucú); Nimuendajú 1919–20, 1008 (Shipaya); Caspar 1956, 210–11 (Tupari); Preuss 1921–23 1, 167 (Witoto); Orbigny 1844, 214 (Yuracaré). See also all other regions except Far South.

Page 36/Kaingang double chants: Henry 1964, 126 & 148; Urban 1986, 373 & 375. Double chants in other tribes: ibid., 372–76; Sherzer 1979, 145–51 (Cuna); Sherzer 1983, 72–95 (Cuna).

Page 38/Daughter of the Sun: Reichel-Dolmatoff 1971, 35–36.

Pages 38–40/Why we are poor: FLSAI 7, 77–79 (Bororo); Ehrenreich 1891, 40 (Carayá); Murphy 1958, 81 (Mundurucú); HSAI 3, 360 (Paressí); Hildebrand 1975 (Ufaina).

Page 40/On the Bororo today: Crocker 1985, 330–31; "For Brazil's Tribes: A New Will to Live," *New York Times,* 8/2/74, 29 & 42.

Page 41/*Kúwai* of the Cubeo: Goldman 1963, 147–48 & 160 & 182 & 193; Koch-Grünberg 1967 2, 159–60 & 162 & 164–65

* Pages 44–48/Origin of Male Domination: Biocca 1965–66 1, 419–25 (Baniwa); Hugh-Jones 1979, 263–66 (Barasana); Goldman 1963, 193 (Cubeo); Reichel-Dolmatoff 1971, 169–70 (Desana); Villas Boas and Villas Boas 1973, 119–21 (Kamayurá); Trupp 1977, 71–75 (Makuna); Gregor 1985, 112–13 (Mehinaku); Murphy and Murphy 1974, 88–89 (Mundurucú); Stradelli 1890 (Tariana); Biocca 1965–66 1, 230–31 (Tucano); Hildebrand 1975, 326 (Ufaina myth noted but not published); Huxley 1957, 150 (Urubú); Koch-Grünberg 1967 2, 292–93 (Yahuna). See also Gran Chaco and Far South.

Page 49/"Let us put on these garments of hair": Stradelli 1890, 813.

Page 49/Incident of October 23, 1883: Biocca 1965–66 1, 26–30.

Page 49/Ritual wailing of the women: Murphy and Murphy 1974, 93.

* Pages 50–52/Amazon myth: HSAI 1, 516 (Carayá); Basso 1985, 262–85 (Kalapalo); Villas Boas and Villas Boas 1973, 123–25 (Kamayurá); Leach and Fried 1972, 42 (Macurap); HSAI 1, 516 (Tupinamba); Schultz 1966, 136–42 (Waurá); HSAI 3, 762 (Witoto). In the Brazilian Highlands: FLSAI 4, 335–38 (Apinayé); FLSAI 8, 521 (Shikrí Cayapó). In the Central Andes: Cieza de León 1883, 3 (Aymara). See also Guiana.

Page 50/Columbus and Orellana: sources cited in Alexander 1920, 19 & 281.

Page 54/Ufaina mythmaker "thinks well": Hildebrand 1975, 326.

Page 54/"Our Great Father came alone": Nimuendajú 1914, 393.

Page 55/"When earth did not yet exist": Biocca 1965–66 1, 269–81.

Page 56/*Romi Kumu*: Hugh-Jones 1979, 204 & 263–66 (Barasana); Trupp 1977, 73 (Makuna).
Page 56/"In the beginning there was nothing": ibid., 31.
Page 57/"Was it not an illusion?": Preuss 1921–23 1, 166–67 as translated in Bierhorst 1976, 40–41.
Page 58/"Our First Father, the absolute": Cadogan 1959, 13–15 as translated in Bierhorst 1976, 37–38.
Page 59/Mbyá paradise: Cadogan 1959, 29 & 30.
Page 59/Guaraní migrations: Espíndola 1961, 313 & 316.
Page 59/Messianism in the Northwest Amazon: Biocca 1965–66 1, 25–26; Nimuendajú 1952, 137–40.
Page 60/Messianic myths of the Guaraní: Nimuendajú 1914, 400–3 (Apapocúva); Cadogan 1959, 86 (Mbyá); Riester 1970, 468–69 (Guarayú).

Part Two : Guiana

Page 66/Emergence story: Bourne 1906, 12ff. as cited in Radin 1942, 13 (Taino). See also all other regions except Far South.
* Pages 66–68/Guiana myths of sky descent: Brett 1880, 179 (Arawak) cited in Roth 1915, 142; Im Thurn 1967, 377 (Carib); HSAI 4, 564 (Island Carib); Brett 1880, 55–60 (Warrau); FLSAI 1, 216–20 & 290–311 (Warrau); Couture-Brunette and Saffirio 1985, 9 (Yanomamo); Civrieux 1980, 23–24 & 48 (Yekuana).
Page 70/Shamanism in Yekuana mythology: Civrieux 1980, 164; Guss 1985, 55–75.
Page 70/Levels of the universe: Fock 1963, 101–2 (Waiwai); Chagnon 1968, 44–45 (Yanomamo); Guss 1985, 57 (Yekuana).
Page 71/Yekuana spirit brides and husbands: Guss 1985, 58 & 63 & 69–70.
* Pages 71–72/Vulture Wife: Brett 1880, 29–30 (Arawak); van Coll 1908, 482–84 (Caliña); Goeje 1943, 96 (Caliña, Carib, and Makushí); Simpson 1944, 268–73 (Camaracoto); Koch-Grünberg 1916, 81–91 (Taulipáng); FLSAI 1, 118–20 (Warrau).
* Pages 72–73/Underwater Woman: Roth 1915, 245–46 (Arawak); ibid., 251–52 (Carib); Civrieux 1974, 112–13 (Cariña); FLSAI 1, 96–98 (Warrau); Civrieux 1980, 34–35 (Yekuana). See also Central Andes.
Page 74/Anaconda becomes rainbow: Civrieux 1974, 109.
Page 74/*Amana*: Goeje 1943, 63.
Page 74/Carib version with several women: Gillen 1936, 170.
Page 74/"Fair Maid" or "Water Momma" stories: Roth 1915, 154; Drummond 1977, 858 & 865.
Page 75/Wapishana story of *Kasum*: Farabee 1967, 119–20.
Page 75/Spells of the Taulipáng: Koch-Grünberg 1923, 219–74; Armellada 1972.
Page 75/*Tarén* about the hawks and the wasps: ibid., 236–37.
Page 78/David Guss: personal communication 1986; cf. Guss 1986, 416–17.
Page 78/*Tarén* came from the Makushí: Armellada 1972, 180.
Page 78/Narrative incantations among the Ayoreo: Bórmida 1978.

Page 78/In California and Oregon: Bierhorst 1985, 147–49.

* Pages 79–80/Tree and the Flood: Im Thurn 1967, 379 (Acawai and Carib); Koch-Grünberg 1916, 33–38 (Arekuna and Taulipáng); Gillen 1936, 189–90 (Carib); Farabee 1967, 83–84 (Makushí); ibid. (Wapishana); Ogilvie 1940, 65–67 (Wapishana); Civrieux 1980, 132–37 (Yekuana). See also Greater Brazil, Gran Chaco, and Northwest.

* Page 80/Gourd and the Flood: Simpson 1944, 264–65 (Camaracoto); Civrieux 1974, 77–79 (Kariña); Bourne 1906, 20ff. (Taino) cited in Radin 1942, 17–18.

* Pages 81–82/Origin of the Carib Warrior: Armellada and Bentivenga 1975, 234–36 (Piaroa creation story); Walde-Waldegg 1936, 41 (Sáliva version); Brett 1880, 62–74 (Warrau story of serpent and young woman); Roth 1915, 144 (told by the Caribs themselves).

Page 82/Yanomamo myth of Moon: Chagnon 1968, 47–48; Armellada and Bentivenga 1975, 205–6.

* Page 83/Amazon myth: Roth 1915, 222 & 365 (Arawak, Carib, and Makushí); Shoumatoff 1986, 106–7 (Kaxúyana); Alexander 1920, 19 (Taino); Koch-Grünberg 1916, 124 (Taulipáng). See also Greater Brazil.

* Pages 83–87/Twin Myth: Roth 1915, 133–35 (Carib); Civrieux 1974, 82–84 (Kariña); Roth 1915, 135 (Makushí); Armellada 1972, 46–50 (Taulipáng); Fock 1963, 38–40 (Waiwai); Roth 1915, 130–33 (Warrau); Chagnon 1968, 46 (Yanomamo); Civrieux 1980, 51–82 (Yekuana). See also Greater Brazil, Northwest, and Central Andes.

Page 87/Origin of tribes from the two women who were fished up: Farabee 1967, 159 (Mapidian); ibid., 143–45 (Taruma); ibid., 172–73 (Waiwai); Fock 1963, 38–42 (Waiwai); Couture-Brunette and Saffirio 1985, 9 (Yanomamo).

Part Three : Brazilian Highlands

Page 94/Emergence stories virtually nonexistent; but for simple emergence motifs, see FLSAI 4, 157 & 249 (Cayapó); Maybury-Lewis 1974, 285–86 (Shavante). See also all other regions except Far South.

Page 94/Attitude toward ceremony and myth: HSAI 1, 509 & 514; Maybury-Lewis 1974, 240 & 286.

Page 94/Origin of laughter: FLSAI 4, 329 (Cayapó).

Page 94/Noisy vegetables: FLSAI 8, 219 (Krahó).

Page 94/Nighthawk's wings: FLSAI 4, 273 (Cayapó).

Page 96/Why didn't you come sooner?: FLSAI 8, 33 (Sherente).

* Pages 96–98/Star Woman: FLSAI 4, 194–223 (Apinayé, Canela, Cayapó, and Krahó); FLSAI 8, 175–90 (Cayapó, Shavante, Sherente, and Shikrí Cayapó). See also Gran Chaco.

Page 97/Antti Aarne: Stith Thompson 1946, 435–46.

* Pages 98–99/Corn Tree: FLSAI 4, 216 (Apinayé); ibid., 224–27 (Cayapó); ibid., 196–98 (Krahó); FLSAI 8, 137–47 (Shavante and Shikrí Cayapó).

Page 100/Lévi-Strauss and "transformations": Lévi-Strauss 1969, 63 and passim (see especially 307).

* Pages 101–102/Bird Nester and the Jaguar: FLSAI 4, 160–88 (Apinayé, Canela, Cayapó, Krahó, and Krenye); FLSAI 8, 108–35 (Cayapó, Krahó, Shavante, Sherente, Shikrí Cayapó, and Suyá).

Page 103/"My brother-in-law, let's go": Giaccaria and Heide 1975, 15, translated in FLSAI 8, 111, quoted by permission of the UCLA Latin American Center.

Page 104/"There are some baby macaws a long way over there": text recorded by Anthony Seeger and published in FLSAI 8, 108, quoted with minor alterations by permission of Anthony Seeger and the UCLA Latin American Center.

Page 106/Humans created by throwing gourds: FLSAI 4, 75 (Apinayé).

Pages 107–8 *Kokrít* myths: FLSAI 4, 239 (Canela); FLSAI 8, 247–50 (Shikrí Cayapó and Txukahamai).

Page 108/Suyá myth of cannibal spirits: FLSAI 8, 203–8.

Page 110/"Oh, give it to my brother-in-law": Maybury-Lewis 1974, 101–2.

* Pages 110–11/Sun and Moon cycle: see following eight notes.

Page 111/Hot meat: FLSAI 4, 34 (Apanyekra) & 53 (Apinayé) & 59 (Canela) & 65 (Cayapó) & 39–40 (Krahó) & 67 (Krenye); FLSAI 8, 35 (Sherente).

Page 111/Fiery headdress: FLSAI 4, 33 (Apanyekra) & 51–52 (Apinayé) & 58–59 (Canela) & 41 (Krahó).

Page 111/Palm fruits: FLSAI 4, 33 (Apanyekra) & 53–54 (Apinayé) & 60 (Canela) & 230–31 (Cayapó).

Page 111/Self-working tools: FLSAI 4, 32 (Apanyekra) & 54–55 (Apinayé) & 59–60 (Canela) & 68–72 (Krahó). Variants outside the Brazilian Highlands: Weiss 1975, 269 & 487 (Campa); Nordenskiöld 1912, 260–70 (Chiriguano); Murphy 1958, 80 (Mundurucú); Koch-Grunberg 1916, 124–28 (Taulipáng); Wagley and Galvão 1949, 132 (Tenetehara).

Page 111/Deaths and revivals: FLSAI 4, 35 (Apanyekra) & 47–48 (Krahó); FLSAI 8, 27–28 (Canela).

Page 112/Sun and Moon took their fire with them: FLSAI 4, 160.

Page 112/Radin on trickster myths: Radin 1942, 155; cf. Radin 1972, 132–46.

Pages 112–15/Sun and Moon cycle of the Apinayé: FLSAI 4, 51–55.

Part Four : Gran Chaco

Page 119/*Chacu* means "hunting ground": Bravo 1967, 65–66; HSAI 1, 197.

Page 120/Pleiades as hunters who climbed to sky: FLSAI 5, 45 (Mataco); Rivera de Bianchi 1973, 701 (Mocoví).

Page 120/Southern Cross as ostrich chased to sky: FLSAI 5, 37 (Mataco); Rivera de Bianchi 1973, 703 (Mocoví); FLSAI 6, 27 (Toba).

Page 120/Pleiades as people around campfire: Mashnshnek 1973, 118 & 138.

Page 122/"The beginning, when people were animals": FLSAI 5, 140.

Page 122/Fox stories in Greater Brazil: Nordenskiöld 1912, 26off. (Chiriguano); Kruse 1946–49, 631–33 (Mundurucú); Preuss 1921–23 1, 574–78 (Witoto). In the Central Andes: La Barre 1950 (Aymara); see Chapter Seventeen, above (Quechua); Hissink and Hahn 1961, 421–22 (Tacana); HSAI 2, 582 (Uro-Chipaya). In the Far South: HSAI 2, 753 (Mapuche); FLSAI 9 (Tehuelche).

* Pages 122–23/Toba Fox stories: FLSAI 6, 227 (tree-sitting contest with vulture) & 223 (origin of fox tripes) & 224–25 (tries to imitate skunks) & 261–62 (watermelons from vomit) & 233–35 (Fox and Jaguar) & 237–39 (Fox and his sister-in-law) & 241 (marries a man) & 248–49 (baby-sitter) & 255–56 (missionary).

* Page 123/Tree and the Flood: HSAI 1, 369 (Ashluslay); Leach and Fried 1972, 123 (Chané); FLSAI 10, 92 (Chorote); FLSAI 5, 146–68 (Mataco). See also Greater Brazil, Guiana, and Northwest.

* Page 123/Fox plants the first algarroba: Nordenskiöld 1912, 26off. (Chané); FLSAI 10, 50–51 (Chorote).

* Page 124/*Tokwah* is a little man: Alvarsson 1984, 96–97.

* Page 124/*Tokwah* steals fire: FLSAI 5, 103.

* Page 125/*Tokwah* gives men their "milk": Mashnshnek 1973, 139; Alvarsson 1985, 169; FLSAI 5, 80–81.

* Page 125/*Tokwah* introduces adultery: FLSAI 5, 145.

* Page 125/*Tokwah* makes death permanent: FLSAI 5, 17 & 90; Mashnshnek 1973, 147–48.

* Page 125/Carancho insists that honey be placed inside of trees: Lévi-Strauss 1973, 74n.

* Page 125/Carancho advised people to steal and murder: FLSAI 5, 32.

* Page 125/Carancho the fire bringer: HSAI 1, 368 (Chamacoco); FLSAI 10, 92–93 (Chorote); FLSAI 6, 161–66 (Toba).

* Page 125/Carancho spoils easy hunting: FLSAI 6, 172–73.

* Page 126/Carancho rescues people surrounded by water: FLSAI 6, 163–65.

* Page 126/Fox and Carancho treat snakebite: FLSAI 6, 152–56.

* Pages 128–29/Bird Nester's Wife: FLSAI 10, 221–24 (Chorote); FLSAI 5, 239 (Mataco); Lévi-Strauss 1969, 100 (Tereno); FLSAI 6, 309–13 (Toba).

Page 129/"In ancient times the jaguar was a woman": FLSAI 5, 98.

Pages 129–30/Woman shaman: FLSAI 6, 340–41.

Page 130/Mother of birds: FLSAI 10, 116–23.

* Pages 131–33/Star Woman: Métraux 1943, 118 (Chamacoco); FLSAI 10, 254–67 (Chorote); Mashnshnek 1973, 137–39 (Mataco); FLSAI 6, 51–60 (Toba). See also Brazilian Highlands.

Page 133/First people created by Morning Star: FLSAI 10, 26.

Page 133/Creator is beetle: HSAI 1, 36.

* Page 133/Emergence stories: FLSAI 5, 59–60 & 62–63 (Mataco); Sánchez Labrador 1910 2, 50–51 (Mbayá); HSAI 1, 367 (Tereno); FLSAI 6, 129 (Toba). See also all other regions except Far South.

* Pages 134–35/Women from the Sky: FLSAI 10, 29–35 (Chorote); Métraux 1946, 106 (Lengua); FLSAI 5, 67–77 (Mataco); FLSAI 6, 111–44 (Toba).

Pages 136–37/Origin of Male Domination: Métraux 1943 (*Anáposo* ceremony and myth). See also Greater Brazil and Far South.

Page 139/Trance-journeys: Barabas and Bartolomé 1979, 83–84; Palavecino 1979, 67–69 & 72. For *yulo*, see Bravo 1967, 318.

Pages 139–40/Myth of a visit to the fire master: Mashnshnek 1973, 139–40. Cf. FLSAI 5, 129–30; Barabas and Bartolomé 1979, 77.

Page 140/World fire caused by women leaving their husbands: FLSAI 5, 126–27.

Pages 140–42/World fire caused by fall of moon or sun: FLSAI 6, 68 (Toba); Métraux 1946, 34–35 (Mocoví).

Page 142/Origin of various constellations: FLSAI 6, 25–26.

Page 142/Flood myths: FLSAI 10, 38–39 (Chorote); FLSAI 5, 126 (Mataco); FLSAI 6, 88–90 (Toba).

Page 143/Myth of *Asin*: FLSAI 6, 98–99.

Page 144/Myths of the great darkness: FLSAI 6, 94–96 (Toba); Métraux 1946, 32 (Vilela).

Page 145/Myths of the restoration of life: FLSAI 10, 38 & 47–48 (Chorote); Mashnshnek 1973, 141–42 (Mataco); Barabas and Bartolomé 1979, 78–79 (Mataco); FLSAI 5, 128–29 (Mataco).

Page 145/"There was a bird called *Tus*": Mashnshnek 1973, 141.

Part Five : Far South

Page 152/Mapuche flood myth: Faron 1963; Faron 1971; Casamiquela 1982; Fernández 1982.

* Page 154/High god or supreme deity: Gusinde 1923–24, 544–45 (*Kólas* of the Alacaluf); FLSAI 9, 8–9, and HSAI 1, 157–58 (*Kóoch* of the Tehuelche); Faron 1968, 63, and Faron 1971, 50–52, and HSAI 2, 742–47 (*Nyenéchen* of the Mapuche and Pehuenche); HSAI 1, 167–68 (*Soychu* of the Puelche); HSAI 1, 123 (*Temáukel* of the Selknam); HSAI 1, 99 & 102–3 (*Watawinéwa* of the Yamana).

Pages 154–55/Myths of *Kóoch*: FLSAI 9, 17–18 & 23.

Page 155/Deeds of *Kenós* and *Yoáloh* in response to deity's orders: FLSAI 2, 21 (Selknam); Gusinde 1961 4, 1099 & 1121 (Yamana).

Pages 155–57/*Yoáloh* myths: FLSAI 3, 30–61.

Page 157/Hero myths of the Selknam and the Alacaluf: FLSAI 2, 21–39; Gusinde 1930, 697; Gusinde 1974, 542.

Pages 157–59/*Elal* of the Tehuelche: FLSAI 9, 23–102.

Page 159/*Cónkel* and *Pedíu*: Lehmann-Nitsche 1930.

Page 161/"Be affectionate with your wives": Chapman 1982, 108.

Page 164/*Yoáloh-tárnuhipa* and Moon directed the other women: FLSAI 3, 36 (Yamana); FLSAI 2, 149 (Selknam).

Page 164/"We do not know how children came into being": Gusinde 1961 4, 1119.

Page 164/*Hálpen*: Bridges 1950, 416–17.

Page 164/*Tánuwa*: Gusinde 1961 5, 1238–39.

Page 165/"The moon woman caused the great flood": Gusinde 1961 4, 1114–15.

Page 166/"The men themselves were the ones who kindled the flames": Gusinde 1974, 487.

Page 166/"There was a time when the men turned against the women": Keller 1962, 528.

Page 167/Origin of birds and animals: Gusinde 1974, 487; FLSAI 3, 187–88 & 192; FLSAI 2, 149–50; Bridges 1950, 435.

* Page 168/Origin of Male Domination: see preceding nine notes. See also Greater Brazil and Gran Chaco.

Page 168/Manner in which Fuegian myths were collected: FLSAI 3, 9–10.
Page 168/"Maybe they suspected": Bridges 1950, 425.
Page 168/"On one occasion, when Angela": Chapman 1982, 75.

Part Six : Northwest

Page 174/Peter Martyr on Dabaiba myths: Anglería 1964–65 2, 328 & 645 & 647 & 650–52.

* Page 174/Moon and His Sister: ibid., 647 (Dabaiba); Wassén 1934b, 5–7 (Cuna). See also Greater Brazil.

Page 176/"They said that their origin had been from a man called *Mechión*": Simón 1892, 366.
Page 176/Tolú Old Woman: Wassén 1933, 117.
Pages 176–78/Myths of the Muisca: Simón 1891, 279–90.
Page 177/Ritual of the golden man: ibid., 242–43.
Page 178/Alfred Kroeber on *Bochica:* HSAI 2, 908–9.
Page 178/Names and attributes of the Kogi goddess: Preuss 1919–20, 378; Preuss 1921–22, 460.
Page 178/Kogi ancestry traced to jaguar or "fathers of the world": Reichel-Dolmatoff 1975, 55; Reichel-Dolmatoff 1949–50, 162.
Page 179/*Gaulchováng* imagined as fat and beautiful: Reichel-Dolmatoff 1951, 86.
Page 179/"The sea existed first": ibid., 9–18.
Page 180/Origin of the sun: Preuss 1921–22, 737–46.
Page 180/Trickster obtains fire: Reichel-Dolmatoff 1951, 60.
Page 180/"Mother, I was very afraid": ibid., 15.
Page 182/Yaruro mythology: Petrullo 1939.
Page 182/Emergence story (*Hatchawa* finds people in hole): ibid., 239. Cf. Guajiro emergence motif: HSAI 4, 382. See also all other regions except Far South.

* Page 183/Tree and the Flood: Wassén 1934b, 3–4 & 22–25 (with Cuna earth mother); Wassén 1933, 109–10 & 131 (Chocó and Catío). See also Greater Brazil, Guiana, and Gran Chaco.

* Page 184/Twin Myth: Perrin 1976, 103–6 & 121–22 (Guajiro). Cf. Wassén 1933, 116 (Chocó); Wassén 1934b, 119–20 (Cuna). See also Greater Brazil, Guiana, and Central Andes.

Pages 184–86/Story of *Pulówi* and the hunter: Perrin 1976, 62–72.
Page 186/"Late in the evening *Pulówi* appeared": Perrin 1976, 66–67, translated from the French by permission of the University of Texas Press. (Perrin's work has been published in English as *The Way of the Dead Indians: Guajiro Myths and Symbols*, trans. Michael Fineberg, copyright © 1987, University of Texas Press, Austin.)
Page 186/*Pulówi* drinks human blood: Perrin 1976, 40.
Page 186/*Pulówi* of the sea hurls the surf: ibid., 40.
Page 187/Cuna narratives with interrupted flow: Sherzer 1979; Sherzer 1983, 46–47.
Page 187/"You have written well what we have narrated": Perrin 1976, 19.

Page 189/Newspaper accounts of giants: "Tall Story from the Jungle" (Agence France-Presse dispatch), *New York Post* 2/26/73 (cf. "Brazil's Kreen-Akarores: Requiem for a Tribe?," *National Geographic*, Feb. 1975, 254–69); "Peru's Hunched Back Giants . . . Are They Stone Age Aborigines?" (UPI dispatch), *The Freeman* (Kingston, N.Y.), 5/20/76.

Page 190/Attempt to collect Cayapa myths: Barrett 1925 2, 355–56.

* Page 190/Male giants without women: ibid., 371–72 (Cayapa); Cieza de León 1947, 405 (Manta); Zárate 1947, 465 (Manta); Simón 1892, 366 (Tolú); Wavrin 1937, 518 (Yupa).

* Pages 191–93/Food-Inhaler Bride: Wilbert 1974, 15 (Catío and Chocó); Barrett 1925 2, 376 (Cayapa); Calazacon and Orazona 1982, 274 (Colorado); Wilbert 1974, 86–89 (Yupa). Food-inhaler or anus-less motif in Greater Brazil: Nimuendajú 1919–20, 1021–22 (Shipaya); Murphy and Quain 1966, 74 (Trumaí); Nimuendajú 1952, 119 (Tukuna); Huxley 1957, 171 (Urubú). In Guiana: Gillen 1936, 155 (Carib); Koch-Grünberg 1916, 77 (Taulipáng); Wilbert 1974, 15 (Warrau and Yanomamo). In the Far South: FLSAI 9, 20 & 134 (Tehuelche). In the Central Andes: Hissink and Hahn 1961, 88 & 352–54 (Tacana).

Pages 193–94/Northwest folk beliefs: Barrett 1925 2, 376–77 (*palámbele* of the Cayapa); Wassén 1933, 116 (blood drinkers of the Chocó); Reichel-Dolmatoff 1975, 52 (blood drinkers of the Páez); Calazacon and Orazona 1982, 284–86 (*ulili* of the Colorado); Wilbert 1974, 139 (*Mashíramu* of the Yupa).

Page 194/*Kurupira*: Huxley 1957, 181–82 (among Urubú, comparison with anteater); Métraux 1928, 64–67 (early sources, rarity among modern Indians); Niles 1981, 57 & 162 (Guaraní); Nimuendajú 1919–20, 1037–38 (Shipaya); Hildebrand 1975, 374 (Ufaina); Wagley 1964, 77 & 225 (rural Brazil); Smith 1983 (rural Brazil); Teschauer 1906, 24–30 (rural Brazil).

Part Seven : Central Andes

Page 200/Gods of the Incas: HSAI 2, 293–95.

Page 200/Painted document pertaining to Manco Capac: Molina 1873, 4–6.

Pages 202–3/Variants of *Wirakocha* myth: Bendezú Aybar 1980, 33–36 (Betanzos' version); Molina 1873, 6–7; Lara 1973, 38 (version recorded by Pedro Sarmiento de Gamboa); Cieza de León 1883, ch. 5.

Pages 203–4/Legend of *Tonapa:* Pachacuti 1873, 70–73; Osborne 1968, 86–89.

Pages 204–5/Myth of *Koniraya Wirakocha:* Urioste 1983, ch. 2.

Page 205/Variants of the main part of the story: Métraux 1931, 169 (Chiriguano and Uro-Chipaya); Métraux 1928, 232–33 (Tupinamba).

Page 205/Medieval legend of how Christ was chased: Dähnhardt 1909, 51–58.

Page 206/Old gods and new gods: Pachacuti 1873, 72 (female idol destroyed by *Tonapa*); Urioste 1983, chs. 1 & 5 (cannibal god defeated by *Pariakaka*); Osborne 1968, 107 (*Kon* defeated by *Pachacamah*); Mishkin 1940, 225–26 (*Pachacamah* defeated by Sun).

Pages 206–7/Egg-birth motif: Chumap Lucía and García-Rendueles 1979 1, 39 (Aguaruna); Mishkin 1940, 226 (Chincha); Primeros Agustinos 1865, 22–23 (Huamacucho); Urioste 1983, ch. 5 (Huarochirí); Pellizzaro 6,

19–22 (Shuar). In Greater Brazil: Balzano 1984, 30 (Chacobo); Hilde-brand 1975, 359 (Ufaina). In Guiana: Armellada 1972, 47–48 (Tau-lipáng); Fock 1963, 40 (Waiwai); Civrieux 1980, 48–54 (Yekuana). In the Gran Chaco: Rivera de Bianchi 1973, 720 (Mbayá).

Page 207/World ages: Howard-Malverde 1981, 25 (Cañar); Stein 1982, 251 (Hualcán); Gow and Condori 1982, 20–24 (Pinchimuro); Núñez del Prado 1974, 239 (Qotobamba).

* Page 208/*Chullpa* myth: HSAI 2, 571 (Aymara); Stein 1982, 251 (Hualcán); Mishkin 1940, 235–36 (Kauri); Gow and Condori 1982, 26 & 28 (Pinchi-muro); Núñez del Prado 1974, 239–41 (Q'ero and Qotobamba); HSAI 2, 585 (Uro-Chipaya).

Page 208/*Chullpa* sickness: HSAI 2, 568.

Page 208/Christ in *chullpa* myth: Mishkin 1940, 235; Núñez del Prado 1974, 241.

Page 209/Christ as culture hero: Waman Puma in Lara 1973, 44 (Huánuco); Parsons 1945, 147 (Imbabura).

Page 209/Christ as trickster: ibid., 146.

Pages 209–10/Version of Christ's life from the Cañar: Howard-Malverde 1981, 197–208.

Page 211/European tale types: Dähnhardt 1909, 12–16 (Cow and the Mule); ibid., 61–66 (Sown Field); ibid., 95–97 (Christ and the Farmer). South American variants of Christ and the Farmer: FLSAI 7, 86–87 (Bororo); Howard-Malverde 1981, 205 (Cañar); Müller 1934, 444 (Mbyá); Cháves 1958, 134 (Siona); Nimuendajú 1915, 281 (Tenetehara).

Page 213/*Avíreri* of the Campa: Weiss 1975, 310–28 & 407–8 & 492.

Page 213/*Varinkoshi* of the Shipibo: Girard 1958, 252.

Page 213/*Pachacamah:* Weiss 1972, 163 (Machiguenga); Weiss 1975, 266 (Campa).

Page 214/*Pachamama:* Hissink and Hahn 1961, 154–55 & 333–35 (Tacana); Núñez del Prado 1974, 245–46 (Quechua).

Page 214/Crop mother: Brown 1985, 50–51 (Aguaruna); Whitten 1978, 843–45 (Canelos); Harner 1972, 70 (Shuar); Hissink and Hahn 1961, 223–25 (Tacana).

Pages 214–15/Myth of *Nunkwi:* Guallart 1978 (Aguaruna); Chumap Lucía and García-Rendueles 1979 2, 377–415 (Aguaruna); Pellizzaro 8 (Shuar); Karsten 1935, 513–16 (Shuar); Rueda 1983, 82–87 (Shuar).

* Page 216/Twin Myth: Chumap Lucía and García-Rendueles 1979 1, 39–73 (Aguaruna); Métraux 1931, 149–50 (Amuesha); Weiss 1975, 483 (Campa); Primeros Agustinos 1865, 22–23 (Huamacucho); Pellizzaro 6, 15–141 (Shuar); Karsten 1935, 523–26 (Shuar); Barrueco 1985, 36–41 (Shuar); HSAI 3, 650 (Záparo). See also Greater Brazil, Guiana, and Northwest.

* Pages 216–17/Parrot Brides: Howard-Malverde 1981, 11–12 (Cañar and Imbabura); Molina 1873, 8–9 (16th-century Cañar); Jiménez de la Espada 1965, 201–2 (Maina); Roe 1982, 49–51 (Shipibo); Stirling 1938, 122 (Shuar); Hissink and Hahn 1961, 42–45 (Tacana). Variants from other regions: FLSAI 4, 54 (Apinayé); Ehrenreich 1891, 39–40 (Carayá); Magaña and Jara 1985, 25–26 (Caliña); HSAI 1, 516 ("Rio Yamunda").

* Pages 217–18/Underwater Woman: Chumap Lucía and García-Rendueles

1979 2, 650 (Aguaruna); Brown 1985, 52 (Aguaruna); Pellizzaro 2 (Shuar); Hissink and Hahn 1961, 55–58 & 211–12 (Tacana). See also Guiana.

Page 220/Quechua beliefs regarding ancient artifacts and architectural remains: Stein 1982, 251; Allen 1983, 44–45.

Pages 221–22/Feline god: HSAI 2, 171–72; Benson 1972, ch. 2.

Page 222/Tacana story of Grandfather Lightning: Hissink and Hahn 1961, 77.

Pages 222–24/Revolt of the utensils: Urioste 1983 1, 19 (Huarochirí); Hissink and Hahn 1961, 40 & 84–85 & 364 (Tacana). In Greater Brazil: Hugh-Jones 1979, 263 (Barasana); Métraux 1931, 158 (Chiriguano); Nimuendajú 1952, 125 (Tukuna). In Mochica art: Kutscher 1950, 44–45; Métraux 1931, 126; Métraux 1946, 33; Lyon 1981.

Page 226/Shipibo myth of the serpent bridge: Roe 1982, 120–21.

Page 226/Claude Lévi-Strauss: Lévi-Strauss 1967, 264–68.

Page 226/Toba myth of *Lik:* Métraux 1946, 58–59.

Page 228/Ufaina myth of fish-filled boa: Hildebrand 1975, 337–39.

Page 228/Staff God: Mefford 1980; HSAI 2, 117; Mason 1973, 92; Molina 1873, 5 (Tiahuanuco as *Wirakocha*'s residence).

Page 230/Stuttgart fox head: Disselhoff and Linné 1961, 174.

Page 230/Sheaths for litter poles: HSAI 2, 239.

Page 232/Endurance contest: Arguedas and Carrillo 1967, 92–93.

Page 232/Big mouth: Borja 1937, "El zorra y el huaychao"; cf. FLSAI 6, 229–30.

Page 232/Disguised suitor: Paredes 1949, 69–70; cf. FLSAI 6, 239–40.

* Pages 233–37/Rod-of-gold or *Inkarrí* legend: Bendezú Aybar 1980, 277–88 (Andamarca, Ayacucho, Cuzco, Puquio, and Q'ero); Garcilaso 1959, bk. 1, chs. 15–17 (16th-century Cuzco); Stein 1982, 251–52 (Hualcán); Mishkin 1940, 235 (Kauri); Núñez del Prado 1974, 239–40 (Q'ero); Allen 1983, 44 (Sonqo).

* Page 235/Emergence motif: Cieza de León 1947, ch. 100 (Aymara); HSAI 2, 800–801 (Cañar); Garcilaso 1959, ch. 15 (Cuzco); Primeros Agustinos 1865, 23 (Huamacucho); Simón 1891, 278 (Jauja); HSAI 3, 550 (Machiguenga); HSAI 2, 796 (Panzaleo). See also all other regions except Far South.

Page 235/Cabello de Balboa: Mishkin 1940, 229; HSAI 2, 196 & 318.

Page 237/*Pachakuti:* Allen 1983, 45; Gow 1982, 216.

Page 237/Story of the old bearded man and the Cuzco earthquake: ibid., 209.

Page 238/"*Campesino!* The *patrón* will no longer eat": Bendezú Aybar 1980, 431; Gow 1982, 219.

Page 238/*Pishtaco:* Oliver-Smith 1969, 367; Weiss 1975, 292; Brown 1985, 183.

Page 240/Shuar mythology "is being forgotten": HSAI 3, 627.

Page 240/Bilingual edition of Aguaruna myths: Chumap Lucía and García-Rendueles 1979.

References

Far from a complete list of works on South American mythology, the following serves mainly to amplify the Notes on Sources, above. Those who need a fuller bibliography should consult Niles' *South American Indian Narrative*, to which Vázquez' "Present State of Research in South American Mythology" makes useful additions. For South American Indian culture in general, O'Leary's *Ethnographic Bibliography*, though published in 1963, remains a standard reference, which may be used together with Welch's recent *Indians of South America: A Bibliography*.

A dagger (†) has been added to any title that contains an important regional or comparative study; an asterisk (*) signifies an unusually full collection of myths from a particular tribe.

The abbreviations JAF and LAIL stand for *Journal of American Folklore* and *Latin American Indian Literatures*.

Alexander, Hartley Burr. *Latin-American* (vol. 11 of *The Mythology of All Races*, ed. Louis Herbert Gray). Boston: Marshall Jones, 1920.

Allen, Catherine J. "Of Bear-Men and He-Men," LAIL 7 (1983): 38–51.

Alvarsson, Jan-Åke. "How the Matacos Found Their Fish," LAIL 8 (1984): 92–98.

Anglería, Pedro Mártir de. *Decadas del Nuevo Mundo*. 2 vols. Mexico: José Porrúa, 1964–65.

Arguedas, José María, and Francisco Carrillo. *Poesía y prosa quechua*. Lima: Biblioteca Universitaria, 1967.

Armellada, Cesáreo de. *Pemonton taremaru*. Caracas: Universidad Católica Andrés Bello, 1972.

———, and Carmela Bentivenga Napolitano. *Literaturas indígenas venezolanas*. Caracas: Monte Avila, 1975.

Balzano, Silvia. "Káko: A Cultural Hero from the Chacobos," LAIL 8 (1984): 26–34.

Barabas, Alicia M., and Miguel A. Bartolomé. "The Mythic Testimony of the Mataco," LAIL 3 (1979): 76–85.

Barrett, S. A. *The Cayapa Indians of Ecuador*. 2 vols. New York: Museum of the American Indian, 1925.

Barrueco, Domingo. *Mitos y leyendas shuar*. [Quito, Ecuador]: Mundo Shuar, 1985.

Basso, Ellen B. *The Kalapalo Indians of Central Brazil*. New York: Holt, Rinehart and Winston, 1973.

———. *A Musical View of the Universe: Kalapalo Myth and Ritual Performance*. Philadelphia: University of Pennsylvania Press, 1985.

Bendezú Aybar, Edmundo, ed. *Literatura quechua*. Caracas: Biblioteca Ayacucho, 1980.

Benson, Elizabeth P. *The Mochica*. New York: Praeger, 1972.

Bierhorst, John. *The Mythology of North America*. New York: Morrow, 1985.

———. *The Red Swan*. New York: Farrar, Straus and Giroux, 1976.

Biocca, Ettore. *Viaggi tra gli indi*. 3 vols. Rome: Consiglio Nazionale delle Ricerche, 1965–66.

Bórmida, Marcelo. "Ayoreo Myths," LAIL 2 (1978): 1–13.

Borja, Arturo Jiménez. *Cuentos peruanos*. Lima, [1937].

Bourne, E. G. *Columbus, Ramón Pané and the Beginnings of American Anthropology*. Worcester, 1906.

Bravo, Domingo A. *Diccionario quichua santiagueño castellano*. Buenos Aires: Instituto Amigos del Libro Argentino, 1967.

Brett, W. H. *The Indian Tribes of Guiana*. London, 1868.

———. *Legends and Myths of the Aboriginal Indians of British Guiana*. London, [1880].

Bridges, E. Lucas. *Uttermost Part of the Earth*. New York: E. P. Dutton, 1950.

Brown, Michael F. *Tsewa's Gift*. Washington: Smithsonian, 1985.

† Brundage, Burr Cartwright. "Peruvian Myths of Creation," ch. 4 of Brundage's *Empire of the Inca*. Norman: University of Oklahoma Press, 1963.

Cadogan, León. *Ayvu rapyta*. Universidade de São Paulo, Faculdade de Filosofia, Ciências e Letras. Boletim 227, Antropologia 5. São Paulo, Brazil, 1959.

———. "Baiõ Kará Wachú y otras mitos guayakíes," *América Indígena* 22 (1962): 39–82.

Calazacon, Catalina, and Dolores Orazona. *Yo imin tsachi*. Guayaquil, Ecuador: Banco Central del Ecuador, 1982.

Casamiquela, Rodolfo M. "The Deluge Myth in Patagonia," LAIL 6 (1982): 91–101.

Caspar, Franz. *Tupari*. London: G. Bell, 1956.

Chagnon, Napoleon A. *Yanomamo*. New York: Holt, Rinehart and Winston, 1968.

Chapman, Anne. *Drama and Power in a Hunting Society*. Cambridge: Cambridge University Press, 1982.

Chaumeil, J., and J. P. Chaumeil. "Los mellizos y la lupuna," *Amazonía Peruana*, vol. 2, no. 3 (1978): 159–84.

Cháves, Milcíades. "Mítica de los siona del alto Putomayo," *Miscellanea Paul Rivet Octogenario Dicata*, vol. 2. Mexico: 23rd International Congress of Americanists/Universidad Nacional Autónoma de México, 1958.

* Chumap Lucía, Aurelio, and Manuel García-Rendueles. *"Duik múun . . .": Universo mítico de los aguaruna*. 2 vols. Lima: Centro Amazónico de Antropología y Aplicación Práctica, 1979.

Cieza de León, Pedro de. "La [primera parte de la] crónica del Perú." In *Biblioteca de autores españoles*, vol. 26, pt. 2. Madrid: Atlas, 1947.

———. *Second Part of the Chronicle of Peru* (Clements R. Markham, trans.). Hakluyt Society, 1883.

Civrieux, Marc de. *Religión y magia kari'ña*. Caracas: Universidad Católica Andrés Bello, 1974.

* ———. *Watunna* (David Guss, ed. and trans.). San Francisco: North Point Press, 1980.

Couto de Magalhães, [J. Viera.] *O Selvagem*. Rio de Janeiro, 1876.

Couture-Brunette, Lorraine, and Giovanni Saffirio. "Yanomama Drawings: New Art by an Old People," *Carnegie Magazine*, May/June 1985: 1 and 6–12.

Crocker, Jon Christopher. *Vital Souls*. Tucson: University of Arizona Press, 1985.

Dähnhardt, Oskar. *Natursagen*, vol. 2: Sagen zum Neuen Testament. Leipzig and Berlin: B. G. Teubner, 1909.

Disselhoff, Hans-Dietrich, and Sigvald Linné. *The Art of Ancient America*. New York: Crown, 1961.

Dockstader, Frederick J. *Indian Art in South America*. Greenwich, Conn.: New York Graphic Society, 1967.

Drummond, Lee. "Structure and Process in the Interpretation of South American Myth: The Arawak Dog Spirit People," *American Anthropologist* 79 (1977): 842–68.

Ehrenreich, Paul. *Beiträge zur Völkerkunde Brasiliens*. Berlin: Spemann, 1891.

Espíndola, Julio César. "A propósito del mesianismo en las tribus guaraní," *América Indígena* 21 (1961): 307–25.

Farabee, William Curtis. *The Central Arawaks*. New York: Humanities Press, 1967.

Faron, Louis C. *Hawks of the Sun*. Pittsburgh: University of Pittsburgh Press, 1971.

———. "The Magic Mountain and Other Origin Myths of the Mapuche of Central Chile," *JAF* 76 (1963): 245–48.

———. *The Mapuche Indians of Chile*. New York: Holt, Rinehart and Winston, 1968.

Fernández G., Germán M. A. "The Araucanian Deluge Myth," *LAIL* 6 (1982): 102–13.

Fock, Neils. *Waiwai: Religion and Society of an Amazonian Tribe*. Copenhagen: National Museum, 1963.

Garcilaso de la Vega. *Comentarios reales de los incas*. Lima: Librería Internacional del Perú, [1959?].

Giaccaria, Bartolomeu, and Adalberto Heide. *Jerônimo Xavante Conta*. Campo Grande, Brazil: Museu Regional Dom Bosco, 1975.

Gillen, John. *The Barama Caribs of British Guiana*. Papers of the Peabody Museum of American Archaeology and Ethnology, Harvard University, vol. 14, no. 2. 1936.

Girard, Rafael. *Indios selváticos de la Amazonía peruana*. Mexico: Libro Mex Editores, 1958.

† Goeje, C. H. de. *Philosophy, Initiation and Myths of the Indians of Guiana and Adjacent Countries*. International Archives for Ethnography, vol. 44. 1943.

Goldman, Irving. *The Cubeo*. Urbana: University of Illinois Press, 1963.

Gow, Rosalind C. "Inkarri and Revolutionary Leadership in the Southern Andes," *Journal of Latin American Lore* 8 (1982): 197–221.

————, and Bernabé Condori. *Kay pacha.* Cuzco, Peru: Centro de Estudios Rurales Andinos Bartolomé de las Casas, 1982.

Gregor, Thomas. *Anxious Pleasures.* Chicago: University of Chicago Press, 1985.

Guallart, J. M. "El mito de Nunkui," *Amazonía Peruana,* vol. 2, no. 3 (1978): 7–8.

Gusinde, Martin. "Das Brüderpaar in der südamerikanischen Mythologie," *Proceedings* (23rd International Congress of Americanists, New York, 1928), 1930: 687–98.

————. *Die Feuerland Indianer,* vol. 3: Die Halakwulup. Vienna: St. Gabriel, 1974.

————. *The Yamana: The Life and Thought of the Water Nomads of Cape Horn* (Frieda Schütze, trans.). 5 vols. New Haven: Human Relations Area Files, 1961.

Guss, David. "Keeping It Oral: A Yekuana Ethnology," *American Ethnologist* 13 (1986): 413–29.

————, ed. *The Language of Birds.* San Francisco: North Point Press, 1985.

Harner, Michael J. *The Jívaro.* Garden City, N.Y.: Doubleday/Natural History Press, 1972.

Hartmann, Gunther. *Masken südamerikanischer Naturvölker.* Berlin: Museum für Völkerkunde, 1967.

Henry, Jules. *Jungle People.* New York: Vintage/Random House, 1964.

Hildebrand, Martín von. "Origen del mundo según los ufaina," *Revista Colombiana de Antropología* 18 (1975): 321–82. Bogotá.

* Hissink, Karin, and Albert Hahn. *Die Tacana,* vol. 1: Erzählungsgut. Stuttgart: W. Kohlhammer, 1961.

Howard-Malverde, Rosaleen. "Dioses y diablos: Tradición oral de Cañar Ecuador," *Amerindia: Revue d'Ethnolinguistique Amérindienne,* numéro spécial 1, 1981. Paris.

Hugh-Jones, Stephen. *The Palm and the Pleiades.* Cambridge, England: Cambridge University Press, 1979.

Huxley, Francis. *Affable Savages.* New York: Viking, 1957.

Im Thurn, Everard F. *Among the Indians of Guiana.* New York: Dover, 1967.

Jiménez de la Espada, Don Marcos. "Relaciones geográficas de Indias: Perú," *Biblioteca de autores españoles,* vols. 183–85. Madrid: Atlas, 1965.

Karsten, Rafael. *The Head-Hunters of Western Amazonas.* Helsingfors: Societas Scientiarum Fennica, 1935.

Keller, Carlos. "Der Ursprungsmythus der Kloketen-Feier der Selknam-Indianer auf Feuerland," *Anthropos* 57 (1962): 524–28.

Koch-Grünberg, Theodor. *Indianermärchen aus Südamerika.* Jena: Eugen Diederichs, 1920.

* ————. *Vom Roroima zum Orinoco,* vol. 2. (Berlin: Dietrich Reimer, 1916) and vol. 3 (Stuttgart: Strecker and Schröder, 1923).

————. *Zwei Jahre unter den Indianern.* 2 vols. in 1. Graz, Austria: Akademische Druck, 1967.

Kruse, Albert. "Erzählungen der Tapajoz-Mundurukú," *Anthropos* 41–44 (1946–49): 314–30, 614–56.

————. "Karusakaybë, der Vater der Mundurukú," *Anthropos* 46 (1951): 915–32, and 47 (1952): 992–1018.

Kutscher, Gerdt. *Chimu: Eine altindianische Hochkultur.* Berlin: Gebr. Mann, 1950.

La Barre, Weston. "Aymara Folktales," *International Journal of American Linguistics* 16 (1950): 40–45.

Lara, Jesús, ed. *Mitos, leyendas y cuentos de los quechuas.* La Paz and Cochabamba, Bolivia: Editorial Los Amigos del Libro, 1973.

† Lévi-Strauss, Claude. *From Honey to Ashes.* New York: Harper and Row, 1973.

† ———. *The Raw and the Cooked.* New York: Harper and Row, 1969.

———. *Structural Anthropology.* Garden City, N.Y.: Anchor Books/Doubleday, 1967.

Leach, Maria, and Jerome Fried. *Standard Dictionary of Folklore, Mythology and Legend.* New York: Funk and Wagnalls, 1972.

Lehmann-Nitsche, Robert. "Mitología sudamericana XIV: El viejo Tatrapai de los araucanos," *Revista del Museo de La Plata* 32 (1930): 41–56, 307–16. La Plata, Argentina.

Loukotka, Čestmír. *Classification of South American Indian Languages.* Los Angeles: UCLA Latin American Center, 1968.

Lyon, Patricia J. "Arqueología y mitología: La escena de 'los objetos animados' y el tema de 'el alzamiento de los objetos,' " *Scripta Ethnologica* 6 (1981): 105–8. Buenos Aires.

Magaña, Edmundo, and Fabiola Jara. "Carib Myths on the Origin of Some Animal Species," *Latin American Indian Literatures Journal* 1 (1985): 13–27.

Mashnshnek, Celia Olga. "Seres potentes y héroes míticos de los mataco del Chaco central," *Scripta Ethnologica* 1 (1973): 105–54. Buenos Aires.

Mason, J. Alden. *The Ancient Civilizations of Peru.* Harmondsworth, England: Penguin, 1973.

Maybury-Lewis, David. *Akwẽ-Shavante Society.* New York: Oxford University Press, 1974.

Mefford, Jill. "Threads from the Past," *Symbols,* summer 1980: 1 and 6–7. Peabody Museum and Department of Anthropology, Harvard University.

Métraux, Alfred. "Mitos y cuentos de los indios chiriguano," *Revista del Museo de la Plata,* 33 (1931): 119–84. La Plata, Argentina.

———. "A Myth of the Chamacoco Indians and Its Social Significance," JAF 56 (1943): 113–19.

* ———. *Myths of the Toba and Pilagá Indians of the Gran Chaco.* Memoirs of the American Folklore Society, vol. 40. 1946.

———. *La religion des tupinamba.* Paris: Librairie Ernest Leroux, 1928.

† ———. "Twin Heroes in South American Mythology," JAF 59 (1946): 114–23. Not cited ("Métraux 1946" in Notes on Sources refers to Métraux's *Myths of the Toba and Pilagá*).

Mishkin, Bernard. "Cosmological Ideas among the Indians of the Southern Andes," JAF 53 (1940): 225–41.

Molina, Cristóbal de. "An Account of the Fables and Rites of the Yncas." In Clements R. Markham, ed., *Narratives of the Rites and Laws of the Yncas,* Hakluyt Society, 1873.

Müller, Franz. "Beiträge zur Ethnographie der Guaraní-Indianer in östlichen

Waldgebiet von Paraguay," *Anthropos* 29 (1934): 177–208, 441–60, 695–702.

Murphy, Robert F. *Mundurucú Religion*. Berkeley: University of California Press, 1958.

———, and Buell Quain. *The Trumaí Indians of Central Brazil*. Seattle: University of Washington Press, 1966.

Murphy, Yolanda, and Robert F. Murphy. *Women of the Forest*. New York: Columbia University Press, 1974.

Niles, Susan A. *South American Indian Narrative: Theoretical and Analytical Approaches: An Annotated Bibliography*. New York: Garland, 1981.

Nimuendajú, Curt. "Bruchstücke aus Religion and Uberlieferung der Šipáia-Indianer," *Anthropos* 14–15 (1919–20): 1002–1039.

———. "Die Sagen von der Erschaffung und Vernichtung der Welt als Grundlagen der Religion der Apapocúva-Guaraní," *Zeitschrift für Ethnologie* 46 (1914): 284–403. Berlin.

———. "Sagen der Tembé-Indianer (Pará und Maranhão)," *Zeitschrift für Ethnologie* 47 (1915): 281–301.

———. "Social Organization and Beliefs of the Botocudo of Eastern Brazil," *Southwestern Journal of Anthropology* 2 (1946): 93–115.

———. *The Tukuna*. Berkeley: University of California Press, 1952.

Nordenskiöld, Erland. *Indianerleben: El Gran Chaco*. Leipzig: Albert Bonnier, 1912.

Núñez del Prado B., Juan Víctor. "The Supernatural World of the Quechua of Southern Peru as Seen from the Community of Qotobamba," *Native South Americans: Ethnology of the Least Known Continent* (Patricia J. Lyon, ed.), 238–51. Boston: Little, Brown, 1974.

Ogilvie, John. "Creation Myths of the Wapisiana and Taruma," *Folk-Lore* 51 (1940): 64–72.

O'Leary, Timothy. *Ethnographic Bibliography of South America*. New Haven: Human Relations Area Files, 1963.

Oliver-Smith, Anthony. "The Pishtaco," JAF 82 (1969): 363–68.

Orbigny, Alcide d'. *Voyage dans l'Amérique méridionale*, vol. 3, pt. 1. Paris: P. Bertrand, 1844.

Osborne, Harold. *South American Mythology*. London: Paul Hamlyn, 1968.

Pachacuti Yamqui Salcamayhua, Juan de Santa Cruz. "An Account of the Antiquities of Peru." In Clements R. Markham, ed., *Narratives of the Rites and Laws of the Yncas*," Hakluyt Society, 1873.

Palavecino, Enrique. "The Magic World of the Mataco," LAIL 3 (1979): 61–75.

Paredes, M. Rigoberto. *El arte folklórico de Bolivia*. 2d. ed. La Paz, Bolivia, [1949].

Parsons, Elsie Clews. *Peguche*. Chicago: University of Chicago Press, 1945.

* Pellizzaro, Siro. [*Mitología shuar*.] Vol. 1: Arútam, [1976?]. Vol. 2: Tsunki, 1980. Vol. 3: Uwishin, 1978. Vol. 4: Wee, 1980. Vol. 5: Ayumpúm, 1980. Vol. 6: Etsa, defensor del pueblo shuar, n.d. Vol. 7: Etsa, el modelo del hombre shuar, 1982. Vol. 8: Nunkui, 1978. Vol. 9: La tsantsa, 1980. Vol. 10: Shakaim, 1977. Vol. 11: Celebración de la vida y de la fecundidad, 1983. Vol. 12: Iwianch', n.d. Sucua, Ecuador: Mundo Shuar. Note: The series title, *Mitología shuar*, does not appear in all the volumes.

Perrin, Michel. *Le chemin des indiens morts*. Paris: Payot, 1976.

Petrullo, Vincenzo. "The Yaruros of the Capanaparo River, Venezuela," Bureau of American Ethnology, Bulletin 123, 161–290. 1939.

Povos e culturas. Lisbon: Museu de Etnologia do Ultramar, 1972.

Preuss, Konrad Theodor. "Forschungsreise zu den Kágaba-Indianern der Sierra Nevada de Santa Marta in Kolumbien," *Anthropos* vols. 14–15 (1919–20): 314–404, 1040–79; vols. 16–17 (1921–22): 459–80, 737–64.

———. *Monumentale vorgeschichtliche Kunst*. Göttingen: Vandenhoeck and Ruprecht, 1929.

* ———. *Religion und Mythologie der Uitoto*. 2 vols. Göttingen: Vandenhoeck and Ruprecht, 1921–23.

Primeros Agustinos. "Relación de la religión y ritos del Perú." In *Colección de documentos inéditos, relativos al descubrimiento, conquista y colonización de las posesiones españolas en América y Oceania*, vol. 3, Madrid, 1865.

Radin, Paul. *The Indians of South America*. Garden City, N.Y.: Doubleday, 1942.

———. *The Trickster*. New York: Schocken, 1972.

Reichel-Dolmatoff, Gerardo. *Amazonian Cosmos*. Chicago: University of Chicago Press, 1971.

———. *Beyond the Milky Way*. Los Angeles: UCLA Latin American Center, 1978.

———. *Los Kogi*. 2 vols. [Vol 1] published as *Revista del Instituto Etnológico Nacional*, vol. 4, nos. 1 and 2, Bogotá, 1949–50. Vol. 2, Bogotá: Editorial Iqueima, 1951.

———. *The Shaman and the Jaguar*. Philadelphia: Temple University Press, 1975.

Riester, Jürgen. "Zur Religion der Pauserna-Guarasug'wa in Ostbolivien," *Anthropos* 65 (1970): 466–79.

Rivera de Bianchi, Mabel. "Mitología de los pueblos del Chaco, según visión de los autores de los siglos XVII y XVIII," *América Indígena* 23 (1973): 695–733.

Roe, Peter G. *The Cosmic Zygote*. New Brunswick, N.J.: Rutgers University Press, 1982.

†* Roth, Walter Edmund. "An Inquiry into the Animism and Folk-lore of the Guiana Indians," *30th Annual Report of the Bureau of American Ethnology, 1908–1909*, 103–386. 1915.

* Rueda, M. V. *Setenta mitos shuar*. Quito, Ecuador: Mundo Shuar, 1983.

Sánchez Labradór, José. *El Paraguay católico*. 2 vols. Buenos Aires: Universidad Nacional de La Plata, 1910.

Schmidt, Max. *Kunst und Kultur von Peru*. Berlin: Propyläen-Verlag, 1929.

Schultz, Harald. "The Waurá," *National Geographic Magazine*, Jan. 1966: 130–52.

Seeger, Anthony. *Nature and Society in Central Brazil*. Cambridge: Harvard University Press, 1981.

Sherzer, Joel. *Kuna Ways of Speaking*. Austin: University of Texas Press, 1983.

———. "Strategies in Text and Context: Cuna *kaa kwento*," JAF 92 (1979): 145–63.

Shoumatoff, Alex. "Amazons," *The New Yorker*, Mar. 24, 1986: 85–107.

Simón, Pedro. *Noticias historiales de las conquistas de tierra firme en las indias occidentales.* Vol. 2 (1891): Segunda Parte. Vol. 3 (1892): Partes Segunda y Tercera. Bogotá: Medardo Rivas.

Simpson, George Gaylord. "A Carib (Kamarakoto) Myth from Venezuela," JAF 57 (1944): 263–79.

Siskind, Janet. *To Hunt in the Morning.* New York: Oxford University Press, 1975.

Smith, Nigel. "Enchanted Forest," *Natural History,* Aug. 1983: 14–20.

Stein, William W. "Myth and Ideology in a Nineteenth Century Peruvian Peasant Uprising," *Ethnohistory* 29 (1982): 237–64.

Steinen, Karl von den. *Unter den Naturvölkern Zentral-Brasiliens.* Berlin: Dietrich Reimer, 1894.

Steward, Julian H., ed. *Handbook of South American Indians.* 7 vols. New York: Cooper Square, 1963.

Stirling, M. W. *Historical and Ethnographical Material on the Jivaro Indians.* Bureau of American Ethnology, Bulletin 117. 1938.

Stradelli, Ermano. "Leggenda dell-Jurupary," *Bollettino della Società Geografica Italiana* 28 (1890): 659–89 and 798–835.

Teschauer, Carl. "Mythen und alte Volkssagen aus Brasilien," *Anthropos* 1 (1906): 185–93 and 731–44.

Thompson, J. Eric S. *Ethnology of the Mayas of Southern and Central British Honduras,* Anthropological Series, vol. 17, no. 2. Chicago: Field Museum of Natural History, 1930.

Thompson, Stith. "Analogues and Borrowings in North and South American Indian Tales." In Earl H. Swanson, Jr., ed., *Languages and Cultures of Western North America,* Idaho State University Press, Pocatello, 1970.

———. *The Folktale.* New York: Holt, Rinehart and Winston, 1946.

———. *Tales of the North American Indians.* Bloomington: Indiana University Press, 1929.

Trupp, Fritz. *Mythen der Makuna.* Acta Ethnologica et Linguistica 40. Vienna, 1977.

Urioste, George L. *Hijos de Pariya Qaqa: La tradición oral de Waru Chiri.* 2 vols. Syracuse: Maxwell School of Citizenship and Public Affairs, Syracuse University, 1983.

van Coll, P. C. "Contes et légendes des Indiens de Surinam," *Anthropos* 2 (1907): 682–89, and 3 (1908): 482–88.

Vázquez, Juan Adolfo. "The Present State of Research in South American Mythology," *Numen* 25 (1978): 240–76.

———. "The Reconstruction of the Myth of Inkarri," *Latin American Indian Literatures Journal* 2 (1986): 92–109.

Villas Boas, Orlando, and Claudio Villas Boas. *Xingu.* New York: Farrar, Straus and Giroux, 1973.

Wagley, Charles. *Amazon Town.* New York: Knopf, 1964.

———. *Welcome of Tears.* Prospect Heights, Ill.: Waveland Press, 1983.

———, and Eduardo Galvão. *The Tenetehara Indians of Brazil.* New York: Columbia University Press, 1949.

Walde-Waldegg, Hermann von. "Notes of the Indians of the Llanos of Casanare and San Martin (Colombia)," *Anthropological Quarterly* 9 (1936): 38–45.

Wassén, Henry. "Cuentos de los indios chocós," *Journal de la Société des Américanistes*, n.s. vol. 25 (1933): 103–37. Paris.

———. "The Frog in Indian Mythology and Imaginative World," *Anthropos* 29 (1934): 613–58. Cited as Wassén 1934a.

———. "Mitos y cuentos de los indios cunas," *Journal de la Société des Américanistes* n.s. vol. 26 (1934): 1–35. Paris. Cited as Wassén 1934b.

Wavrin, Marquis de. *Moeurs et coutumes indiens sauvages de l'Amérique du Sud.* Paris: Payot, 1937.

Weiss, Gerald. "Campa Cosmology," *Ethnology* 11 (1972): 157–72.

† ———. *Campa Cosmology.* New York: American Museum of Natural History, 1975.

Welch, Thomas L. *The Indians of South America: A Bibliography.* Washington, D.C.: Columbus Memorial Library, Organization of American States, 1987.

Whitten, Norman E., Jr. "Ecological Imagery and Cultural Adaptability: The Canelos Quichua of Eastern Ecuador," *American Anthropologist* 80 (1978): 836–59.

Wilbert, Johannes. *Yupa Folktales.* Los Angeles: UCLA Latin American Center, 1974.

†* ———, [and Karin Simoneau, eds.] [The Folk Literature of South American Indians.] [No. 1:] *Folk Literature of the Warao Indians*, 1970. [No. 2:] *Folk Literature of the Selknam Indians*, 1975. [No. 3:] *Folk Literature of the Yamana Indians*, 1977. [No. 4:] *Folk Literature of the Gê Indians*, vol. 1, 1978. [No. 5:] *Folk Literature of the Mataco Indians*, 1982. [No. 6:] *Folk Literature of the Toba Indians*, vol. 1, 1982. [No. 7:] *Folk Literature of the Bororo Indians*, 1983. [No. 8:] *Folk Literature of the Gê Indians*, vol. 2, 1984. [No. 9:] *Folk Literature of the Tehuelche Indians*, 1984. [No. 10:] *Folk Literature of the Chorote Indians*, 1985. [Nos. 11 and 12:] *Folk Literature of the Guajiro Indians*, vols. 1 and 2, 1986. Los Angeles: UCLA Latin American Center. Note: Simoneau is coeditor beginning with No. 5.

Zárate, Agustín de. "Historia del descubrimiento y conquista de la provincia del Perú." In *Biblioteca de autores españoles*, vol. 26, pt. 2. Madrid: Atlas, 1947.

Index

Also available from Quill:

Gods and Heroes of the New World / volume one
The Mythology of North America

"Bierhorst's descriptions of the background and history, the connections and crossovers, of the myths and mythologies, and his glimpses of the world views of various peoples and regions are lucid and thoughtful."
The New York Times Book Review

"The book fulfills its purpose, constituting a much-needed overview."
American Anthropologist

"Noted folklorist Bierhorst first discusses characteristic patterns and themes, then defines eleven mythological regions, and examines the sacred stories of each. . . . He enlivens his general analysis with examples of particular stories, making this useful for both browsing and reference."
ALA Booklist